SIGN R
(signs used in tl

Good footpath - - - - - -
(sufficiently distinct to be followed in mist)

Intermittent footpath
(difficult to follow in mist)

**Route recommended
 but no path**
(if recommended one way only, arrow indicates direction)

Wall ∞∞∞∞∞∞∞ **Broken wall** °°°°°°°°°°°°°°

Fence ┼┼┼┼┼┼┼┼ **Broken fence** ''''''''''''''''

Marshy ground ⚘⚘⚘⚘ **Trees** 🜨🜨🜨🜨

Crags 🏔🏔🏔 **Boulders** ▫▫▫▫

Stream or River
(arrow indicates direction of flow)

Waterfall ∿⌁ **Bridge** ∿

Buildings ▪▫▪ **Unenclosed road** ▦▦▦▦

Contours (at 100' intervals)
1900
1800
1700

Summit-cairn ▲ **Other** (prominent) **cairns** △

THE
NORTHERN
FELLS

REVISED EDITIONS

PUBLISHER'S NOTE

Fell walking can be dangerous, especially
in wet, windy, foggy or icy conditions.
Please be sure to take sensible precautions
when out on the fells. As A. Wainwright himself
frequently wrote: use your common sense
and watch where you are putting your feet.

A PICTORIAL GUIDE

TO THE

LAKELAND FELLS

SECOND EDITION

REVISED BY CHRIS JESTY

being an illustrated account
of a study and exploration
of the mountains in the
English Lake District
by

A Wainwright

BOOK FIVE
THE NORTHERN FELLS

Frances Lincoln Limited
4 Torriano Mews
Torriano Avenue
London NW5 2RZ
www.franceslincoln.com

First edition published by Henry Marshall, Kentmere, 1962
First published by Frances Lincoln 2003
Second (revised) edition published by Frances Lincoln 2008
Reprinted with minor corrections 2009

Printed and bound in China

A CIP catalogue for this book is
available from the British Library

ISBN 978 0 7112 2667 8

9 8 7 6 5 4

THIS REVISED AND UPDATED EDITION PUBLISHED BY
FRANCES LINCOLN, LONDON

FOREWORD
BY BETTY WAINWRIGHT

FOREWORD

The Pictorial Guides have never before been revised, for the reasons given by AW in his concluding remarks to the third volume, *The Central Fells*, where he wrote that by the time he had finished Book Seven, age would prevent him undertaking the 'joyful task' of revising the series himself. He went on to write:

> ... Substantially, of course, the books will be useful for many years to come, especially in the detail and description of the fell tops, while the views will remain unaltered for ever, assuming that falling satellites and other fancy gadgets of man's invention don't blow God's far worthier creations to bits. But, this dire possibility apart, the books must inevitably show more and more inaccuracies as the years go by. Therefore, because it is unlikely that there will ever be revised editions, and because I should just hate to see my name on anything that could not be relied on, the probability is that the books will progressively be withdrawn from publication after a currency of a few years.

This was written in 1958, when the oldest volume was only three years old and by the time he had completed Book Seven in 1965 he was even more conscious of the little things that had gone out of date in the previous volumes — cairns demolished or built, screes eroded, woods felled or grown up, new paths made. As the years passed and it became apparent that the books were still in demand, despite these inaccuracies, he was occasionally approached by people asking for revised editions. But the core of the problem was that, as old age approached, he knew he could not undertake the changes himself, nor did he trust anyone to do the work as he would have wished.

When, in 1980, Chris Jesty broached the idea to him, he was told 'after my lifetime'. This was half the battle won — AW knew Chris's work well, and did trust him. Now, given the continuing popularity and use of the Pictorial Guides, I am delighted that, due to Chris's commitment, the guides are being revised and I give them my blessing. It is with pleasure that I picture Chris re-walking and checking and, where necessary, correcting every route, every ascent and every path. Although most of the individual corrections are minor, the overall impact is huge, and I feel proud and confident — as I am sure AW would be too — that the revised guides will satisfy the needs of the 21st-century walker.

Betty Wainwright
Kendal, January 2005

INTRODUCTION
TO THE
SECOND EDITION
BY CHRIS JESTY

INTRODUCTION TO THE SECOND EDITION

In 1959 I went on an Outward Bound course at Eskdale Green, which involved a lot of walking in the mountains. I found that the depiction of paths on Ordnance Survey maps left definite room for improvement, and I had the idea of producing a guide book that would make it easier for people to find their way around. But in 1961 I was given one of Wainwright's Pictorial Guides to the Lakeland Fells and discovered that he had beaten me to it.

It occurred to me that one day the books would become out of date, and that, as I was presumably much younger than the author, the time might arrive when I would be allowed to revise them. It has taken more than forty years for that dream to turn into a reality.

In the meantime I had made the acquaintance of the author. I collaborated with him on *A Guide to the View from Scafell Pike*, and later on, when his eyesight was failing, I drew the maps for two of his other books (*Wainwright in the Limestone Dales* and *Wainwright's Favourite Lakeland Mountains*). Shortly before he died he requested that if ever the Lakeland Guides were to be revised I should be offered the job.

When, in 2003, following a change of publisher, the proposal was revived, I threw myself into the job with enthusiasm. I had a number of advantages over the author. I had a car, I had satellite navigation equipment, I was able to work on enlargements of the pages, and as I didn't have a job I was able to devote all my time and all my energy to this vast project.

Every feature on the maps and ascent diagrams and every word of text have been checked, but I have not checked every recommended route without a path. Descriptions of natural features and views are virtually unaltered, but the number of changes that have been made to maps and ascent diagrams is enormous. The decision was taken to print the paths in a second colour so that they stand out from other details, and also so that readers can tell at a glance that it is the revised edition they are using.

Summit altitudes have been corrected where they differ by five feet or more from the latest Ordnance Survey figures. Parking information has been added where appropriate. I have also taken the liberty of adding other information that seems to me to be of interest. No changes have been made to drawings of landscapes, natural features or buildings, or, of course, to Wainwright's 'Personal Notes in Conclusion'.

Occasional references will be found in the books to Bartholomew's maps. These are still available, but they are now published by Collins.

In order to keep the books as accurate as possible and in anticipation of future revised editions, readers are invited to write to me (c/o the publishers) about any errors they find in the revised Pictorial Guides. Emails to chrisj@frances-lincoln.com and letters sent to me c/o Frances Lincoln, 4 Torriano Mews, Torriano Avenue, London NW5 2RZ, will be passed on regularly. Amendments and information about changes that have taken place since publication are available on the Frances Lincoln website (www.franceslincoln.com) on the page for *The Northern Fells*, Second Edition.

Chris Jesty
Kendal, October 2007

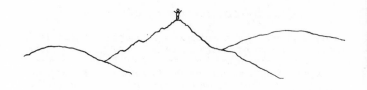

BOOK FIVE
is dedicated to
those who travel alone

THE SOLITARY WANDERERS
ON THE FELLS
who find contentment
in the companionship of the mountains
and of the creatures of the mountains

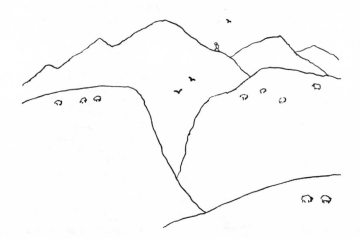

Classification and Definition

Any division of the Lakeland fells into geographical districts must necessarily be arbitrary, just as the location of the outer boundaries of Lakeland must always be a matter of opinion. Any attempt to define internal or external boundaries is certain to invite criticism, and he who takes it upon himself to say where Lakeland starts and finishes, or, for example, where the Central Fells merge into the Southern Fells and *which* fells are the Central Fells and which the Southern and *why* they need be so classified, must not expect his pronouncements to be generally accepted.

Yet for present purposes some plan of classification and definition must be used. County and parochial boundaries are no help, nor is the recently-defined area of the Lakeland National Park, for this book is concerned only with the high ground.

First, the external boundaries. Straight lines linking the extremities of the outlying lakes enclose all the higher fells very conveniently. There are a few fells of lesser height to the north and east, however, that are typically Lakeland in character and cannot properly be omitted: these are brought in, somewhat untidily, by extending the lines in those areas. Thus:

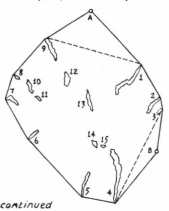

1 : *Ullswater*
2 : *Hawes Water*
3 : proposed *Swindale Resr*
4 : *Windermere*
5 : *Coniston Water*
6 : *Wast Water*
7 : *Ennerdale Water*
8 : *Loweswater*
9 : *Bassenthwaite Lake*
10: *Crummock Water*
11: *Buttermere*
12: *Derwent Water*
13: *Thirlmere*
14: *Grasmere*
15: *Rydal Water*
A : *Caldbeck*
B : *Longsleddale (church)*

continued

Classification and Definition

continued

The complete Guide includes all the fells in the area enclosed by the straight lines of the diagram. This is an undertaking quite beyond the compass of a single volume, and it is necessary, therefore, to divide the area into convenient sections, making the fullest use of natural boundaries (lakes, valleys and low passes) so that each district is, as far as possible, self-contained and independent of the rest.

This division gives seven areas, each with a well-defined group of fells, and each area is the subject of a separate volume

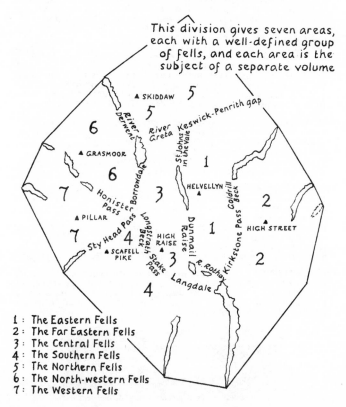

1 : The Eastern Fells
2 : The Far Eastern Fells
3 : The Central Fells
4 : The Southern Fells
5 : The Northern Fells
6 : The North-western Fells
7 : The Western Fells

INTRODUCTION

Notes on the Illustrations

THE MAPS................ Many excellent books have been written
about Lakeland, but the best literature of all for the walker
is that published by the Director General of Ordnance Survey,
the 1" map for companionship and guidance on expeditions, the
2½" map for exploration both on the fells and by the fireside.
These admirable maps are remarkably accurate topographically
but there is a crying need for a revision of the paths on the hills:
several walkers' tracks that have come into use during the past
few decades, some of them now broad highways, are not shown at
all; other paths still shown on the maps have fallen into neglect
and can no longer be traced on the ground.

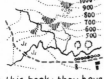

The popular Bartholomew 1" map is a
beautiful picture, fit for a frame, but this
too is unreliable for paths; indeed here the
defect is much more serious, for routes are
indicated where no paths ever existed, nor
ever could — the cartographer has preferred
to take precipices in his stride rather than
deflect his graceful curves over easy ground.

Hence the justification for the maps in this book: they have
the one merit (of importance to walkers) of being dependable as
regards delineation of paths. They are intended as supplements
to the Ordnance Survey maps, certainly not as substitutes.

THE VIEWS.............. Various devices have
been used to illustrate the views from the
summits of the fells. The full panorama
in the form of an outline drawing is most
satisfactory generally, and this method
has been adopted for the main viewpoints.

THE DIAGRAMS OF ASCENTS.................. The routes of ascent
of the higher fells are depicted by diagrams that do not pretend
to strict accuracy: they are neither plans
nor elevations; in fact there is deliberate
distortion in order to show detail clearly:
usually they are represented as viewed
from imaginary 'space-stations.' But it is
hoped they will be useful and interesting.

THE DRAWINGS....... The drawings at least are honest attempts
to reproduce what the eye sees: they illustrate features of
interest and also serve the dual purpose of breaking up the
text and balancing the layout of the pages, and of filling up
awkward blank spaces, like this:

Thirlmere

THE
NORTHERN
FELLS

Circular in plan, the area of the Northern Fells is completely severed from all other mountainous parts of the Lake District by Bassenthwaite Lake, the Vale of Keswick and the low country of the Glenderamackin River, which extend like a wide moat around the southern base of the group. West and north these fells are bounded by the coastal plain of Cumbria and east by the valley of the Eden. Thus they rise in isolation as an independent and separate geographical unit.

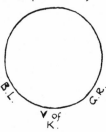

This circle of high ground is divided naturally into three almost equal segments by the main valleys draining the area, the headwaters of which spring from the vast upland basin of Skiddaw Forest. The south-western sector is occupied by the mass of Skiddaw, the south-eastern by Blencathra and its satellites, and the northern, which is of lower elevation and consequently hidden in views from the south by the other two, is a tract of rolling hills comprising the Caldbeck and Uldale Fells.

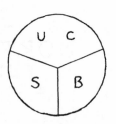

Journeys around the perimeter and into the silent interior along the three valleys forming the segments (the Dash, Caldew and Glenderaterra) give an excellent idea of the composition and character of these fells and are recommended as a preliminary to the exploration of the group.

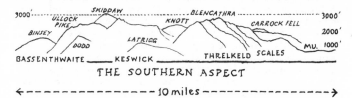

THE SOUTHERN ASPECT

← - - - - - - - - - - - 10 miles - - - - - - - - - - - →

The vertical scale in these diagrams is exaggerated.
(The hills don't *really* look as good as this!)

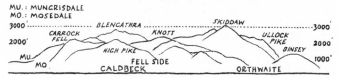

THE NORTHERN ASPECT

The southern aspects of Skiddaw and Blencathra are familiar to frequenters of the Lake District, and the usual approaches on this side are well known. Their northern slopes, falling to the unseen and undefiled hollow of Skiddaw Forest, are less in favour and rarely visited.

Skiddaw Forest is a remarkable place, unique in Lakeland. Common geographical concepts are upset here: the Forest occupies a central position amongst the Northern Fells, but instead of being a concentration of lofty ground from which descending ridges radiate it is actually an upland depression rimmed by summits. The Forest is uncultivated, a desert of heather, trees being entirely absent save for a windbreak at the one solitary building.

The Caldbeck and Uldale Fells are more appropriately classed as hills than as rough mountains, having smooth rounded slopes, an absence of rock and few defined ridges. The whole of these uplands is a vast sheep pasture, without the obstruction of walls and fences and free from natural hazards. (Carrock Fell wishes to be disassociated from this general description). Although relatively unexciting in scenic quality, however, these hills afford excellent tramping and an exhilarating freedom to wander at will, with added interest provided by the evidences, now decaying, of centuries of mining activity. The Caldbeck and Uldale Fells, remote, quieter and lonelier now than they have ever been since men first made their homes nearby, have never received much attention from visitors.   Guide books have ignored them completely. It is true that for excitement of outline and challenging situations and beauty of scenery they fall far short of the mountains to the south, yet there is a strong appeal about them not found in (or lost to) the more popular areas of Lakeland — they are unspoilt, serene and restful, a perfect sanctuary for birds and animals and fellwalkers who prefer to be away from crowds, even though this means also being away from ice-cream and pop and crisps. Oh, and juke-boxes.

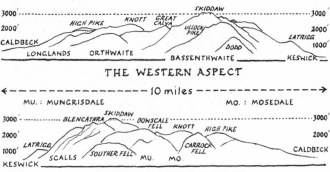

THE WESTERN ASPECT

THE EASTERN ASPECT

Roads of one sort or another completely encircle the Northern Fells, ringing their bases but touching 1000' in the north, and these have been adopted in this book as defining the limits of the territory to be described. Outside, all around, is a richly wooded, fertile countryside, everywhere occupied by little communities who are busily engaged in farming their land, not in providing caravan sites, refreshment and lodging for holiday makers. Back o' Skidda' especially is another world, a place that hasn't changed.

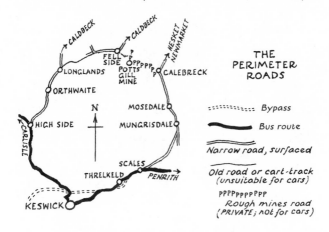

THE
PERIMETER
ROADS

:::::::::::: Bypass

—— Bus route

Narrow road, surfaced

Old road or cart-track
(unsuitable for cars)

PPPPpppPPPP
Rough mines road
(PRIVATE; not for cars)

Keswick is, with the help of buses, the best single base of operations, and there is no lack of accommodation elsewhere around the southern arc of these fells, from the foot of Bassenthwaite to Scales. Around the northern arc, however, there is very little — and even this little is not adequately brought to the notice of those who are seeking a refuge, the reason being that so few are. There are no hotels, no guest houses. It should therefore be mentioned that *limited* accommodation *may* be found on the perimeter *by enquiry* at Mosedale and at the Mill Inn in Mungrisdale, and, a short distance away, at Ireby, Hesket Newmarket and Whelpo (which is near Caldbeck).

THE NORTHERN FELLS
Natural Boundaries

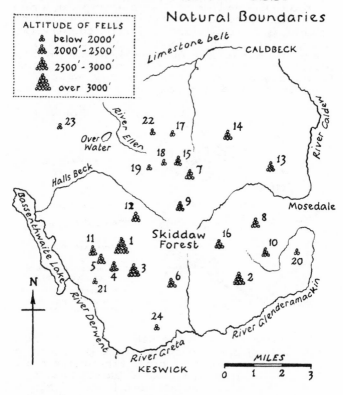

ALTITUDE OF FELLS
- 🔺 below 2000'
- 🔺 2000'-2500'
- 🔺 2500'-3000'
- 🔺 over 3000'

CALDBECK

Limestone belt

River Ellen

Over Water

Halls Beck

Bassenthwaite Lake

River Derwent

River Caldew

Mosedale

Skiddaw Forest

N

River Glenderamackin

River Greta

KESWICK

MILES
0 1 2 3

1: SKIDDAW
2: BLENCATHRA
3: SKIDDAW LITTLE MAN
4: CARL SIDE
5: LONG SIDE
6: LONSCALE FELL
7: KNOTT
8: BOWSCALE FELL
9: GREAT CALVA
10: BANNERDALE CRAGS
11: ULLOCK PIKE
12: BAKESTALL
13: CARROCK FELL
14: HIGH PIKE
15: GREAT SCA FELL
16: MUNGRISDALE COMMON
17: BRAE FELL
18: MEAL FELL
19: GREAT COCKUP
20: SOUTHER FELL
21: DODD
22: LONGLANDS FELL
23: BINSEY
24: LATRIGG

THE NORTHERN FELLS

in the order of their appearance in this book

<table>
<thead>
<tr><th colspan="4">Reference to map opposite</th><th></th><th>Altitude in feet</th></tr>
<tr><th>over 3000'</th><th>2500-3000'</th><th>2000-2500'</th><th>below 2000'</th><th></th><th></th></tr>
</thead>
<tbody>
<tr><td></td><td></td><td>12</td><td></td><td>.. BAKESTALL ..</td><td>2208</td></tr>
<tr><td></td><td></td><td>10</td><td></td><td>.. BANNERDALE CRAGS ..</td><td>2241</td></tr>
<tr><td></td><td></td><td></td><td>23</td><td>.. BINSEY ..</td><td>1466</td></tr>
<tr><td></td><td>2</td><td></td><td></td><td>.. BLENCATHRA ..</td><td>2847</td></tr>
<tr><td></td><td></td><td>8</td><td></td><td>.. BOWSCALE FELL ..</td><td>2306</td></tr>
<tr><td></td><td></td><td></td><td>17</td><td>.. BRAE FELL ..</td><td>1920</td></tr>
<tr><td></td><td></td><td>4</td><td></td><td>.. CARL SIDE ..</td><td>2447</td></tr>
<tr><td></td><td></td><td>13</td><td></td><td>.. CARROCK FELL ..</td><td>2169</td></tr>
<tr><td></td><td></td><td></td><td>21</td><td>.. DODD ..</td><td>1647</td></tr>
<tr><td></td><td></td><td>9</td><td></td><td>.. GREAT CALVA ..</td><td>2265</td></tr>
<tr><td></td><td></td><td></td><td>19</td><td>.. GREAT COCKUP ..</td><td>1726</td></tr>
<tr><td></td><td></td><td>15</td><td></td><td>.. GREAT SCA FELL ..</td><td>2136</td></tr>
<tr><td></td><td></td><td>14</td><td></td><td>.. HIGH PIKE ..</td><td>2157</td></tr>
<tr><td></td><td></td><td>7</td><td></td><td>.. KNOTT ..</td><td>2329</td></tr>
<tr><td></td><td></td><td></td><td>24</td><td>.. LATRIGG ..</td><td>1203</td></tr>
<tr><td></td><td></td><td></td><td>22</td><td>.. LONGLANDS FELL ..</td><td>1585</td></tr>
<tr><td></td><td></td><td>5</td><td></td><td>.. LONG SIDE ..</td><td>2405</td></tr>
<tr><td></td><td></td><td>6</td><td></td><td>.. LONSCALE FELL ..</td><td>2344</td></tr>
<tr><td></td><td></td><td></td><td>18</td><td>.. MEAL FELL ..</td><td>1804</td></tr>
<tr><td></td><td></td><td>16</td><td></td><td>MUNGRISDALE COMMON</td><td>2077</td></tr>
<tr><td>1</td><td></td><td></td><td></td><td>.. SKIDDAW ..</td><td>3053</td></tr>
<tr><td></td><td>3</td><td></td><td></td><td>SKIDDAW LITTLE MAN</td><td>2837</td></tr>
<tr><td></td><td></td><td></td><td>20</td><td>.. SOUTHER FELL ..</td><td>1713</td></tr>
<tr><td></td><td></td><td>11</td><td></td><td>.. ULLOCK PIKE ..</td><td>2230</td></tr>
<tr><td>1</td><td>2</td><td>13</td><td>8</td><td></td><td></td></tr>
<tr><td colspan="4">24</td><td></td><td></td></tr>
</tbody>
</table>

Each fell is the subject of a separate chapter

Bakestall

2208'

Orthwaite
Bassenthwaite
High
Side
GREAT
CALVA
BAKESTALL
Skiddaw
House
SKIDDAW

MILES
0 1 2 3 4

from Brockle Crag

NATURAL FEATURES

Even the most diligent student of maps of Lakeland is not likely to have noticed the name of Bakestall and few walkers will have heard of it. Bakestall (the name of a summit rather than of a fell) is a rough raised platform on the sprawling north flank of Skiddaw, merely a halt in the easy slopes and barely qualifying for recognition as a separate top. It would pass almost without comment but for its command of a scene of extra-ordinary interest: a unique combination of natural features that arrests the attention all the more because it is unexpected, startling and seemingly out of place amongst the smooth heathery uplands all around. The summit is perched high above a steepening slope from which has been scooped an enormous hollow, as though a giant hand had clawed at and ripped away the fellside, leaving a rim of crags along the line of cleavage. This escarpment, a rising horseshoe of cliffs half-a-mile in length, is Dead Crags, a dark yet colourful rampart of buttresses and jutting aretes patched a vivid green with bilberry and brown and purple with ling. But grander even than this strange and silent crater are the magnificent waterfalls in the precipitous wooded ravine at its base, where Dash Beck, issuing from the vast waste of Skiddaw Forest, leaps exultantly at its first glimpse of gentle pastures and plunges over the lip in a series of falls, one following another in a mighty torment of roaring and thrashing waters — the finest spectacle of its kind in the district. This is Whitewater Dash, also known as Dash Falls, a tremendous sight in spate, when the thunder of its great cataracts can be heard miles away down the valley. The brave little road to Skiddaw House, climbing sinuously in and out of the hollow to disappear over the skyline, is the one evidence of man, but instead of intruding, as roads so often do, this desolate track merely adds to the loneliness of the scene. On the west, Bakestall is clearly defined by Dead Beck, which flows down a rough and rocky gutter to join Dash Beck en route for Bassenthwaite Lake.

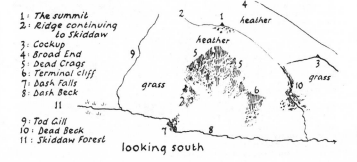

1 : The summit
2 : Ridge continuing to Skiddaw
3 : Cockup
4 : Broad End
5 : Dead Crags
6 : Terminal cliff
7 : Dash Falls
8 : Dash Beck
9 : Tod Gill
10 : Dead Beck
11 : Skiddaw Forest

looking south

MAP

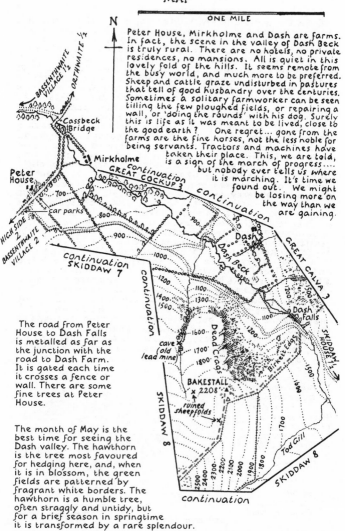

ONE MILE

Peter House, Mirkholme and Dash are farms. In fact, the scene in the valley of Dash Beck is truly rural. There are no hotels, no private residences, no mansions. All is quiet in this lovely fold of the hills. It seems remote from the busy world, and much more to be preferred. Sheep and cattle graze undisturbed in pastures that tell of good husbandry over the centuries. Sometimes a solitary farmworker can be seen tilling the few ploughed fields, or repairing a wall, or 'doing the rounds' with his dog. Surely this is life as it was meant to be lived, close to the good earth? One regret... gone from the farms are the fine horses, not the less noble for being servants. Tractors and machines have taken their place. This, we are told, is a sign of the march of progress.... but nobody ever tells us where it is marching. It's time we found out. We might be losing more on the way than we are gaining.

BASSENTHWAITE VILLAGE 1½

ORTHWAITE ½

Cassbeck Bridge

Mirkholme

Peter House

continuation GREAT COCKUP 3

continuation

car parks

700

800

900

HIGH SIDE 2

BASSENTHWAITE VILLAGE 2

continuation SKIDDAW 7

900

1000

continuation

1200

1100

1300

1400

1500

1600

cave (old lead mine)

1700

1800

Dead Crags

Dash

Dash Beck

GREAT CALVA 3

Dash Falls

SKIDDAW 11

1200

1100

1200

1500

Birkett Edge

BAKESTALL × 2208

ruined sheepfolds

SKIDDAW 8

2400

2500

2300

2200

2100

2000

1900

1800

1700

1600

Tod Gill

SKIDDAW 8

continuation

The road from Peter House to Dash Falls is metalled as far as the junction with the road to Dash Farm. It is gated each time it crosses a fence or wall. There are some fine trees at Peter House.

The month of May is the best time for seeing the Dash valley. The hawthorn is the tree most favoured for hedging here, and, when it is in blossom, the green fields are patterned by fragrant white borders. The hawthorn is a humble tree, often straggly and untidy, but for a brief season in springtime it is transformed by a rare splendour.

ASCENT FROM THE ROAD TO SKIDDAW HOUSE
900 feet of ascent : ⅔ mile from Dash Falls
(1750 feet, 4⅔ miles from High Side or Bassenthwaite Village)

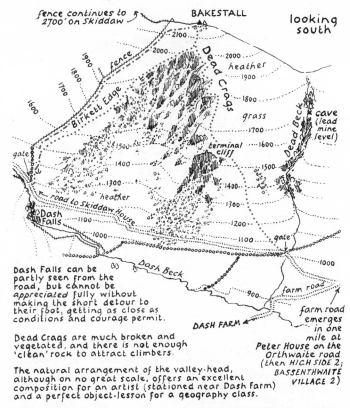

fence continues to 2700' on Skiddaw

BAKESTALL

looking south

Dead Crags

fence

Birkett Edge

heather

grass

terminal cliff

Dead Beck

cave (lead mine level)

gate

heather

road to Skiddaw House

Dash Falls

gate

Dash Beck

farm road

farm road emerges in one mile at Peter House on the Orthwaite road (then HIGH SIDE 2; BASSENTHWAITE VILLAGE 2)

DASH FARM

Dash Falls can be partly seen from the road, but cannot be *appreciated* fully without making the short detour to their foot, getting as close as conditions and courage permit.

Dead Crags are much broken and vegetated, and there is not enough 'clean' rock to attract climbers.

The natural arrangement of the valley-head, although on no great scale, offers an excellent composition for an artist (stationed near Dash farm) and a perfect object-lesson for a geography class.

Two routes are given, that by Birkett Edge being the better for views of Dead Crags, and convenient for an easy visit to Dash Falls. (This is also, incidentally, the best way to Skiddaw from any point on the rough Skiddaw House road) The more direct route, going up steeply between the terminal cliff and Dead Beck from the gate in the intake wall, is less interesting; note that this route should not be used for descent in mist, when only sheer good luck could prevent one from running foul of crags.

THE SUMMIT

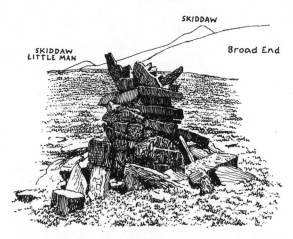

The summits of the Northern Fells are not, as a rule, distinguished by handsome and imposing cairns, due more to a lack of suitable building material in the vicinity, no doubt, than to a lack of industry on the part of visitors. The summit of Bakestall, where good rough rock outcropping amongst the heather served to provide the cairn illustrated (which has now become a pile of stones), is uncharacteristic. A smaller cairn to the north-west of the main cairn indicates a better viewpoint overlooking a very pleasant pastoral scene: the Dash Valley. A third cairn marks the highest point of the summit, which occurs 100 yards south of the main cairn at the angle of the fence.

DESCENTS : All descents must of necessity be to the road to Skiddaw House skirting the base of the fell, and this is quickly reached by following first the fence down Birkett Edge (detour to the left to see the combe of Dead Crags) and then a short wall. *In mist*, there is no safe alternative, but in clear weather the steep slope may be descended directly to the rim of Dead Crags (taking care not to panic the sheep grazing there) where the cliff-top may be followed down to the right to Birkett Edge.

If it is desired to locate the old mine level in the Dead Beck ravine on the way down to the road descend the easy slope of heather north-west to the beck. The 'cave' is in the far bank directly beneath the first

A : Dead Crags
B : Birkett Edge
C : Dead Beck
D : to Skiddaw

rowan trees and a few feet above the stream-bed. The ravine becomes too rough to follow in comfort lower down but the road may be reached by a detour on the steep grass of either bank. It should be noted that on this route nothing will be seen of Dead Crags or Dash Falls, the cave and ravine, although interesting, being poor compensation.

THE VIEW

Bakestall is very much in the shadow of Skiddaw, and the view is circumscribed accordingly, but there is a restricted glimpse of distant fells over the deep Glenderaterra valley.   North-west, however, there is an open view to the Solway and the Scottish hills, a prospect greatly enhanced by the sharp fall of the fellside to the tranquil valley below.

Principal Fells

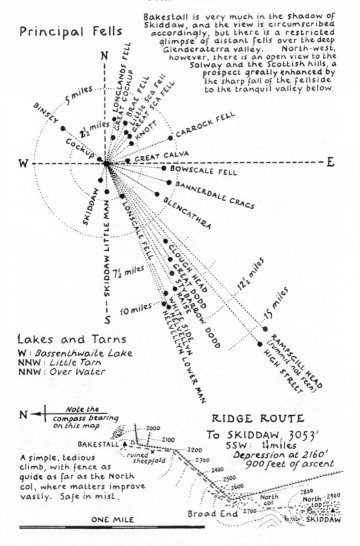

5 miles

BINSEY

2½ miles

Cockup

GREAT LONGLANDS FELL
GREAT COCKUP
BRAE FELL
Little Sca Fell
GREAT SCA FELL
KNOTT

CARROCK FELL

GREAT CALVA

BOWSCALE FELL

BANNERDALE CRAGS

BLENCATHRA

SKIDDAW

SKIDDAW LITTLE MAN

LONSCALE FELL

7½ miles

10 miles

CLOUGH HEAD
GREAT DODD
STYBARROW DODD
RAISE
WHITE SIDE
HELVELLYN
HELVELLYN LOWER MAN

12½ miles

15 miles

RAMPSGILL HEAD
(summit not seen)
HIGH STREET

Lakes and Tarns
W : Bassenthwaite Lake
NNW : Little Tarn
NNW : Over Water

Note the compass bearing on this map

RIDGE ROUTE

To SKIDDAW, 3053'
SSW : 1½ miles
Depression at 2160'
900 feet of ascent

BAKESTALL ▲
ruined sheepfold

A simple, tedious climb, with fence as guide as far as the North col, where matters improve vastly. Safe in mist.

2000
2100
2200
2300
2400
2500
2600
2700
2800
2900

North col

North top

Broad End

SKIDDAW ▲

ONE MILE

a *Bakestall* portfolio

Dead Crags, from *Birkett Edge*

as seen on the approach along the Skiddaw House road

The head of the Dash valley

as seen from the top of Dead Crags

The Terminal
Cliffs of
Dead Crags
from Birkett Edge;
Binsey in the
background

Blencathra from the summit of Bakestall

The old mine level
in the ravine
of Dead Beck
(Cave entrance
5' x 3', but
flooded)

Dash Falls
(Whitewater Dash
on Ordnance maps)

There are many finer
individual waterfalls
in Lakeland, but for
a grand succession of
falls the first place
must undoubtedly be
given to Dash Falls.
  Little more than half
the total height is shown
in the illustration.

Bannerdale Crags

2241'

east ridge

BOWSCALE FELL ▲
Mungrisdale ●
▲ BANNERDALE
CRAGS
▲ BLENCATHRA
● Scales
● Threlkeld

MILES

0 1 2 3 4

*from the ridge leading
to Bowscale Fell*

NATURAL FEATURES

Bannerdale Crags, to be appreciated fully, should be approached from the pleasant village of Mungrisdale, for only in this direction, eastwards, is revealed the mile-long rim of cliffs that gives the fell a name and is its one great scenic attraction. This escarpment is interrupted by a pronounced spur, the east ridge, but otherwise falls very steeply to the little side-valley of Bannerdale, which is uninhabited, uncultivated and — since the closing of the Lead Mine — unfrequented, much of it being a swamp. Few traces now remain of the old mine at the foot of the crags, nature having cloaked the ravages of man with her own processes.

Westwards and southwards mainly grassy slopes, with one extensive fan of scree, fall steeply from the plateau to the headwaters of the River Glenderamackin; beyond is the towering mass of Blencathra.   The river pursues an erratic course and bounds the fell on three sides, but to the north high land continues to Bowscale Fell.

Few visitors to Lakeland will have seen the crags, which turn their back on the district and are quite concealed from all places and viewpoints of popular resort.   They are worth a visit, as is delightful Mungrisdale, an alpine old-world village that has so far escaped the invasions of tourists. But one must choose between stout boots and wet feet on the lonely march to Bannerdale.

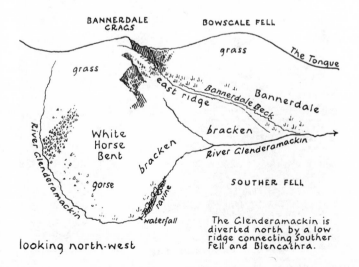

looking north-west

The Glenderamackin is diverted north by a low ridge connecting Souther Fell and Blencathra.

MAP

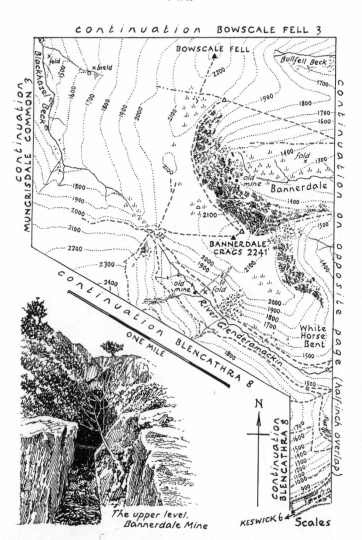

continuation BOWSCALE FELL 3

BOWSCALE FELL

Bullfell Beck

continuation MUNGRISDALE COMMON 3

Blackhazel Beck

x fold

x field

old mine

Bannerdale

fold

BANNERDALE CRAGS 2241

old mine

x fold

River Glenderamackin

White Horse Bent

continuation on opposite page (half-inch overlap)

continuation BLENCATHRA 8

ONE MILE

N

continuation BLENCATHRA 8

KESWICK 6

Scales

The upper level, Bannerdale Mine

MAP

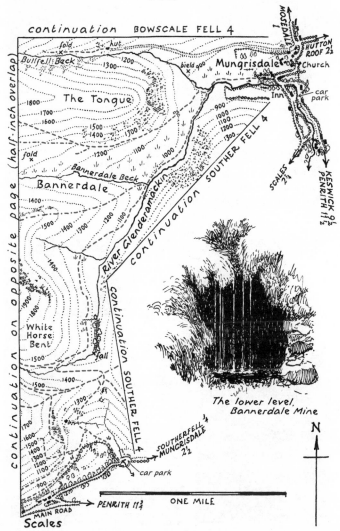

continuation   BOWSCALE FELL 4

continuation on opposite page (half-inch overlap)

MOSEDALE

HUTTON ROOF 2½

Church

Mungrisdale

car park

fold   hut

Bullfell Beck

The Tongue

bield

Inn

Bannerdale Beck

Bannerdale

River Glenderamackin

continuation SOUTHER FELL 4

SCALES 2¼

KESWICK 11½

PENRITH

White Horse Bent

fall

continuation SOUTHER FELL 4

The lower level,
Bannerdale Mine

SOUTHERFELL ¾
MUNGRISDALE 2½

car park

PENRITH 11¾   ONE MILE

MAIN ROAD

Scales

N

Bannerdale Crags from Mungrisdale

right :
*The east ridge,
with the summit
to the right*

below :
*The summit from
the final tower of
the east ridge*

Between the east ridge and the main
mass of the summit is a long, steep
and rough scree-gully, to which the
attention of experienced scramblers
is directed. It looks interesting.

ASCENT FROM MUNGRISDALE
1500 feet of ascent : 2 (or 3) miles

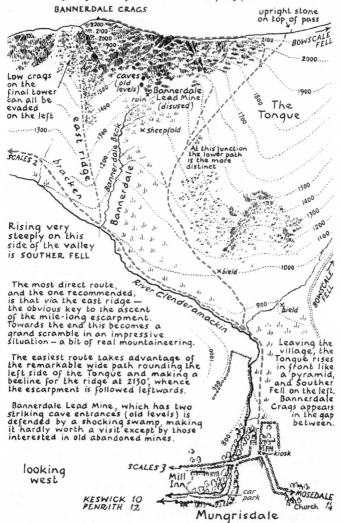

BANNERDALE CRAGS

upright stone on top of pass

2200
2100
2000
1900

BOWSCALE FELL

2100

2000

Low crags on the final tower can all be evaded on the left

1900

1500

caves (old levels)

Bannerdale Lead Mine (disused)

ruin

1800

The Tongue

1400

east ridge

1700

× sheepfold

At this junction the lower path is the more distinct

1300

bracken

1200

Bannerdale Beck

Bannerdale

1500

1400

1300

1200

1100

SCALES 2

Rising very steeply on this side of the valley is SOUTHER FELL

River Glenderamackin

× bield

1000

900

× bield

BOWSCALE FELL

The most direct route, and the one recommended, is that via the east ridge — the obvious key to the ascent of the mile-long escarpment. Towards the end this becomes a grand scramble in an impressive situation — a bit of real mountaineering.

The easiest route takes advantage of the remarkable wide path rounding the left side of the Tongue and making a beeline for the ridge at 2150', whence the escarpment is followed leftwards.

Bannerdale Lead Mine, which has two striking cave entrances (old levels) is defended by a shocking swamp, making it hardly worth a visit except by those interested in old abandoned mines.

Leaving the village, the Tongue rises in front like a pyramid, and Souther Fell on the left. Bannerdale Crags appears in the gap between.

1000

900

800

looking west

SCALES 3

Mill Inn

car park

kiosk

KESWICK 10
PENRITH 12

MOSEDALE
Church 1¼

Mungrisdale

ASCENT FROM SCALES
1550 feet of ascent : 2½ miles

After crossing the footbridge keep to the left when ascending White Horse Bent to enjoy the fine end-on view of Sharp Edge with the wild hollow of Scales Tarn below to the left. This is one of the best mountain scenes in the district, and is exclusive to this unfrequented viewpoint.

From the col *descend left* by a good wide path (not shown in the diagram) to cross the Glenderamackin at a footbridge. *Note well that the path is not clear at the col.* Ignore the obvious path curving left and rising; instead take a grassy trod bifurcating right 20 paces beyond the second rockstep. In 40 yards turn left to the col. Then go straight ahead along a clear path going down to the footbridge.

Scales (760')

looking north-east

This is a tedious climb, fully justified by the striking and unusual views of Blencathra during the ascent and by the final surprising rim of crags.

THE SUMMIT

BOWSCALE FELL

This summit is distinguished by the Ordnance Survey's rare use of the word *Curricks* (on their large-scale maps), but the patient enquirer who, having searched his dictionary and drawn a blank, has toiled up here to find out what exactly a currick is will discover only two quite ordinary cairns. The main cairn is made of flat stones laid horizontally around a vertical stone which is leaning slightly.   Currick or no currick, it is excellently sited near the edge of the great downfall into Bannerdale, and the crater-like rim in view to the north is magnificent. There is a second cairn on the highest point which is no more than a pile of stones.

DESCENTS : Two paths leave the summit to the north-east. The one to the right is more spectacular, but the one to the left is safer.   The two paths eventually reunite, and from this point onwards there is a continuous path all the way to Mungrisdale.   For Scales look for the path that heads west to the Glenderamackin col and turn left. The broad south slope is everywhere easy, and a quick way off. Descent by the east ridge is also practicable, and safe in mist if the top of it can be located, but the ridge can be dangerous when under snow or ice.

PLAN OF SUMMIT

THE VIEW

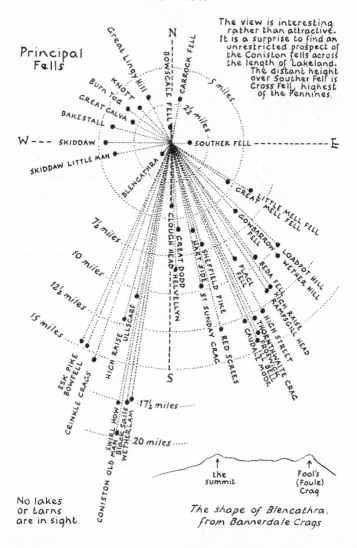

The view is interesting rather than attractive. It is a surprise to find an unrestricted prospect of the Coniston fells across the length of Lakeland. The distant height over Souther Fell is Cross Fell, highest of the Pennines.

Principal Fells

N
BOWSCALE FELL
CARROCK FELL
5 miles
Great Lingy Hill
KNOTT
Burn Tod
GREAT CALVA
2½ miles
BAKESTALL
W --- SKIDDAW
SOUTHER FELL ------------ E
SKIDDAW LITTLE MAN
BLENCATHRA

LITTLE MELL FELL
GREAT MELL FELL
GOWBARROW FELL
LOADPOT HILL
WETHER HILL
BEDA FELL
HIGH RAISE
RAMPSGILL HEAD
PLACE FELL
HIGH STREET
THORNTHWAITE CRAG
FROSWICK
ILL BELL
CAUDALE MOOR

GREAT DODD
CLOUGH HEAD
HELVELLYN
SHEFFIELD PIKE
HART SIDE
ST SUNDAY CRAG
RED SCREES

7½ miles
10 miles
12½ miles
15 miles
HIGH RAISE
ULLSCARF

ESK PIKE
BOWFELL
CRINKLE CRAGS

S

17½ miles
SWIRL HOW
CONISTON OLD MAN
BLACK SAILS
WETHERLAM
20 miles

No lakes or tarns are in sight.

the summit
Fool's (Foule) Crag

The shape of Blencathra, from Bannerdale Crags

RIDGE ROUTES

To BOWSCALE FELL, 2306':
1¼ miles : NW, then NNE
Depression at 2060'
250 feet of ascent

An easy stroll, calling for some skill
in negotiating swampy ground. Keep
to the edge of the escarpment, which
is drier and has striking views.

To BLENCATHRA, 2847'
1½ miles : W, then SW and S
Depression at 2010'
850 feet of ascent

A direct line is not practicable.
Aim for the Glenderamackin col
and ascend the grassy ridge
rising directly opposite: this
has an interesting 'back' view
of Sharp Edge, but the great
feature of the route is Foule
Crag, which is skirted to
the right, the saddle
above being reached
by a stiff pull.

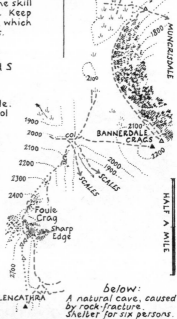

below:
A mature tree grows out
of the chimney-breast of
the ruined hut.

below:
A natural cave, caused
by rock-fracture.
Shelter for six persons.

Odd features at Bannerdale Mine

Binsey

1466'

from Robin Hood, near Bassenthwaite

Private path in Binsey Plantation

• Ireby

High
Ireby •   Uldale •

▲ BINSEY
• Bewaldeth

Bassenthwaite

MILES
0   1   2   3

NATURAL FEATURES

Binsey is the odd man out. This gentle hill rises beyond the circular perimeter of the Northern Fells, detached and solitary, like a dunce set apart from the class. It is of no great height, is well within the category of Sunday afternoon strolls, has an easy slope just right for exercising the dog or the children, is without precipices and pitfalls, never killed or injured anybody, breeds hares instead of foxes, and is generally of benign appearance. Yet it is much too good to be omitted from these pages.

For one thing it is a most excellent station for appraising the Northern Fells as a preliminary to their exploration. For another, it is a viewpoint of outstanding merit. For another, it possesses a grand little summit with a once-important but now-forgotten history. For another, its rocks are volcanic, not slate as are those of all neighbour fells.

Binsey occupies the extreme north-west corner of the Lake District. Beyond is the coastal plain, then the sea, then Scotland; nothing intervenes to interrupt this sweeping panorama. What a domain, and what a throne to view it from!

the summit ridge, looking east

West Crag

MAP

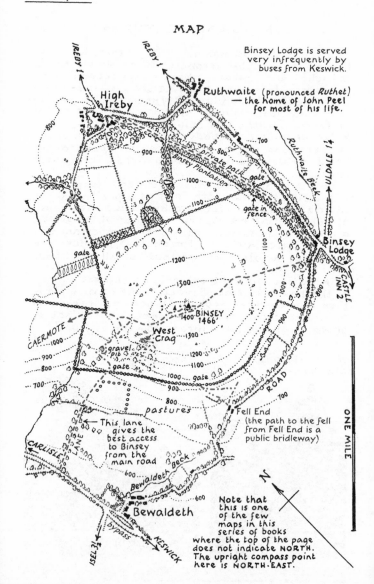

Binsey Lodge is served very infrequently by buses from Keswick.

Ruthwaite (pronounced *Ruthet*) — the home of John Peel for most of his life.

High Ireby

IREBY 1
IREBY 1
ULDALE 1¼

Ruthwaite Beck

Binsey Plantation

private path

gate
gate in fence

Binsey Lodge

CASTLE INN 2

gate

CAERMOTE

West Crag

BINSEY 1466'

gravel pit

gate
gate

ROAD

pastures

Fell End
(the path to the fell from Fell End is a public bridleway)

This lane gives the best access to Binsey from the main road

CARLISLE

ONE MILE

Bewaldeth Beck

Bewaldeth

bypass
KESWICK
ISEL 2¼

N

Note that this is one of the few maps in this series of books where the top of the page does not indicate NORTH. The upright compass point here is NORTH-EAST.

ASCENT FROM BEWALDETH
950 feet of ascent : 1¾ miles

The summit of Binsey is remarkable for the ancient tumulus
crowning the highest point: this is now accompanied
by a modern cairn. An Ordnance Survey column
stands between the two, and no fewer
than four wind-shelters have been
fashioned from the abundant
stones of the tumulus.

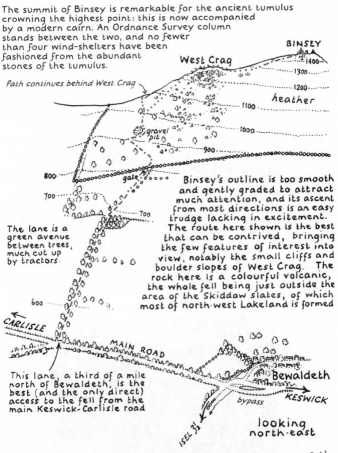

Path continues behind West Crag

Binsey's outline is too smooth
and gently graded to attract
much attention, and its ascent
from most directions is an easy
trudge lacking in excitement.
The route here shown is the best
that can be contrived, bringing
the few features of interest into
view, notably the small cliffs and
boulder slopes of West Crag. The
rock here is a colourful volcanic,
the whole fell being just outside the
area of the Skiddaw slates, of which
most of north-west Lakeland is formed

The lane is a
green avenue
between trees,
much cut up
by tractors.

This lane, a third of a mile
north of Bewaldeth, is the
best (and the only direct)
access to the fell from the
main Keswick-Carlisle road

looking
north-east

This is a pleasant little climb at any season of the
year, but on a warm clear day in August the purple
heather and glorious panoramic view together make
Binsey one of the best places for spending an hour of
undisturbed peace and enjoyment. Or take the family.

ASCENT FROM BINSEY LODGE
620 feet of ascent : 1 mile

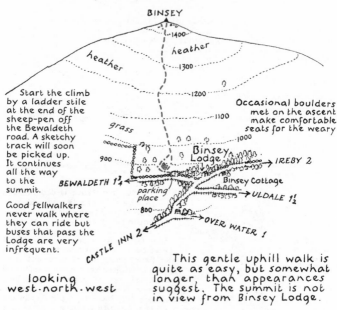

BINSEY

1400

heather

heather

1300

1200

heather

1100

grass

1000

900

Binsey Lodge

IREBY 2

Start the climb by a ladder stile at the end of the sheep-pen off the Bewaldeth road. A sketchy track will soon be picked up. It continues all the way to the summit.

Occasional boulders met on the ascent make comfortable seats for the weary

BEWALDETH 1¾

parking place

Binsey Cottage

ULDALE 1½

Good fellwalkers never walk where they can ride but buses that pass the Lodge are very infrequent.

800

CASTLE INN 2

OVER WATER 1

looking
west·north·west

This gentle uphill walk is quite as easy, but somewhat longer, than appearances suggest. The summit is not in view from Binsey Lodge.

Binsey Lodge

ASCENT FROM HIGH IREBY
700 feet of ascent · 1½ miles

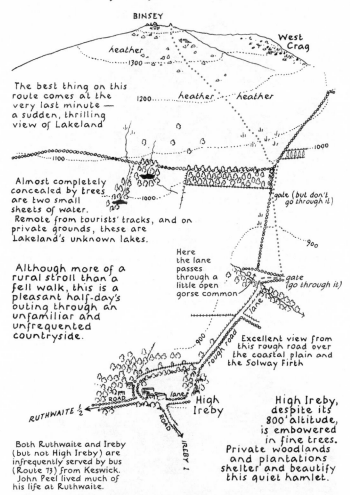

BINSEY

West Crag

heather
1300

The best thing on this route comes at the very last minute — a sudden, thrilling view of Lakeland

1200   heather   heather

1000

1100

Almost completely concealed by trees are two small sheets of water.
Remote from tourists' tracks, and on private grounds, these are Lakeland's unknown lakes.

1000

gate (but don't go through it)

900

Here the lane passes through a little open gorse common

gate (go through it)

Although more of a rural stroll than a fell walk, this is a pleasant half-day's outing through an unfamiliar and unfrequented countryside.

lane

900

Excellent view from this rough road over the coastal plain and the Solway Firth

rough road

RUTHWAITE ½ ←

ROAD

lane

High Ireby

ROAD

IREBY 1

High Ireby, despite its 800' altitude, is embowered in fine trees. Private woodlands and plantations shelter and beautify this quiet hamlet.

Both Ruthwaite and Ireby (but not High Ireby) are infrequently served by bus (Route 73) from Keswick. John Peel lived much of his life at Ruthwaite.

looking south-south-west

THE SUMMIT

The summit is the best part of the fell, taking the form of a small ridge surmounted by a great heap of stones (in fact a tumulus) with an Ordnance Survey column alongside and a modern cairn beyond it. The column bears a plaque dated 1999 saying that it forms part of the O.S. National G.P.S. Network. There is a lower cairn to the north-west. With the added attraction of an excellent view, this summit is worthy of a greater mountain than Binsey.

DESCENTS : All routes of descent are simple. At West Crag there is a little roughness. In mist, bearings can be taken at the summit: the modern cairn is east of the Survey column. Binsey Lodge (which is not in sight) is reached by aiming for Over Water (which is).

On the top of Binsey..........

..... Prehistoric Tumulus and Ancient Briton

THE VIEW

The Lakeland segment is only a third of the whole, but is full of interest, especially to the south, where again the surprising fact is demonstrated, by the unobstructed view of the faraway Coniston fells, that the central part of the district is generally of lower altitude than the perimeter.

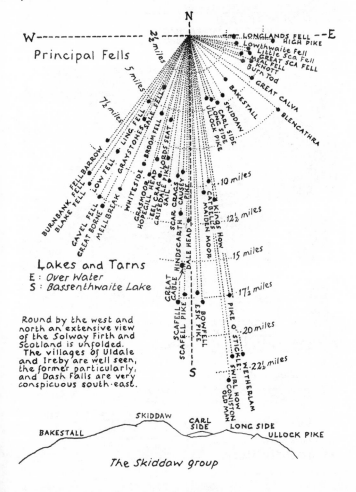

Principal Fells

Lakes and Tarns
E : Over Water
S : Bassenthwaite Lake

Round by the west and north an extensive view of the Solway Firth and Scotland is unfolded.
The villages of Uldale and Ireby are well seen, the former particularly, and Dash Falls are very conspicuous south-east.

The Skiddaw group

Blencathra

2847'

from Mungrisdale road end

better known,
until recently,
as Saddleback

MUNGRISDALE 2
HESKET NEWMARKET 9

BOWSCALE FELL ▲
Mungrisdale ●
SKIDDAW ▲
● Skiddaw
House
SOUTHER FELL ▲
▲ BLENCATHRA
LONSCALE
FELL ▲
● Scales
● Threlkeld

MILES
0 1 2 3 4

NATURAL FEATURES

Blencathra is one of the grandest objects in Lakeland. And one of the best known.   Seen from the south-west, the popular aspect, the mountain rises steeply and in isolation above the broad green fields of Threlkeld, a feature being the great sweeping curve leaping out of the depths to a lofty summit-ridge, where the skyline then proceeds in a succession of waves to a sharp peak before descending, again in a graceful curve, to the valley pastures far to the east.

This is a mountain that compels attention, even from those dull people whose eyes are not habitually lifted to the hills.   To artists and photographers it is an obvious subject for their craft; to sightseers passing along the main road or former railway between Keswick and Penrith, its influence is magnetic; to the dalesfolk it is the eternal background to their lives, there at birth, there at death. But most of all it is a mountaineers' mountain.

continued

from Castlerigg Stone Circle

NATURAL FEATURES

continued

The supreme feature of Blencathra, the one that invests the mountain with special grandeur, is the imposing southern front, a remarkable example of the effect of elemental natural forces. It forms a tremendous facade above the valley, and makes a dark, towering backcloth to a stage of farmsteads and cottages, of emerald pastures and meadows and woodlands along its base. There is nothing inviting in these shattered cliffs and petrified rivers of stone that seem to hold a perpetual threat over the little community below: the scene arrests attention, but intimidates and repels. Few who gaze upon these desolate walls are likely to feel any inclination and inspiration to scramble up through their arid, stony wildernesses to the contorted skyline so high above. Consequently the area has remained a no-man's-land for walkers, even though closely within sight of road and railway travellers. Blencathra is ascended thousands of times a year but rarely by ways up the southern front. This is a pity. Here is the greatness of the mountain. Its detail is a fascinating study.

west   east

THE SOUTHERN FRONT
3¼ miles

The outer slopes, rising on the west and east flanks from valley level to the uppermost escarpment below the summit ridge, are smoothly curved, massive and yet so symmetrical that they might well have been designed by a master architect to supply a perfect balance to the structure. These two outliers are Blease Fell and Scales Fell.

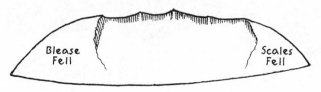

Blease
Fell   Scales
Fell

continued

NATURAL FEATURES

continued

From their extremities the slopes of Blease Fell and Scales Fell extend uneventfully towards each other across the front until, suddenly and dramatically, they are halted at the edge of a scene of devastation, the wreckage of what appears to have been, in ages past, a tremendous convulsion that tore the heart out of the mountain and left the ruins seemingly in a state of tottering collapse. The picture is chaotic: a great upheaval of ridges and pinnacles rising out of dead wastes of scree and penetrated by choked gullies and ravines, the whole crazily tilted through 2000' of altitude. Even in this area of confusion and disorder, however, Nature has sculptured a distinct pattern.
Four watercourses emerge from surrounding debris to escape to the valley:

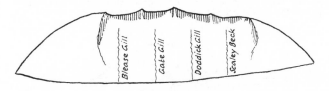

Between the four ravines, three lofty spurs, alike in main characteristics, thrust far out; narrow and frail where they leave the solid mass of the mountain, they widen into substantial buttresses as they descend to the valley. It is as though a giant hand had clawed at the mountain, each finger scooping out a deep hollow, with narrow strips of ground left undisturbed between.

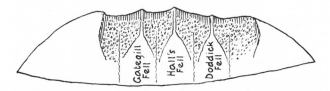

There are thus five buttresses on the southern front, each named as a separate fell. The two outer are grassy, with flat tops; the three in the middle are heathery and rise to distinct peaks, the central one being Blencathra's summit. Such is the pattern of the southern front.

continued

NATURAL FEATURES
continued

The other flanks of the mountain are mainly smooth and rounded, although on the east side Scales Fell breaks its curve to form the hollow of Mousthwaite Comb. But, from the summit, high ground continues north across a slight depression (the Saddle) to the prominent top of Foule Crag, this being the outline from which the alternative name, Saddleback, derives. A distinct ridge curves away to the Glenderamackin col from Foule Crag, while a rocky spur goes off to the east, this latter being the well-known Sharp Edge, second in fame to Striding Edge on Helvellyn as a test for walkers. Deepset in the hollow between Sharp Edge and the main ridge is one of the most characteristic mountain tarns in the district, Scales Tarn.

It is interesting to note that although Blencathra lies well to the east of the axis of Lakeland, approximately 99% of its drainage joins the Derwent in the west, only a few drops being gathered by the Eden catchment.

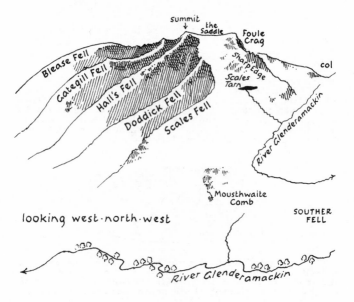

looking west·north·west

Blencathra joins Bowfell in the author's best half-dozen.

The summit escarpment

looking
west

from
Scales Fell
to the
summit

from
the summit
to Gategill
Fell Top

from
Gategill
Fell Top
to
Blease Fell

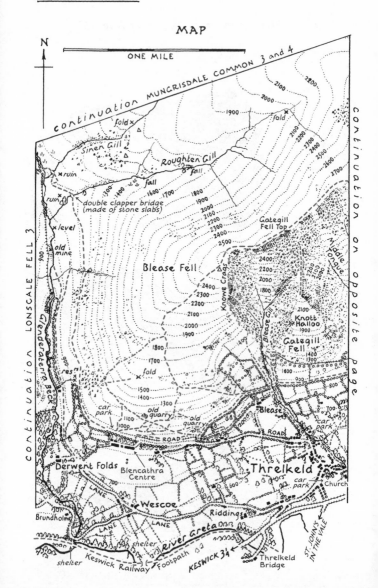

MAP

N

ONE MILE

continuation MUNCRISDALE COMMON 3 and 4

continuation on opposite page

continuation LONSCALE FELL 3

fold

Sinen Gill

Roughten Gill

fall

1900

fold

ruin

fall

2000
2100
2200
2400
2500
2600
2700

double clapper bridge
(made of stone slabs)

300
1400
1600
1700
1800
1900
2000
2100
2200
2300
2400
2500

ruin

level

old
mine

Gategill
Fell Top

Blease Fell

Knowe Crags

2400
2200
2000
1800

2400
2200
2000

Middle Tongue

900

2100

Knott
Halloo
1900

Glenderaterra Beck

res'r

fold

Blease G.

1400

Gategill
Fell
1400
1300

1600

1800
1700
1600
1500
1400
1300

800

700

car
park

old
quarry

old
quarry

Blease

ROAD

car
park

700

600

ROAD

continuation

Derwent Folds

Blencathra
Centre

700

Threlkeld

car
park
Church

LANE

Brundholm

Wescoe

Riddings

LANE

LANE

shelter

River Greta

ST. JOHN'S
IN THE VALE

shelter

Keswick Railway

Footpath

KESWICK 3¼

Threlkeld
Bridge

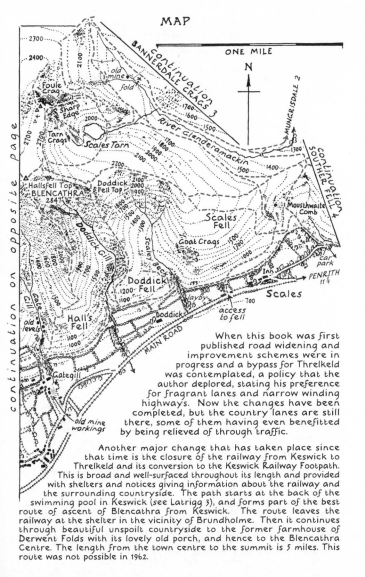

MAP

When this book was first published road widening and improvement schemes were in progress and a bypass for Threlkeld was contemplated, a policy that the author deplored, stating his preference for fragrant lanes and narrow winding highways. Now the changes have been completed, but the country lanes are still there, some of them having even benefitted by being relieved of through traffic.

Another major change that has taken place since that time is the closure of the railway from Keswick to Threlkeld and its conversion to the Keswick Railway Footpath. This is broad and well-surfaced throughout its length and provided with shelters and notices giving information about the railway and the surrounding countryside. The path starts at the back of the swimming pool in Keswick (see Latrigg 3), and forms part of the best route of ascent of Blencathra from Keswick. The route leaves the railway at the shelter in the vicinity of Brundholme. Then it continues through beautiful unspoilt countryside to the former farmhouse of Derwent Folds with its lovely old porch, and hence to the Blencathra Centre. The length from the town centre to the summit is 5 miles. This route was not possible in 1962.

ASCENT FROM THRELKELD
via ROUGHTEN GILL
2400 feet of ascent : 5 miles

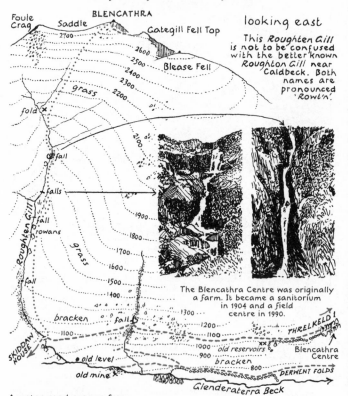

looking east

This *Roughten Gill* is not to be confused with the better known *Roughton Gill* near Caldbeck. Both names are pronounced 'Rowt'n'.

BLENCATHRA

Foule Crag

Saddle

Gategill Fell Top

2700

2600

2500

2400

2300

2200

Blease Fell

grass

fold ✕

2100

fall

falls

2000

fall

1900

rowans

1800

grass

1700

1600

1500

1400

Roughten Gill

fall

The Blencathra Centre was originally a farm. It became a sanitorium in 1904 and a field centre in 1990.

bracken

fall

1300

1200

1100

THRELKELD

SKIDDAW HOUSE

1100

1000 old reservoirs

900

bracken

xx

Blencathra Centre

• old level

800

old mine ✕

DERWENT FOLDS

Glenderaterra Beck

A motor-road goes up from Threlkeld to the car park at the Blencathra Centre and ends there. Its direction is continued by a public bridleway along the side of a wall. Use this.

For walkers who panic at the proximity of precipices and cannot face steep slopes, the roundabout route by Roughten Gill, which holds no terrors at all, is a good way to the top, but most people will find it unexciting and dreary. The best thing about it is delayed until the very end : the sudden thrilling view of Lakeland, which has been hidden during the climb.

ASCENT FROM THRELKELD
via BLEASE FELL
2450 feet of ascent : 2½ miles

looking north

Blease Fell

Gategill Fell Top

BLENCATHRA

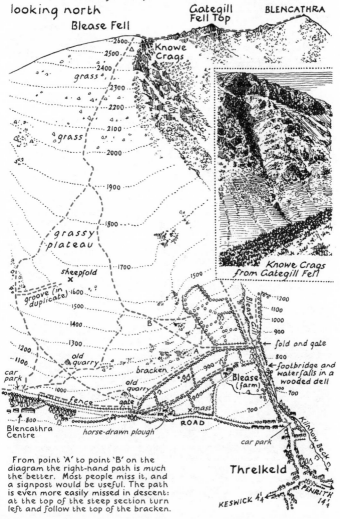

2600
2500
2400
grass
2300
2200
2100
grass
2000
1900
1800
grassy plateau
1700

Knowe Crags

sheepfold ×

groove (in duplicate)
1600
1500
1400
1300
1200
1100
old quarry
bracken
old quarry
gate
car park
1000
fence
800
Blencathra Centre

horse-drawn plough

B

A

ROAD

×mast

Knowe Crags
from Gategill Fell

1500

Blease Gill

1200
1100
1000
900
← fold and gate

800
← footbridge and waterfalls in a wooded dell

Blease
(farm)

700

700

Kilnhow Beck

car park

Threlkeld

KESWICK 4¼

PENRITH 14¼

From point 'A' to point 'B' on the
diagram the right-hand path is much
the better. Most people miss it, and
a signpost would be useful. The path
is even more easily missed in descent:
at the top of the steep section turn
left and follow the top of the bracken.

Blease Gill

ASCENT FROM THRELKELD
via BLEASE GILL
2400 feet of ascent : 2 miles

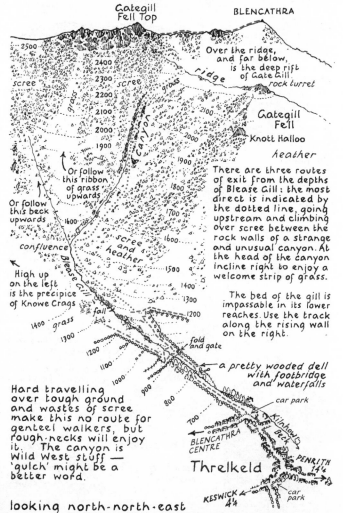

Gategill
Fell Top

BLENCATHRA

2500
2400
2300
2200
2100
2000
1900

scree
grass
scree
scree
grass

ridge

Over the ridge,
and far below,
is the deep rift
of Gate Gill
rock turret

canyon

2100
2000

Gategill
Fell

Knott Halloo

heather

1900

Or follow
this ribbon
of grass
upwards

1800

There are three routes
of exit from the depths
of Blease Gill: the most
direct is indicated by
the dotted line, going
upstream and climbing
over scree between the
rock walls of a strange
and unusual canyon. At
the head of the canyon
incline right to enjoy a
welcome strip of grass.

Or follow
this beck
upwards

1600

1700

1600

scree
and
heather

confluence

1500

The bed of the gill is
impassable in its lower
reaches. Use the track
along the rising wall
on the right.

Blease Gill

1400

High up
on the left
is the precipice
of Knowe Crags

1300

fall

1200

1400 grass

1300

1200

1100

1000

900

fold
and gate

a pretty wooded dell
with footbridge
and waterfalls

800

car park

Kinhont Beck

Hard travelling
over tough ground
and wastes of scree
make this no route for
genteel walkers, but
rough-necks will enjoy
it. The canyon is
Wild West stuff —
'gulch' might be a
better word.

700

BLENCATHRA
CENTRE

Threlkeld

PENRITH
14¼

KESWICK ←
4¼

car park

looking north-north-east

ASCENT FROM THRELKELD
via GATEGILL FELL
2450 feet of ascent : 2 miles

Bleasa Fell

Gategill Fell Top

BLENCATHRA

Knowe Crags

scree

Note the grassy Middle Tongue rising from the depths

miniature Striding Edge rock turret

Far below on this side is Gate Gill

Knott Halloo

Heather

Blea Crags

Gategill Fell

heather

canyon

remnant of wall

two small rock shelters

bracken

fold

Blease Gill

Blease Fell

This route becomes really enjoyable only when Knott Halloo is reached. There the slope eases to a rock turret, where the ridge, hitherto broad, narrows to an arete (avoided on the left). Then a simple grassy crest leads up the final tower, easily by-passed on scree to the right.

Gategill Fell is the steepest of Blencathra's buttresses in its lower part. Getting up to Knott Halloo is collar-work — an easy but unremitting ascent over stones and heather.

Gategill Fell rises directly above Threlkeld, almost oppressively, and the broad front, tapering to a cap of rock, is a dominant feature in the view of Blencathra from the village

Kilnhow Beck

BLENCATHRA CENTRE

car park

Threlkeld

looking north

PENRITH 14¼

car park

St. Mary's Church

KESWICK 4¼

Knott Halloo

looking up to Gategill Fell Top
from just above Knott Halloo,
with the rock turret
on the right

Gategill Fell

looking up the
ridge from the
rock turret

looking down the ridge
from Gategill Fell Top

The rock turret is at the far end of
the shadow; to the right is Knott
Halloo, the furthest point in view.

Gate Gill

Blencathra's summit is directly ahead.
Gategill Fell rises on the left, and
Hall's Fell on the right.

ASCENT FROM THRELKELD
via MIDDLE TONGUE
2400 feet of ascent : 2 miles

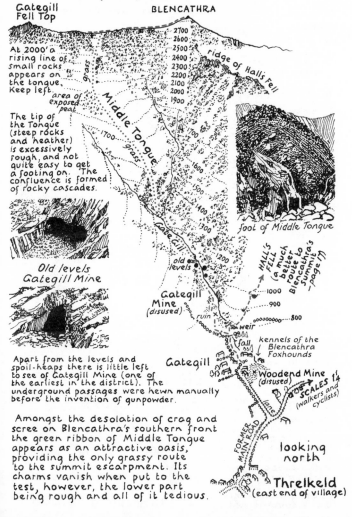

Gategill Fell Top

BLENCATHRA

2700
2600
2500
2400
2300
2200
2100
2000
1900

ridge of Halls Fell

At 2000' a rising line of small rocks appears on the tongue. Keep left.

grass

area of exposed peat

Middle Tongue

The tip of the Tongue (steep rocks and heather) is excessively rough, and not quite easy to get a footing on. The confluence is formed of rocky cascades.

1700

1700

grass

1600

1500

1400

1300

foot of Middle Tongue

Gate Gill

1200

old levels

Old levels Gategill Mine

Gategill Mine (disused)

ruin

HALL'S FELL (a much better route to Blencathra's summit — page 11)

1000

900

800

weir

fall

kennels of the Blencathra Foxhounds

Gategill

Woodend Mine (disused)

SCALES 1¼ (walkers and cyclists)

Apart from the levels and spoil-heaps there is little left to see of Gategill Mine (one of the earliest in the district). The underground passages were hewn manually before the invention of gunpowder.

Amongst the desolation of crag and scree on Blencathra's southern front the green ribbon of Middle Tongue appears as an attractive oasis, providing the only grassy route to the summit escarpment. Its charms vanish when put to the test, however, the lower part being rough and all of it tedious.

FORMER MAIN ROAD

lane

looking north

Threlkeld (east end of village)

ASCENT FROM THRELKELD
via HALL'S FELL
2400 feet of ascent : 2 miles

Gategill Fell Top

BLENCATHRA (Hallsfell Top)

Doddick Fell Top

2700
2600
2500
2400
2300
2200
2100

arete
pinnacle
tower

← care needed in traversing rockface by horizontal crack

From the ridge there are tremendous views down to Doddick and Gate Gills

The last half mile of the ridge, from 2000, is entirely delightful. This section, known as Narrow Edge with good reason, is a succession of low crags, with steps and gateways and towers of rock. A distinct track on grass is available for walkers — at first this keeps mostly on the Doddick side and later prefers the other, occasionally being forced along the crest. Care is needed in places but there are no difficulties. Scramblers will enjoy following the crest throughout.

Under ice and snow the ridge is for experts only

An enchanting track climbs the broad base of the fell. Unseen from below, this track reveals itself in the heather a few yards at a time, beckoning irresistibly upwards to the exciting ridge above.

Middle Tongue

Gategill Fell

Gate Gill

2000
1900
1800
1700
1600
1500
1400
1300
1200
1100
1000
900
800

heather

Doddick Gill

Doddick Fell and Scales Fell come into view →

Hall's Fell
heather
bracken

Doddick Fell

1000

levels

Gategill Mine (disused)

ruin ×
weir
fold
fall

700

Gategill

kennels (the home of the Blencathra Foxhounds)

Woodend Mine (disused)

NO THROUGH ROAD →

600

former drive to THRELKELD HALL (from which Hall's Fell is named)

FORMER MAIN ROAD

LANE

For active walkers and scramblers, this route is *positively* the finest way to any mountain-top in the district. It is direct, exhilarating, has glorious views, and (especially satisfying) scores a bull's-eye by leading unerringly to the summit-cairn.

looking north

Threlkeld (east end of village)

looking down the ridge from the summit

Hall's Fell

the middle section

the curve in the ridge

looking up the ridge to the summit

Doddick Gill

from 1350' on Doddick Fell. On the left is Hall's Fell, rising to Hall's Fell Top (the summit of Blencathra).

ASCENT FROM THRELKELD
via DODDICK GILL
2150 feet of ascent · 2¾ miles

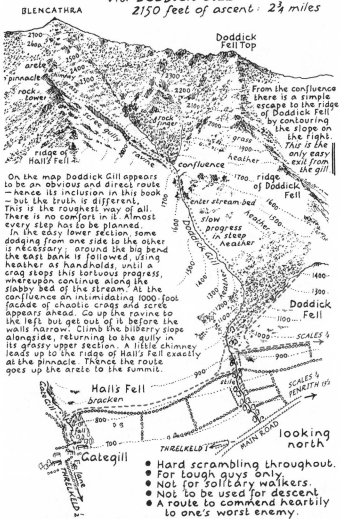

BLENCATHRA

2700
2600

arête

pinnacle

chimney

rock tower

2500
2400
2300

grass

2300

2200

2100

rock finger

2000

1900 grass

heather

1700

ridge of Hall's Fell

scree gully

ravine

confluence

Doddick Fell Top

From the confluence there is a simple escape to the ridge of Doddick Fell by contouring the slope on the right. This is the only easy exit from the gill.

ridge of Doddick Fell

1600

1500

enter stream bed

slow progress in steep heather

heather

heather

1400

1300

Doddick Fell

Doddick Gill

1700
1600
1500
1400
1300
1200
1100
1000

900

SCALES ¾

On the map Doddick Gill appears to be an obvious and direct route — hence its inclusion in this book — but the truth is different. This is the roughest way of all. There is no comfort in it. Almost every step has to be planned.
In the easy lower section, some dodging from one side to the other is necessary; around the big bend the east bank is followed, using heather as handholds, until a crag stops this tortuous progress, whereupon continue along the slabby bed of the stream. At the confluence an intimidating 1000-foot facade of chaotic crags and scree appears ahead. Go up the ravine to the left but get out of it before the walls narrow. Climb the bilberry slope alongside, returning to the gully in its grassy upper section. A little chimney leads up to the ridge of Hall's Fell exactly at the pinnacle. Thence the route goes up the arête to the summit.

Hall's Fell
bracken

Gate Gill

fall

800

700

Gategill

lane THRELKELD 2

stile

SCALES ¾
PENRITH 13½

900

THRELKELD 1

MAIN ROAD

looking north

- Hard scrambling throughout.
- For tough guys only.
- Not for solitary walkers.
- Not to be used for descent
- A route to commend heartily to one's worst enemy.

ASCENT FROM SCALES
via DODDICK FELL
2150 feet of ascent : 1¼ miles

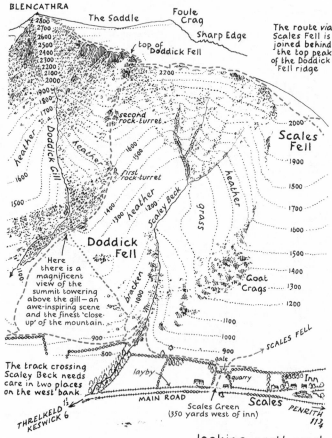

BLENCATHRA

The Saddle

Foule Crag

Sharp Edge

top of Doddick Fell

The route via Scales Fell is joined behind the top peak of the Doddick Fell ridge

2800
2700
2600
2500
2400
2300
2200
2100
2000
1900
1800
1700

2200

Doddick Gill

heather

second rock-turret

heather

first rock-turret

1600

1500

Scales Fell

2000

1900

1800

1700

1600

1500

1600
1500
1400
1300

heather

1200

Scaley Beck

heather

grass

1400

1300

1200

Goat Crags

Doddick Fell

Here there is a magnificent view of the summit towering above the gill — an awe-inspiring scene and the finest 'close-up' of the mountain.

bracken

1000

1100

1000

900

800

900

gate

SCALES FELL

SCALES FELL

The track crossing Scaley Beck needs care in two places on the west bank.

layby

quarry

Inn

MAIN ROAD

Scales Green
(350 yards west of inn)

Scales

THRELKELD 1¾
KESWICK 6

PENRITH 11¾

looking north-west

It is usual, from Scales, to ascend by way of Scales Fell, a very popular route, but better by far is the more direct ridge of Doddick Fell, a grand climb, quite easy, with striking views of the objective. This is a splendid way to the top of Blencathra.

looking up to Doddick Fell Top from 1450'

Doddick Fell

looking down the ridge from Doddick Fell Top

Scaley Beck

Doddick Fell is on the left, rising to the
peak of Doddick Fell Top.   Blencathra's
summit is seen in the top left corner.

ASCENT FROM SCALES
via SCALEY BECK
2150 feet of ascent : 2 miles

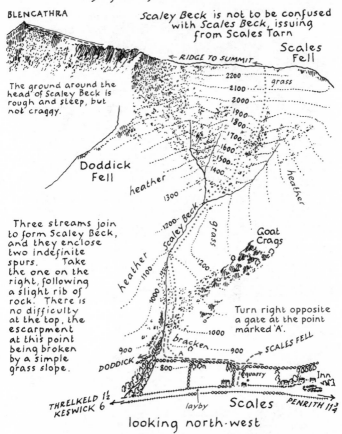

BLENCATHRA

Scaley Beck is not to be confused with Scales Beck, issuing from Scales Tarn

Scales Fell

← RIDGE TO SUMMIT

2200
2100   grass
2000
1900
1800
1700
1600
1500
1400

The ground around the head of Scaley Beck is rough and steep, but not craggy.

Doddick Fell

heather

1300

heather

Three streams join to form Scaley Beck, and they enclose two indefinite spurs. Take the one on the right, following a slight rib of rock. There is no difficulty at the top, the escarpment at this point being broken by a simple grass slope.

1200   Scaley Beck

grass

1100

Goat Crags

1000

1200

Turn right opposite a gate at the point marked 'A'.

1000

heather

bracken

900   900   → SCALES FELL

DODDICK

800   quarry   Inn

A

THRELKELD 1½
KESWICK 6

layby   Scales   PENRITH 11¾

looking north·west

Of the various watercourses on the south front Scaley Beck is the most practicable as a route of ascent, being nowhere too rough to stop progress; the exit, too, is easy. There is little of interest, however, and the route falls far short of that via the adjacent ridge of Doddick Fell.

ASCENT FROM SCALES
via SHARP EDGE
2250 feet of ascent : 2¼ miles

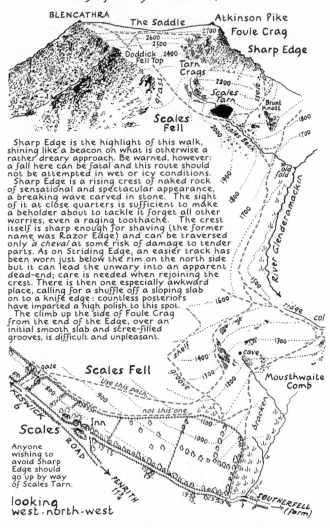

Sharp Edge is the highlight of this walk, shining like a beacon on what is otherwise a rather dreary approach. Be warned, however: a fall here can be fatal and this route should not be attempted in wet or icy conditions.

Sharp Edge is a rising crest of naked rock of sensational and spectacular appearance, a breaking wave carved in stone. The sight of it at close quarters is sufficient to make a beholder about to tackle it forget all other worries, even a raging toothache. The crest itself is sharp enough for shaving (the former name was Razor Edge) and can be traversed only *a cheval* at some risk of damage to tender parts. As on Striding Edge, an easier track has been worn just below the rim on the north side but it can lead the unwary into an apparent dead-end; care is needed when rejoining the crest. There is then one especially awkward place, calling for a shuffle off a sloping slab on to a knife edge: countless posteriors have imparted a high polish to this spot.

The climb up the side of Foule Crag from the end of the Edge, over an initial smooth slab and scree-filled grooves, is difficult and unpleasant.

Anyone wishing to avoid Sharp Edge should go up by way of Scales Tarn.

looking west-north-west

looking down from
Foule Crag

looking east
along the Edge
(the 'awkward
place' in the
foreground)

Sharp Edge

the approach from
Scales Tarn

from Scales Tarn

Foule Crag
Sharp Edge

Brunt
Knott

the path from Scales

ASCENT FROM SCALES
via SCALES FELL
2150 feet of ascent : 2¼ miles

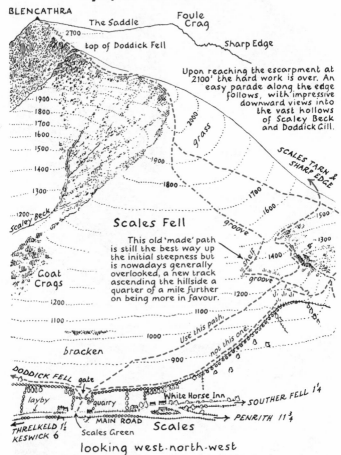

BLENCATHRA

The Saddle

Foule Crag

2700

top of Doddick Fell

Sharp Edge

Upon reaching the escarpment at 2100' the hard work is over. An easy parade along the edge follows, with impressive downward views into the vast hollows of Scaley Beck and Doddick Gill.

1900
1800
1700
1600
1500
1400
1300
1200
Scaley Beck

2000
grass

1900

1800

1700

1600

1500

SCALES TARN & SHARP EDGE

groove

shelf

1300

Coat Crags

Scales Fell

This old 'made' path is still the best way up the initial steepness but is nowadays generally overlooked, a new track ascending the hillside a quarter of a mile further on being more in favour.

1400

groove

1200

1200
1100

1100

1100

Use this path

1000

not this one:

bracken

900

DODDICK FELL

gate

layby

quarry

White Horse Inn

SOUTHER FELL 1¼

MAIN ROAD

PENRITH 11¾

THRELKELD 1½
KESWICK 6

Scales Green

Scales

looking west-north-west

This is the best-known route up Blencathra, and has been in common use for over a century. Until recently, the tough grass of Scales Fell resisted the formation of a continuous track. The climb, tedious up to 2000', becomes excellent in its later stages.

ASCENT FROM MUNGRISDALE
2250 feet of ascent : 4 miles

BLENCATHRA

2700
2600

Atkinson Pike (top of Foule Crag)

Blue Screes (an extensive slope of loose
slate fragments, quite easy
to cross)

Sharp
Edge

2400
2300

2200
2100
2000
1900

Mungrisdale
Common

2000

BOWSCALE
FELL

SCALES

Glenderamackin
col

1900
1800

col

BANNERDALE
CRAGS

2200
2100
2000
1900
1800
1700
1600

The
Tongue

*Alternatively, the Glenderamackin col
may be reached by following the
path alongside the river from
Mungrisdale around the
south end of Bannerdale
Crags and up the west
side. The path, rarely
used, is distinct and
continuous to the col.
This is the natural line of
approach and, although
longer, much the
better in mist.*

Bannerdale

sheepfold

At this junction
the lower path is
the more distinct,
but take the higher.

SCALES 2
COL (in mist)

Bannerdale Beck

1400
1300
1200
1100

**Rising very
steeply on this
side of the valley
is SOUTHER FELL**

River Glenderamackin

bield

1000

Bullfell Beck

x bield

**This is an unusual but
interesting approach,
revealing an aspect of
Blencathra not often seen
and 'saving' the classic view
southwards until the last moment
of the ascent. Passing between
Bannerdale Crags and Bowscale Fell,
the route is a good cross-country
expedition. Easy walking.**

900
1000

800

Mungrisdale

Mill
Inn

x kiosk

KESWICK 10
PENRICH 12

Church

looking west

THE VIEW

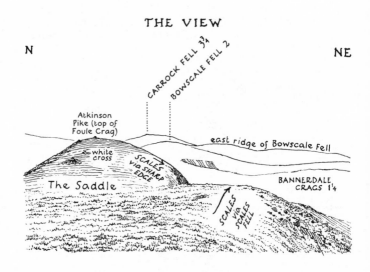

N

NE

THE SUMMIT

The summit is effectively poised above the abyss, precisely at the point where the ridge of Hall's Fell comes up out of the depths to a jutting headland. The summit is, in fact, known as Hallsfell Top. At ground level on the highest point there is an Ordnance Survey trigonometrical station, apparently disused. Otherwise nothing marks the summit but a poor untidy heap of rubble. Much slaty stone is lying exposed here, but it is unsuitable for building cairns, and until somebody carries up a few decent-sized blocks the cairn will continue to disappoint.

The summit is windswept and shelterless and lacks a natural seat, but a few yards down Hall's Fell on the left the lee-side of a small outcrop usually cuts off the prevailing wind.

The excellent turf along the top deserves special mention.

continued

THE VIEW

NE   E

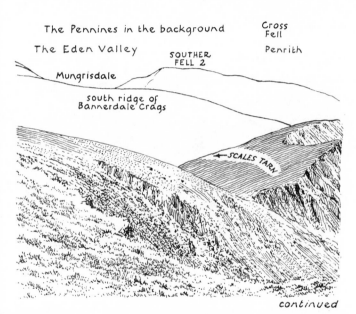

The Pennines in the background   Cross Fell

The Eden Valley   Penrith

SOUTHER FELL 2

Mungrisdale

south ridge of Bannerdale Crags

← SCALES TARN

continued

Descents:

The best *ascents* are by the narrow ridges —— Hall's Fell, Sharp Edge, Doddick Fell and Gategill Fell, *in that order* —— but the best routes of *descent* are those tedious in ascent: Blease Fell, Scales Fell, Glenderamackin col and Roughten Gill, *in that order*. The latter two are roundabout and not suitable in mist, but Blease Fell and Scales Fell, lying at opposite ends of the well-defined summit escarpment, are simple ways off in any weather. The narrow ridges will be found bumpy going down, although Hall's Fell and Doddick Fell are quite practicable and enjoyable, but all may become dangerous under ice and snow.   The gills and ravines on the southern front are much too rough to be considered for descent no matter how good the weather.

THE VIEW

continued

E   SE

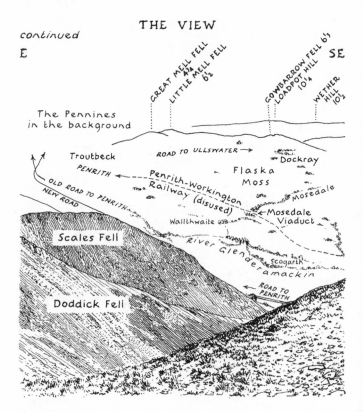

The Pennines
in the background

GREAT MELL FELL 4¼
LITTLE MELL FELL 6½
GOWBARROW FELL 6⅓
LOADPOT HILL 10¼
WETHER HILL 10½

Troutbeck
ROAD TO ULLSWATER →
Dockray
PENRITH
Penrith-Workington
Flaska Moss
OLD ROAD TO PENRITH
Railway (disused)
Mosedale
NEW ROAD
← Mosedale Viaduct
Wallthwaite
Scales Fell
River Glenderamackin
Scogarth
Doddick Fell
← ROAD TO PENRITH

Mosedale ....

The Mosedale appearing in the view above is not the
Mosedale mentioned elsewhere in this book and situated
at the foot of Carrock Fell. There are, in fact, six valleys
of this name (signifying *desolation, dreariness*) in Lakeland
and a pastime that might be adopted to fill in a few minutes
while waiting for the rain to stop is to find them all on the
1" Ordnance Survey map of the district (one of them is spelt
Moasdale). If, having done this, it still looks like raining for
ever, make a list of all the different names on the map in
which "thwaite" (a *clearing*) appears : this occupation will
fill in the rest of the day until bedtime. On the 1" Tourist
Map there are 81 *different*, many of them recurring. Enthusiastic
thwaite-spotters will find several others on larger-scale maps.

THE VIEW

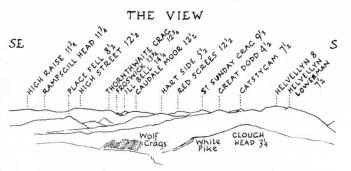

SE   HIGH RAISE 11¾   RAMPSGILL HEAD 11¾   PLACE FELL 8½   HIGH STREET 12½   THORNTHWAITE CRAG 12¾   FROSWICK 13¼   ILL BELL 14¼   CAUDALE MOOR 12½   HART SIDE 5½   RED SCREES 12½   St SUNDAY CRAG 9½   GREAT DODD 4½   CATSTYCAM 7½   HELVELLYN 8   HELVELLYN LOWER MAN 7½   S

Wolf Crags   White Pike   CLOUGH HEAD 3¼

Threlkeld Common

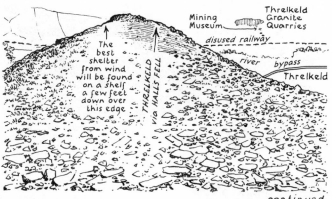

Mining Museum   Threlkeld Granite Quarries

disused railway

river bypass

Threlkeld

The best shelter from wind will be found on a shelf a few feet down over this edge

THRELKELD VIA HALLS FELL

continued

at Threlkeld....

● Look over both parapets of Threlkeld Bridge. Two streams, the River Glenderamackin and St. John's Beck, at this point unite, passing under the bridge individually but emerging as one: the River Greta. The bridge is built over the confluence.

● Visit the Threlkeld Mining Museum. It is situated about half a mile south of the village and is well signposted. It covers mining and quarrying throughout the Lake District, and not just at Threlkeld.

● Visit the little glen of Kilnhow Beck. A pleasant path starts near the Horse and Farrier and proceeds upstream to the open fell at Blease Gill with the help of footbridges. This sylvan dell is not publicised and is a charming surprise.

THE VIEW

continued

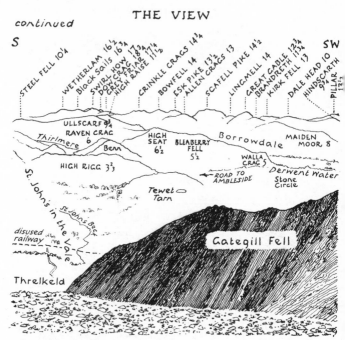

S — STEEL FELL 10¼ — WETHERLAM 16½ — Black Sails 16¾ — SWIRL HOW 17¾ — DOW CRAG 18¼ — GREY FRIAR 17¼ — HIGH RAISE 11½ — CRINKLE CRAGS 14¾ — BOWFELL 14 — ESK PIKE 13½ — ALLEN CRAGS 13 — SCAFELL PIKE 14½ — LINC MELL 14 — GREAT GABLE 12¾ — BRANDRETH 11¾ — KIRK FELL 13 — DALE HEAD 10 — HINDSCARTH 9¾ — PILLAR 13½ — SW

ULLSCARF 9¼ — RAVEN CRAG — Thirlmere 6 — Benn — HIGH SEAT 6½ — BLEABERRY FELL 5½ — Borrowdale — MAIDEN MOOR 8

HIGH RIGG 3⅔ — WALLA CRAG 5 — Derwent Water — ROAD TO AMBLESIDE — Stone Circle

St. Johns in the Vale — St. Johns Beck — Tewet Tarn

disused railway

Threlkeld

Gategill Fell

The White Cross

In view from the summit is a landmark that has aroused the curiosity of visitors for a great many years: a collection of white crystallised stones of high quartz content, laid on the grass in the form of a cross on the easy rise to the top of Foule Crag, north of the Saddle.

This cross owes its existence to the industry of Harold Robinson of Threlkeld. Formerly there was a very small cross of stones here (locally ascribed as a memorial to a walker who lost his life on a rough slope adjacent) and Mr. Robinson, an enthusiastic lone hill-wanderer who has climbed his favourite Blencathra hundreds of times, collected more stones (veins of quartzite occur in the native slate nearby) and extended the cross to its present size of 16' by 10' during a succession of visits from 1945 onwards.

A much smaller but similar white cross on the southern slope of the Saddle is more recent, and the work of persons unknown.

THE VIEW

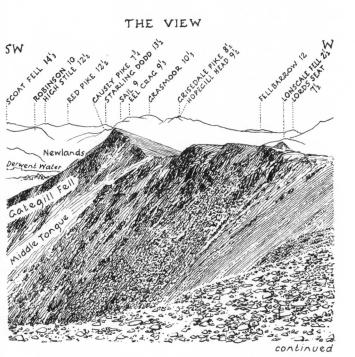

SW

SCOAT FELL 14⅓
ROBINSON 10
HIGH STILE 12½
RED PIKE 12½
CAUSEY PIKE 7¾
STARLING DODD 13½
SAIL 9
EEL CRAG 9⅓
CRASMOOR 10⅓
GRISEDALE PIKE 8½
HOPEGILL HEAD 9½
FELLBARROW 12
LONSCALE FELL 2⅓
LORDS SEAT 7½
W

Newlands
Derwent Water
Gategill Fell
Middle Tongue

continued

Blencathra's old mines

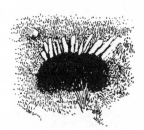

Blencathra has been mined fairly extensively and a variety of ores extracted from workings in the valleys of the Glenderaterra and Glenderamackin and from the adjacent and interlinked Gategill and Woodend mines, the debris of which is still very conspicuous in the Threlkeld landscape. All the mines are now closed, but 100 years ago they were in production and prospering, and finding work for a labour force of 100.

Illustrated is an old level (a little beauty) at the northern workings of the Glenderaterra Mine, as it appeared in 1961. The warning must be repeated that disused mine levels are unsafe because of flooding and collapse and often open into vertical pits.

THE VIEW

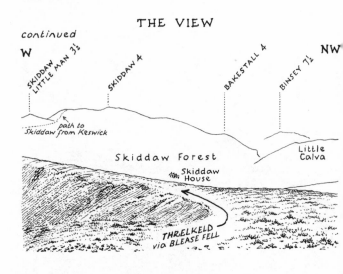

continued

W   NW

SKIDDAW LITTLE MAN 3½   SKIDDAW 4   BAKESTALL 4   BINSEY 7½

path to Skiddaw from Keswick

Little Calva

Skiddaw Forest

Skiddaw House

THRELKELD via BLEASE FELL

RIDGE ROUTE

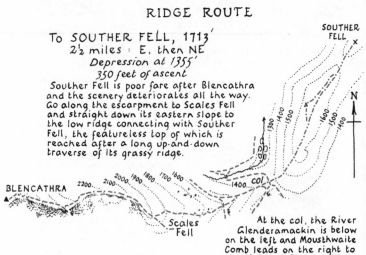

To SOUTHER FELL, 1713′
2½ miles : E, then NE
Depression at 1355′
350 feet of ascent

Souther Fell is poor fare after Blencathra and the scenery deteriorates all the way. Go along the escarpment to Scales Fell and straight down its eastern slope to the low ridge connecting with Souther Fell, the featureless top of which is reached after a long up-and-down traverse of its grassy ridge.

SOUTHER FELL

N

BLENCATHRA   2200   2100   2000   1900   1800   1700   1600   1400   COL

Scales Fell

1300   1400   1500   1600   1500   1400

At the col, the River Glenderamackin is below on the left and Mousthwaite Comb leads on the right to the fields of Scales. There are many tracks hereabouts.

HALF A MILE

THE VIEW

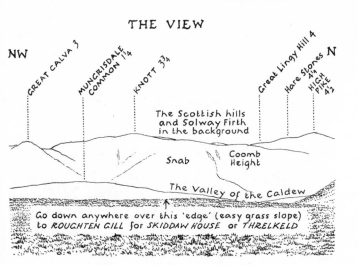

NW

GREAT CALVA 3

MUNGRISDALE COMMON 1¼

KNOTT 3¾

Great Lingy Hill 4

Hare Stones 4½

HIGH PIKE 42

N

The Scottish hills
and Solway Firth
in the background

Snab

Coomb
Height

The Valley of the Caldew

↑
Go down anywhere over this 'edge' (easy grass slope)
to ROUGHTEN GILL for SKIDDAW HOUSE or THRELKELD

RIDGE ROUTE

To BANNERDALE CRAGS, 2241'
1½ miles : N, then NE and E
Depression at 2010'
200 feet of ascent

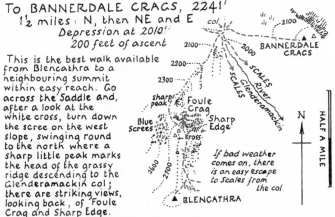

This is the best walk available
from Blencathra to a
neighbouring summit
within easy reach. Go
across the Saddle and,
after a look at the
white cross, turn down
the scree on the west
slope, swinging round
to the north where a
sharp little peak marks
the head of the grassy
ridge descending to the
Glenderamackin col ;
there are striking views,
looking back, of Foule
Crag and Sharp Edge.

col

2100

BANNERDALE
CRAGS

2100

2200

2300

2000

SCALES

SCALES

Glenderamackin

SCALES River

sharp
peak

Foule
Crag

Blue
Screes

Sharp
Edge

cross

If bad weather
comes on, there
is an easy escape
to Scales from
the col.

2600

2700

N

HALF A MILE

▲ BLENCATHRA

From the col, a path heads eastwards over a grassy expanse,
becomes indistinct at one point, and finally peters out shortly
before the summit cairn is reached.

Bowscale Fell

2306'

from the hut on Great Lingy Hill

CARROCK FELL ▲

Mosedale ●
Bowscale ●
▲ BOWSCALE FELL
●
Mungrisdale ●
▲ BANNERDALE CRAGS
▲ BLENCATHRA

MILES
0 1 2 3 4

Point 1876' on the east ridge

NATURAL FEATURES

The Caldew is the greatest watercourse among the
northern fells, and for three miles before the river
escapes to open country it is bounded and deflected
considerably to the north by broad grassy buttresses
descending from the domed summit of Bowscale Fell,
a fine eminence on the eastern perimeter of the group.
Southwards a high link connects with Blencathra and
Bannerdale Crags, and an undistinguished moorland
sprawls away to Skiddaw Forest in the west. It is only
from the valley pastures to the east that Bowscale Fell
really exhibits the proportions of a mountain, this view
revealing two lofty ridges that rise steeply above the
white cottages of Mungrisdale. The finest feature of
the fell, however, is the craggy combe and tarn on the
north flank, overlooking the Caldew: a scene of utter
solitude that can be seen today just as the glacier left
it in ages past.

A topographical curiosity may be noted: it is more
apparent from a study of the map than from a study
of the ground. The Eden-Derwent watershed passes
over the summit; the odd thing about it is that the
western slopes feed the Eden, which is to the east, and
the eastern effluent finds its way into the Derwent, a
river far beyond the mountain barrier to the west.

A glacial combe.....

      tiered crags carved by ice; silent waters
      embanked by moraines; scattered rocks
      in the wake of the departed glacier........
         ..... *Bowscale Tarn from the north*

MAP

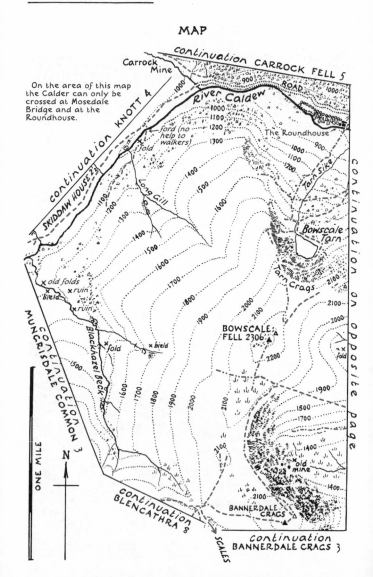

On the area of this map the Calder can only be crossed at Mosedale Bridge and at the Roundhouse.

continuation CARROCK FELL 5

Carrock Mine

River Caldew

continuation KNOTT 4

continuation SKIDDAW HOUSE 2

ROAD

ford (no help to walkers)

The Roundhouse

fold

Long Gill

Tarn Sike

Bowscale Tarn

continuation on opposite page

Tarn Crags

x old folds
bield
x ruin
x ruin

Blackhazel Beck

BOWSCALE FELL 2306

x fold
x bield

continuation MUNGRISDALE COMMON 3

x fold

old mine

ONE MILE

N

continuation BLENCATHRA 8

BANNERDALE CRAGS

SCALES

continuation BANNERDALE CRAGS 3

MAP

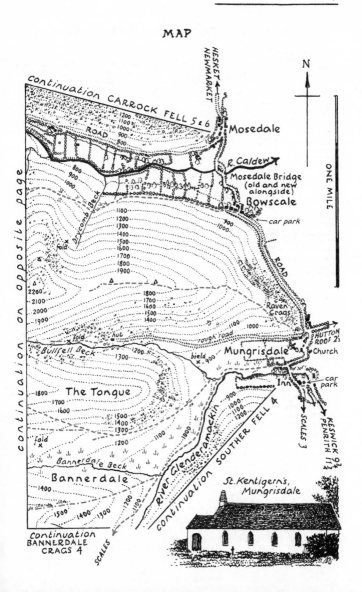

N

continuation CARROCK FELL 5 & 6

HESKET NEWMARKET

ROAD

Mosedale

R. Caldew

Mosedale Bridge (old and new alongside)

Bowscale

car park

ONE MILE

Drycomb Beck

1100
1200
1300
1400
1500
1600
1700
1800
1900

900
1000

ROAD

2200
2100
2000
1900

1800
1700
1600
1500
1400

fold

800
900
1000

Raven Crags

1100

1000

continuation on opposite page

fold

hut

rough road

HUTTON ROOF 2½

Bullfell Beck

1300

1200

bield

900

Mungrisdale

Church

car park

The Tongue

1800
1700
1600

1500
1400
1300

1200

1100

1000

900
1000
1100
1200

Inn

SCALES 3

KESWICK 9¾
PENRITH 11½

fold

Bannerdale Beck

1100

1000

Bannerdale

1400

1500 1400 1300

1200

River Glenderamackin

continuation SOUTHER FELL 4

continuation BANNERDALE CRAGS 4

SCALES

St. Kentigern's, Mungrisdale

ASCENT FROM MUNGRISDALE

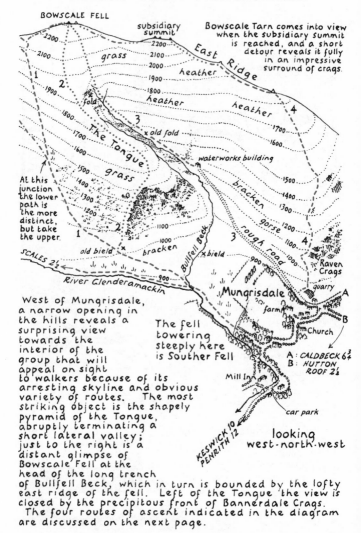

BOWSCALE FELL

subsidiary summit

Bowscale Tarn comes into view when the subsidiary summit is reached, and a short detour reveals it fully in an impressive surround of crags.

East Ridge

grass

heather

heather

heather

fold

The Tongue

x old fold

grass

waterworks building

bracken

gorse

rough road

At this junction the lower path is the more distinct, but take the upper.

old bield

bracken

x bield

Bullfell Beck

Raven Crags

quarry

SCALES 2½

River Glenderamackin

Mungrisdale

farm

Church

A: CALDBECK 6¾
B: HUTTON ROOF 2½

A

B

Mill Inn

car park

KESWICK 10
PENRITH 12

looking west-north-west

The fell towering steeply here is Souther Fell

West of Mungrisdale, a narrow opening in the hills reveals a surprising view towards the interior of the group that will appeal on sight to walkers because of its arresting skyline and obvious variety of routes. The most striking object is the shapely pyramid of the Tongue, abruptly terminating a short lateral valley; just to the right is a distant glimpse of Bowscale Fell at the head of the long trench of Bullfell Beck, which in turn is bounded by the lofty east ridge of the fell. Left of the Tongue the view is closed by the precipitous front of Bannerdale Crags.

The four routes of ascent indicated in the diagram are discussed on the next page.

ASCENT FROM MUNGRISDALE

← Diagram on opposite page

ROUTE 1 : This is the least obvious (it seems to be aiming for Bannerdale Crags) but the easiest route; in fact, the easiest route to any summit over 2000' in Lakeland.   It makes use of an old bridle-path skirting the south flank of the Tongue and rising to the skyline of Bowscale Fell only a simple five-minutes' walk from the top. *1450': 2¼ miles*

ROUTE 2 :   Leave Route 1 at a ruined bield in the bracken and scramble steeply alongside the rising escarpment of the Tongue. Once above this a level ridge continues to the easy final slope of Bowscale Fell. *1470': 2¼ miles.*

ROUTE 3 :   Bullfell Beck offers a direct route, but is deeply enclosed and uninteresting. Its one merit is the shelter it provides in stormy or windy weather. *1450': 2¼ miles.*

ROUTE 4 :   Best of all is the east ridge. Climbing starts at once over a pleasant alp of gorse and bracken and grey rock, after which there is a gentle rise to the heathery ridge, a grouse moor, and two further undulations before the top of the fell is reached. The second of these undulations is big enough and high enough (over 2200') to be regarded as a subsidiary summit. From its slopes Bowscale Tarn is in view below. This is the only route on which the tarn is seen. A prominent cairn on a spur north of this subsidiary summit gives a fine view of Mosedale and the Caldew Valley. *1550': 2½ miles*

Routes 1 and 2 leave Mungrisdale along a short lane with a telephone kiosk at the corner.   Routes 3 and 4 start along a rough lane (gated) at a signposted road-junction at the north end of the village.

For the best 'round tour' ascend by Route 4 and descend by Route 1. Route 4 follows the Eden-Derwent watershed exactly.

Bowscale Tarn and moraine
from the slopes of the subsidiary summit

ASCENT FROM BOWSCALE
1550 feet of ascent : 2½ miles

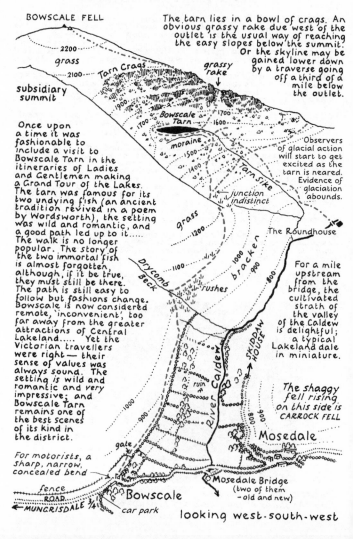

BOWSCALE FELL

subsidiary summit

2200 grass
2100
Tarn Crags

The tarn lies in a bowl of crags. An obvious grassy rake due west of the outlet is the usual way of reaching the easy slopes below the summit. Or the skyline may be gained lower down by a traverse going off a third of a mile below the outlet.

grassy rake

1900

1700 Bowscale Tarn 1700 1600

moraine

1500

1400

Tarn Sike

Observers of glacial action will start to get excited as the tarn is neared. Evidence of glaciation abounds.

junction indistinct

grass

1200

The Roundhouse

Once upon a time it was fashionable to include a visit to Bowscale Tarn in the itineraries of Ladies and Gentlemen making a Grand Tour of the Lakes. The tarn was famous for its two undying fish (an ancient tradition revived in a poem by Wordsworth), the setting was wild and romantic, and a good path led up to it..... The walk is no longer popular. The story of the two immortal fish is almost forgotten, although, if it be true, they must still be there. The path is still easy to follow but fashions change. Bowscale is now considered remote, 'inconvenient', too far away from the greater attractions of Central Lakeland..... Yet the Victorian travellers were right — their sense of values was always sound. The setting is wild and romantic and very impressive; and Bowscale Tarn remains one of the best scenes of its kind in the district.

1100

Drycomb Beck

rushes

bracken

1000

900

800

For a mile upstream from the bridge, the cultivated strath of the valley of the Caldew is delightful; a typical Lakeland dale in miniature.

SKIDDAW HOUSE

River Caldew

ruin

1000

900

800

900

The shaggy fell rising on this side is CARROCK FELL

Mosedale

For motorists, a sharp, narrow, concealed bend

gate

fence
ROAD
←MUNGRISDALE ¾

Bowscale
car park

Mosedale Bridge (two of them – old and new)

looking west-south-west

THE SUMMIT

What appears from a distance to be a big square cairn turns out on closer enquiry to be a roughly-built shelter. A truer cairn stands 100 yards north-east, at a slightly lower level, and points the way to Bowscale Tarn (which is out of sight) and the east ridge. The top of the fell is grassy except for a liberal scattering of small stones on the highest part.

DESCENTS: Gradients are gentle on the top and all routes off are easy. If Bowscale Tarn is to be visited, keep the descending rim of Tarn Crags on the right until a grassy strip can be seen going down to the tarn's outlet — use this.

In bad weather, Mungrisdale is the best place to make for; it can be reached comfortably in an hour. Aim south from the summit to join the path across the col: this may not be distinct at the point reached—keep a lookout for the upright stone.

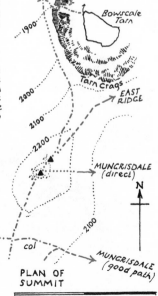

PLAN OF SUMMIT

HALF A MILE

The subsidiary summit

RIDGE ROUTE

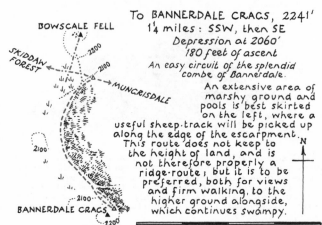

To BANNERDALE CRAGS, 2241'
1¼ miles : SSW, then SE
Depression at 2060'
180 feet of ascent
An easy circuit of the splendid
combe of Bannerdale.

An extensive area of
marshy ground and
pools is best skirted
on the left, where a
useful sheep-track will be picked up
along the edge of the escarpment.
This route does not keep to
the height of land, and is
not therefore properly a
ridge-route; but it is to be
preferred, both for views
and firm walking, to the
higher ground alongside,
which continues swampy.

ONE MILE

looking west to Skiddaw
Skiddaw Little Man (left)   Great Calva (right)

THE VIEW

Bowscale Fell and its near neighbour, Bannerdale Crags, are usually visited during the same walk, and it is especially interesting to note how the distant view southwest changes in the short mile between the two summits, due to the impending mass of Blencathra. From Bowscale Fell the distant skyline appears to the *right* of Blencathra and features the Buttermere fells; from Bannerdale Crags the view is seen to the *left* of Blencathra and is of the Langdale and Coniston fells.

Blencathra is a striking object from Bowscale Fell, appearing as a black tower, and there is a good prospect of the upper Caldew valley.

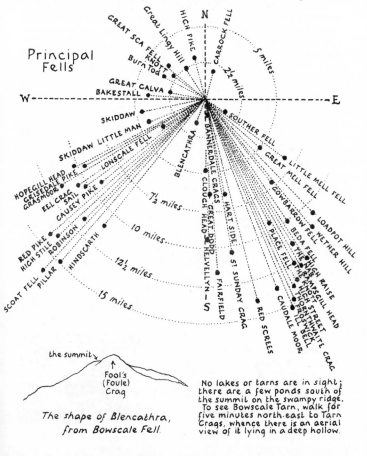

Principal Fells

The shape of Blencathra, from Bowscale Fell.

No lakes or tarns are in sight; there are a few ponds south of the summit on the swampy ridge. To see Bowscale Tarn, walk for five minutes north-east to Tarn Crags, whence there is an aerial view of it lying in a deep hollow.

Brae Fell
1920'

from Fell Side

Caldbeck •

• Fell Side
• Uldale ▲ Green Head
• Longlands
LONGLANDS ▲ ▲ HIGH PIKE
FELL ▲ BRAE FELL
Orthwaite ▲ GREAT SCA FELL

MILES
0 1 2 3 4

from Birk Moss

NATURAL FEATURES

Brae Fell, with a name that seems a marriage of Scottish and Cumbrian influences, is a last outpost of Lakeland in the north and already the typical characteristics of the district are left behind: the outlook is towards the Border——and the name is therefore perhaps not inappropriate.   It is a bare grassy fell of moderate altitude only, though prominent in many views because of its position. A fine cairn crowns the summit, which is a good viewpoint, but there is little else of appeal: if all hills were like Brae Fell there would be far fewer fellwalkers.   On the east side, however, there is a series of ravines going down to Dale Beck, and drift-mining operations have further scarred the flank with artificial gullies and spoil-heaps. Red Gill at one time was mined extensively, producing a rich yield of ores, but the traces are now almost lost in the bracken.

Geographically, Brae Fell is really a buttress of the double-headed Sca Fell, to which it is joined by a high saddle ; on other flanks watercourses define its boundaries clearly.

Charleton Gill, bounding Brae Fell on the west, is an ordinary mountain stream in spite of its rather 'posh' name, but at one place a peculiar formation may be noted on its eastern bank. Here the flank of Brae Fell descends uneventfully, but, almost at valley level, takes the shape of a curved ridge that forces the stream into a sharp detour at its base. This ridge, all grass, has a narrow crest (a favourite sheep-walk); it is probably a glacial moraine of more elegance than is usual: in fact the scene is charming. Few walkers will ever have seen the place, which is not in view from the little-used bridleroad nearby, but it is known to the shepherds and the mapmakers, whose name for it is Saddleback.
In this case there can be no quarrel with the name.

Saddleback, Charleton Gill

MAP

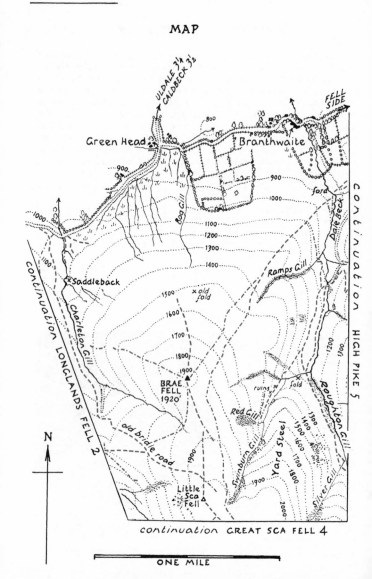

ONE MILE

ASCENT FROM GREEN HEAD
1100 feet of ascent
2 miles

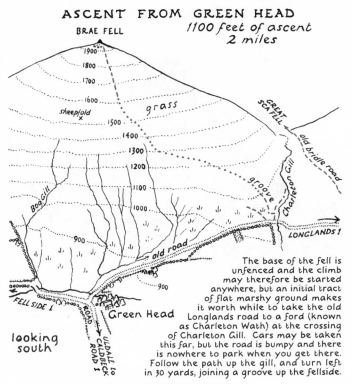

BRAE FELL

1900
1800
1700
1600
sheepfold
×
1500
grass
1400
1300
1200
1100
1000
Bog Gill
900
old road
900
GREAT SCA FELL
old bridle road
Charleton Gill
groove
LONGLANDS 1
FELL SIDE 1
Green Head
ROAD TO CALDBECK
ULDALE TO CALDBECK ROAD 1

looking south

The base of the fell is unfenced and the climb may therefore be started anywhere, but an initial tract of flat marshy ground makes it worth while to take the old Longlands road to a ford (known as Charleton Wath) at the crossing of Charleton Gill. Cars may be taken this far, but the road is bumpy and there is nowhere to park when you get there. Follow the path up the gill, and turn left in 30 yards, joining a groove up the fellside.

One wearies of the search for anything interesting during this overlong and featureless grassy trudge.

ASCENT FROM FELL SIDE
1150 feet of ascent : 2½ miles

The ascent, anywhere up the grass of the north-east slope, is straightforward, and needs no diagram. This is the aspect seen in the title drawing, the prominent ravine there shown being Ramps Gill.

It is impossible to cross Dale Beck at the ford comfortably without wellington boots, and the route to the ford from the north-west is exceedingly marshy. It is therefore best to cross the beck by the footbridge half a mile upstream from the ford, and go up by the south side of Ramps Gill. This gives the eyes something to look at during the ascent other than interminable grass slopes.

THE SUMMIT

Nature left a scattering of stones on the highest part of Brae Fell and Man has tidied up the litter by piling it into a splendid cairn, a landmark for several miles. North of the cairn is a wind-shelter facing east. There is very little fall on the south side, and from this direction the fell is seen to be no more than a shoulder of the Sca Fell mass.

DESCENTS : Many paths radiate from the summit. Those to the north and east peter out within half a mile, and that to the north-east leads to a ford that cannot be crossed dryshod without wellington boots. For Longlands it is best to head south, bearing right in fifty yards to join the old bridle road. For Fell Side it is necessary to find the footbridge over Dale Beck half a mile south of the ford: cut across to the right before the ford is reached, keeping below the bracken.

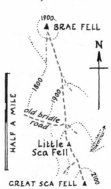

RIDGE ROUTE

TO GREAT SCA FELL, 2136':
1 mile : S
Depression at 1865'

There is now a clear path all the way. It crosses the slight depression to the south and passes over the summit of Little Sca Fell.

THE VIEW

The weariness of the climb to the cairn is dispelled by the beauty of the view, which extends without interruption from the Cumbrian coast near Workington around the northern arc formed by the Solway Firth, the Scottish lowlands and the Border Country, to the Pennines across the Eden Valley in the east. This is a magnificent view, second only in extensiveness, among the northern fells, to that from High Pike.

Principal Fells

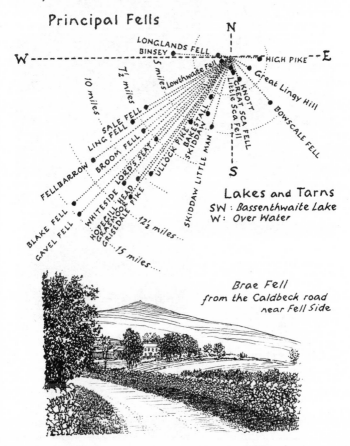

N

W - HIGH PIKE - - E

LONGLANDS FELL
BINSEY
Lowthwaite Fell
5 miles
7½ miles
10 miles
Great Lingy Hill
KNOTT
GREAT SCA FELL
Little Sca Fell
Bowscale Fell
SALE FELL
LING FELL
BROOM FELL
LORD'S SEAT
ULLOCK PIKE
BAKESTALL
SKIDDAW
SKIDDAW LITTLE MAN
FELLBARROW
WHITESIDE
HOPEGILL HEAD
GRASMOOR
GRISEDALE PIKE
BLAKE FELL
GAVEL FELL
12½ miles
15 miles
S

Lakes and Tarns
SW : Bassenthwaite Lake
W : Over Water

Brae Fell
from the Caldbeck road
near Fell Side

Carl Side

2447'
approx.

- Bassenthwaite
- High Side

ULLOCK PIKE ▲   ▲ SKIDDAW
▲ LONG SIDE
● ▲ CARL SIDE   ▲ SKIDDAW LITTLE MAN
DODD ● Millbeck

Little Crosthwaite

Keswick ●

MILES
0   1   2   3

from the main road
near Millbeck

NATURAL FEATURES

Where the steep and stony upper western slope of Skiddaw curves round to the equally steep and stony southern slope there is formed a massive rounded shoulder, which is halted in its descent at 2300' by a grassy saddle, and immediately beyond the dip is the domed summit of Carl Side, a well-defined green plateau. After this interruption, a narrowing ridge resumes the descent southwards to the foothills and fields of Millbeck, this being the natural line of fall of Skiddaw. But also from the summit of Carl Side a sharp ridge, Longside Edge, turns back north-west and finally north, thus circling and concealing Skiddaw's lower western flank: the deep 'moat' thus created is the upland valley of Southerndale, three miles long but so well hidden from popular approaches that walkers in general neither know it nor have even heard the name. This is an unusual geographical arrangement, giving Skiddaw a second wall of defence.

The south ridge, Carl Side proper, is unremarkable except for a distinctive rash of white stones at 1600' extending over several acres, unique in Lakeland and identifying the fell exactly in many distant views. A spur runs off the south ridge to the east and is densely carpeted with heather: this spur, when viewed from the valley, forms the beautiful, symmetrical, dark pyramid of Carsleddam, flanked on the east by the deep trough of Mill Beck, which cleanly severs Carl Side from its towering grey neighbour, Skiddaw Little Man. All streams from the fell go into Bassenthwaite Lake either direct or by way of the main feeder, the River Derwent.

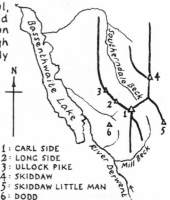

1 : CARL SIDE
2 : LONG SIDE
3 : ULLOCK PIKE
4 : SKIDDAW
5 : SKIDDAW LITTLE MAN
6 : DODD

The Ridges and Watercourses of Carl Side

Carl Side 3

MAP

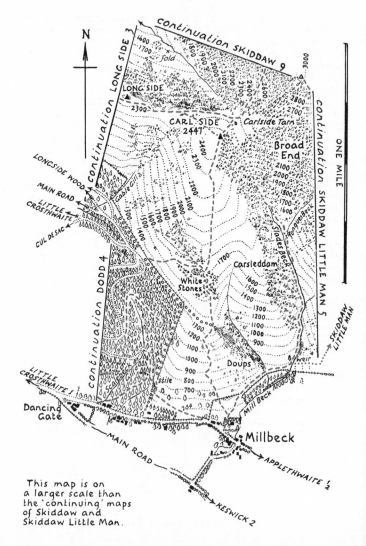

This map is on a larger scale than the 'continuing' maps of Skiddaw and Skiddaw Little Man.

ASCENT FROM LITTLE CROSTHWAITE
2070 feet of ascent : 2¼ miles

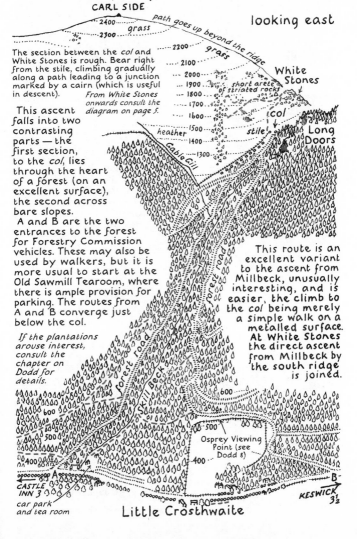

CARL SIDE

looking east

path goes up beyond the ridge

White Stones

short arete of striated rocks

col

stile

Long Doors

heather

Gable Gill

The section between the *col* and White Stones is rough. Bear right from the stile, climbing gradually along a path leading to a junction marked by a cairn (which is useful in descent). *From White Stones onwards consult the diagram on page 5.*

This ascent falls into two contrasting parts — the first section, to the *col*, lies through the heart of a forest (on an excellent surface), the second across bare slopes.

A and B are the two entrances to the forest for Forestry Commission vehicles. These may also be used by walkers, but it is more usual to start at the Old Sawmill Tearoom, where there is ample provision for parking. The routes from A and B converge just below the col.

If the plantations arouse interest, consult the chapter on Dodd for details.

This route is an excellent variant to the ascent from Millbeck, unusually interesting, and is easier, the climb to the col being merely a simple walk on a metalled surface. At White Stones the direct ascent from Millbeck by the south ridge is joined.

forest road

Skill Beck

Osprey Viewing Point (see Dodd 8)

CASTLE INN 3

car park and tea room

KESWICK 3½

Little Crosthwaite

ASCENT FROM MILLBECK
2100 feet of ascent : 1¼ miles (all routes)

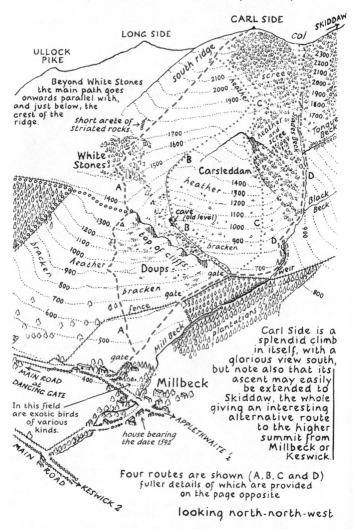

CARL SIDE

SKIDDAW

col

LONG SIDE

ULLOCK PIKE

south ridge

scree

2300
2200
2100
2000
2000
1900
1900
1800
1700.

Beyond White Stones the main path goes onwards parallel with, and just below, the crest of the ridge.

short arete of → striated rocks

C

Heather and scree

Slape Beck

Tongue Beck

1700
1600

White Stones

1500

A

B

Carsleddam

heather

1400
1300
1200

D

1400

1300

1200

1100

900

bracken

cave (old level)

B

1100
1000
900

Black Beck

C

D

1300

1200

1100

top of cliffs

1000

heather

900

Doups

gate

700

weir

800

bracken

gate

800

600

fence

500

bracken

Mill Beck

plantations

gate

400

Carl Side is a splendid climb in itself, with a glorious view south, but note also that its ascent may easily be extended to Skiddaw, the whole giving an interesting alternative route to the higher summit from Millbeck or Keswick.

MAIN ROAD at DANCING GATE

In this field are exotic birds of various kinds.

Millbeck

house bearing the date 1592

APPLETHWAITE ½

MAIN ROAD → KESWICK 2

Four routes are shown (A, B, C and D) fuller details of which are provided on the page opposite

looking north-north-west

ASCENT FROM MILLBECK

continued

A : This is the natural route of ascent, and the best in spite of the tedious initial climb straight up from Millbeck: there is recompense on this section in the glorious view southwards. Turn off the wide path to the weir almost at once after leaving civilisation, by a little embankment (this used to support a fence) and go directly up the brow of the fell, crossing a fence. Higher up a broken wall is reached near the edge of the cliff of Doups (which comes as a surprise). Ahead, a rising path goes through the low crags of White Stones − another surprising place. Some beautiful cairns could be erected here from the plentiful supplies of sparkling quartz, and one or two would be useful. Not all the rocks are white: some are pink; and because many of them are covered in lichens the predominant colour is grey. Above White Stones a remarkably straight track rises up through the heather, keeping just below the ridge until it slants easily to the crest with the summit 300 yards further on over a declining grass slope.

B : This route is more sheltered than A or C, and passes along the foot of the unexpected line of cliffs of Doups, which are quite impressive at such close quarters. Stay on the path to the weir until it crosses a small stream and follow the stream to its source. Here the only sound is the chatter of the stream as it passes over a succession of small waterfalls. Above the source of the stream walking is hampered by knee-high heather and progress is slow. Walking downhill is easier because the deep heather acts like a brake.

CARL SIDE   SKIDDAW →

Carlside col

C : Carsleddam is a most attractive peak when seen from a distance, but it is not easy to get to. There is no sign of the path shown in the illustration or of the cairn shown on the 2½-inch Ordnance Survey map. In addition to heather there is bracken to negotiate in summer and autumn. Nevertheless, the final stages of the climb and its narrow summit are exhilarating, and the view south is superb. Route D may be left anywhere between the small stream and the weir. Then the route is pathless until the south ridge of Carl Side is reached.

The summit of Carsleddam, looking north

D : This route is so obvious and well-defined that it is impossible to stray from it, but two things should be noted. First that the path deteriorates after it passes Black Beck and becomes difficult to follow. Secondly that in the top part of the valley there is nothing but loose scree. It is perhaps significant that the map outside the village hall at Millbeck shows a route to Skiddaw via White Stones, but none via Slades Beck.

It is remarkable how small streams in this area like Black Beck and Tongues Beck, neither of them more than a quarter of a mile long, should have been given names. On the other side of Skiddaw Little Man, in an area that is very rarely visited, there are Slat Gill, Kitbain Gill, Pike Sike and Stile Gill. In many other parts of England, watercourses of this size would be nameless.

ASCENT FROM HIGH SIDE
2050 feet of ascent · 3 miles

looking
south-south-east

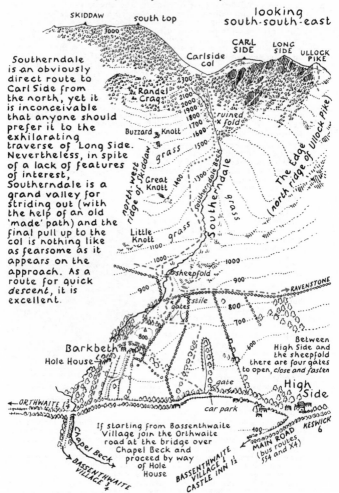

Southerndale is an obviously direct route to Carl Side from the north, yet it is inconceivable that anyone should prefer it to the exhilarating traverse of Long Side. Nevertheless, in spite of a lack of features of interest, Southerndale is a grand valley for striding out (with the help of an old 'made' path) and the final pull up to the col is nothing like as fearsome as it appears on the approach. As a route for quick descent, it is excellent.

Between High Side and the sheepfold there are four gates to open, close and fasten

If starting from Bassenthwaite Village join the Orthwaite road at the bridge over Chapel Beck and proceed by way of Hole House

Southerndale, an unsuspected valley concealed from the popular haunts of tourists, leads naturally to Carl Side and provides an easy route of approach.

THE SUMMIT

The summit is a wide, undistinguished grassy plateau, sloping easily away on three sides but exhibiting a shattered remnant of cliff at the top of the steep, stony and loose east face.

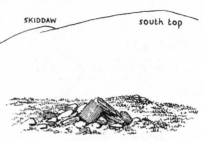

DESCENTS: To MILLBECK (for KESWICK) — The best route, whatever the weather, is along the south ridge and over White Stones. To HIGH SIDE or BASSENTHWAITE —

In clear weather the best route is along the ridge to the west and over Ullock Pike. This is a fine ridge walk, with views of a desolate valley on the right, and in complete contrast, views of mountains, lakes, villages and forests of the left. On a wild or misty day the valley of Southerndale might be preferred.

RIDGE ROUTES

To SKIDDAW, 3053′ : 1 mile : NE, then N
Depression at 2290′ : 780 feet of ascent
Uninviting, but there is no other way

The steep slope of scree rising beyond Carlside Tarn look formidable, but, although toilsome (and longer than it appears to be), there are no difficulties. The best route follows a loose and stony path to the wind-shelter on the middle top.

To LONG SIDE, 2405′ :
½ mile : NW
Depression at 2240′
165 feet of ascent
Make a beeline, joining a track at the depression

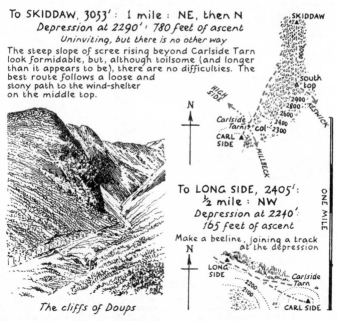

The cliffs of Doups

THE VIEW

The view from the cairn, beautiful though it is to the south, suffers from a broad and uninteresting foreground. Every view is enhanced by a sharp falling away of the foreground, to give it depth as well as distance, but here, unfortunately, too much of the summit-plateau appears in the scene. Two of Carl Side's neighbours, Long Side and Skiddaw Little Man, both abrupt peaks, have an advantage in this respect.

Nevertheless, the prospect southwards over Derwent Water to the mountains around the head of Borrowdale is delightful, and in very marked contrast to the gaunt flanks of Skiddaw and its Little Man near at hand, both rising like mammoth spoil-heaps much higher into the sky. From this grassy belvedere, the massive proportions of Skiddaw are impressed upon the beholder forcibly, almost aggressively. Carl Side is of respectable height yet is quite dwarfed by the tremendous slopes towering above.

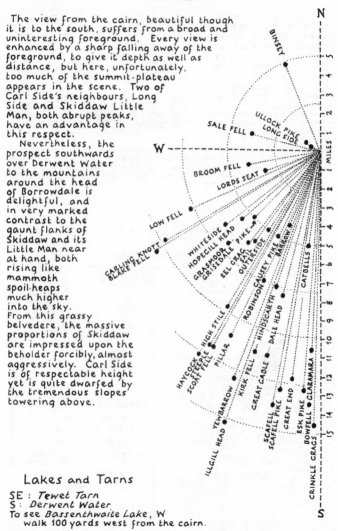

Lakes and Tarns

SE : *Tewet Tarn*
S : *Derwent Water.*
To see *Bassenthwaite Lake*, W
  walk 100 yards west from the cairn.

THE VIEW

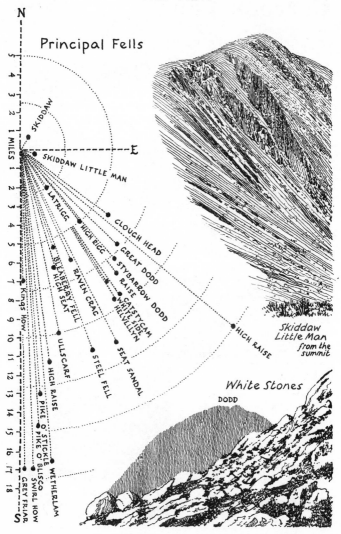

Principal Fells

N

5
4
3
2
1 MILES

Skiddaw

E

SKIDDAW LITTLE MAN

2
3
4
5
6
7
8
9
10
11
12
13
14
15
16
17
18
S

LATRIGG

HIGH RIGG

CLOUGH HEAD

GREAT DODD

BLEABERRY FELL

HIGH SEAT

RAVEN CRAG

STYBARROW DODD

RAISE

CATSTYCAM
WHITE SIDE
HELVELLYN

ULLSCARF

SEAT SANDAL

HIGH RAISE

STEEL FELL

HIGH RAISE

Kings How

PIKE O' STICKLE
PIKE O BLISCO
SWIRL HOW

WETHERLAM

GREY FRIAR

Skiddaw
Little Man
*from the
summit*

White Stones

DODD

Carrock Fell

2169'

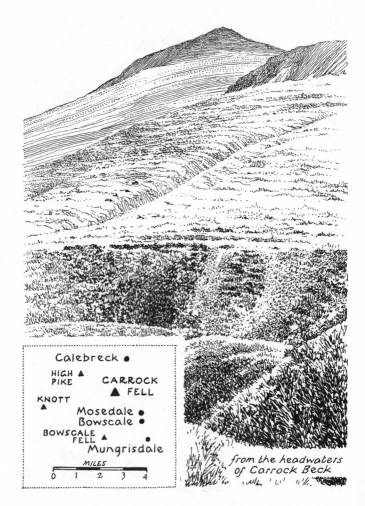

Calebreck ●

HIGH
PIKE ▲   CARROCK
              ▲ FELL ●

KNOTT
▲   Mosedale ●
         Bowscale ●

BOWSCALE ▲
  FELL   ●
      Mungrisdale

MILES
0   1   2   3   4

*from the headwaters
of Carrock Beck*

NATURAL FEATURES

Carrock Fell caters for a wide variety of interests. More than any other fell in the district it attracts people who are not regular walkers or climbers—people, indeed, to whom walking for its own sake has little appeal and is here, on Carrock, only a means to an end and not an end in itself. This rough little height is, first and foremost, a very rich geological field, for here the extensive area of Skiddaw slates and shales, the basic foundation of practically the whole of the Northern Fells, abruptly terminates against a rugged upthrust of igneous or volcanic rocks of different series dovetailed in such a way as to provide an absorbing study for the geologist, while the bed of the Caldew at the western base is notable as one of the few places where the underlying creamy-pink Skiddaw granite is exposed. One need have no special knowledge to see at a glance that Carrock Fell is different from its neighbours: appearance alone is enough, the bouldery slopes contrasting sharply with those of smooth grass all around. Carrock Fell is something of a rebel, a nonconformist, the odd man out—it would look more at home at the head of Borrowdale or Langdale amongst others of like kind.

In the field of mining Carrock is a famous name, having a series of veins that have yielded a variety of rich and rare metals and other minerals. Carrock Mine is especially well known for its supplies of wolfram. Although not now being worked the area is often visited by mineralogists.

Other fells have interesting rocks and minerals also—but Carrock has more than natural attractions on display. Its summit is unique, being ringed by the collapsed walls of an ancient hill-fort of unknown age and origin, thought to be early British, which must, in its time, have been a remarkable stronghold. This in itself is enough to excite the many archaeologists and antiquaries who, individually and in groups, make pilgrimages to the place, but the east base of the fell, too, has scores of artificial mounds that might upon investigation reveal something of the story of Carrock B.C.

continued

Carrock Fell, from the hut on Great Lingy Hill

NATURAL FEATURES

continued

Amongst the igneous rocks of which the fell is formed is gabbro — the stuff the Black Coolin of Skye are made of but a rarity in Lakeland. It is in evidence in the crags of the eastern escarpment and on the boulder-strewn slopes below. Gabbro is an ideal rock for climbing, and here is the one and only climbing-ground in the Northern Fells — very handily situated just above an unenclosed road (the one going *north* out of Mosedale) where cars may be parked. The eastern face of the fell, in fact, everywhere presents attractive scenery.

The heaps of piled boulders on the fell, both on the south and east fronts, provide several safe borrans for foxes in their crevices, these refuges being well-known to followers of the Blencathra pack. When a fox was run to earth on Carrock the hunt was often called off and the frustrated pursuers retired brushless. Cheers for Carrock, therefore, on humane grounds also.

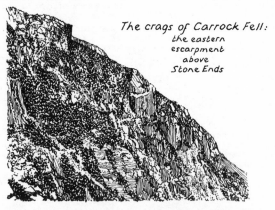

The crags of Carrock Fell:
the eastern
escarpment
above
Stone Ends

Geologists, mineralogists, archaeologists, rock-climbers and foxes : all these are provided for. What is there for the ordinary walker, who simply ascends hills because he likes doing it ? Well, Carrock is a delightful climb, as rough as one cares to make it. In the northern area of Lakeland it ranks next to Blencathra for interest and excitement and beauty of surroundings; in season it has its own special reward for bilberry addicts: there are acres to graze upon. Let others tap rocks with hammers, and dig holes, and prospect with pans, and scale precipices if they wish; heaven for the walker with no special scholarship is at hand in the lush green pastures around the summit. But visit the cairn, of course, for yet another of Carrock's manifold attractions is its glorious view.

Carrock Mine

Carrock Mine is situated at the confluence of Grainsgill Beck and Brandy Gill, in a side-valley of the Caldew. It has been a productive source of mineral wealth in variety, but is best known for its output of the heavy metal *tungsten (wolfram)*, a rare mineral not found elsewhere in Lakeland.

The mine has been closed several times because of falls in world prices. The last time it was reopened was in 1977, after £250,000 had been spent on such things as new buildings. The mine finally closed in 1981, and there is little left to see.

Mineral veins occur in fractures of the rock, commonly following straight courses of varying depth, with branches, and it is usual to find veins running parallel to each other. Carrock Mine offers a good illustration of this. Standing at the head of the artificial 'cut' on the eastern shoulder of Coomb Height one can look directly down its length to Grainsgill Beck and see the line continuing up the opposite slope in a series of levels and shafts – a perfectly straight line over a distance of half a mile. Similarly, on the east side of Brandy Gill another vein is noticeable parallel to the first. The spoil-heaps of mica-quartz are almost white and very conspicuous.

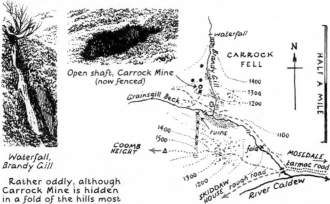

Open shaft, Carrock Mine
(now fenced)

Waterfall,
Brandy Gill

Rather oddly, although Carrock Mine is hidden in a fold of the hills most of its visitors are parties of motorists, their presence being due to the proximity of the mine to the terminus of the surfaced road along the Caldew valley, which is becoming increasingly popular as a Sunday afternoon picnic-place. These visitors are not shod for scrambling over rough ground and often have children and dogs with them: the warning must be repeated that *disused mine-workings are dangerous*, Carrock Mine in fact having some unfenced open shafts. Inspection at a distance is safe; exploration is hazardous.

A source of valuable information on the geology and mineralogy of Lakeland is provided by the book MINES AND MINING IN THE LAKE DISTRICT by *John Postlethwaite* (published 1877; second edition 1889; third edition 1913; reissued 1976; reprinted 1983).

MAP

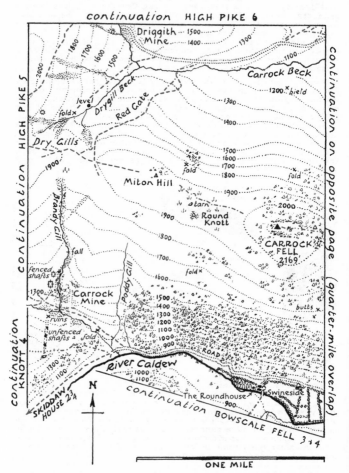

Mosedale means dreary valley, but the name is inappropriate to the mile of emerald pastures watered by the Caldew between the hamlet and Swineside — a charming example of the result of many centuries of patient husbandry, and a typical Lakeland scene.

MAP

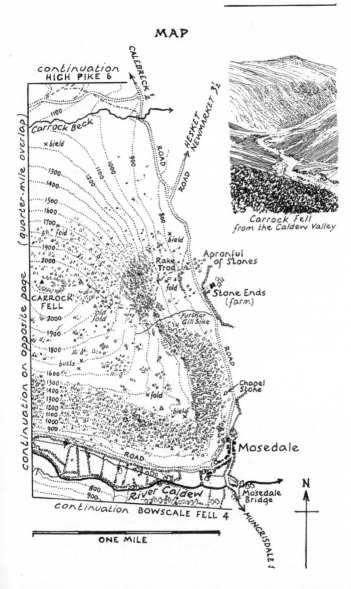

continuation
HIGH PIKE 6

CALEBRECK 2

(quarter-mile overlap)

1100

Carrock Beck

x bield

HESKET NEWMARKET 3½

ROAD

1300
1400
1500
1600
1700
fold
1900
2000

900

800

bield

Rake Trod

Apronful of Stones

fold

Stone Ends (farm)

continuation on opposite page

CARROCK FELL

2000

old fold

Further Gill Sike

1900

1800

butts

1600
1500
1400
1300
1200
1100
1000
900

x fold

bield

ROAD

Chapel Stone

Mosedale

ROAD

River Caldew

800
900

Mosedale Bridge

continuation BOWSCALE FELL 4

MUNGRISDALE 1

N

Carrock Fell
from the Caldew Valley

ONE MILE

ASCENT FROM MOSEDALE
1450 feet of ascent : 2 miles

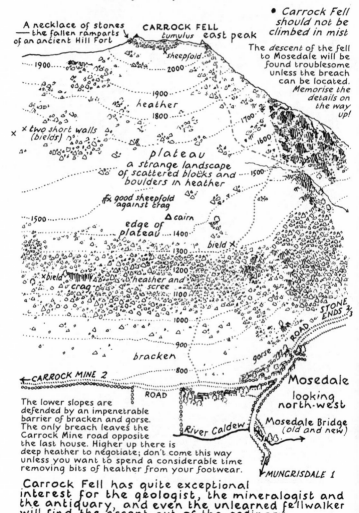

A necklace of stones — the fallen ramparts of an ancient Hill Fort

CARROCK FELL
tumulus east peak

• *Carrock Fell should not be climbed in mist*

The descent of the fell to Mosedale will be found troublesome unless the breach can be located. Memorise the details on the way up!

1900

sheepfold

2000

1900

heather

1800

1700

1600

× × two short walls (bields)

plateau
a strange landscape of scattered blocks and boulders in heather

1500

good sheepfold against crag

△ cairn

1500

edge of plateau   1400

bield ×

1300

×bield

crag   heather and scree

1200

1100

1000

900

bracken

800

gorse

STONE ENDS ¾

ROAD

←CARROCK MINE 2

ROAD

Mosedale
looking north-west

The lower slopes are defended by an impenetrable barrier of bracken and gorse. The only breach leaves the Carrock Mine road opposite the last house. Higher up there is deep heather to negotiate; don't come this way unless you want to spend a considerable time removing bits of heather from your footwear.

River Caldew

Mosedale Bridge (old and new)

↓MUNGRISDALE 1

Carrock Fell has quite exceptional interest for the geologist, the mineralogist and the antiquary, and even the unlearned fellwalker will find the ascent out of the ordinary.

ASCENT FROM STONE ENDS
1400 feet of ascent : 1¼ miles

looking west

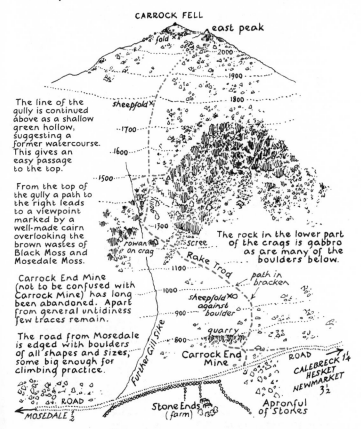

CARROCK FELL

east peak

fold

2000

1900

1800

sheepfold ✗

1700

1600

1500

The line of the gully is continued above as a shallow green hollow, suggesting a former watercourse. This gives an easy passage to the top.

From the top of the gully a path to the right leads to a viewpoint marked by a well-made cairn overlooking the brown wastes of Black Moss and Mosedale Moss.

Carrock End Mine (not to be confused with Carrock Mine) has long been abandoned. Apart from general untidiness few traces remain.

The road from Mosedale is edged with boulders of all shapes and sizes; some big enough for climbing practice.

rowan on crag

1300

scree

Rake Trod

The rock in the lower part of the crags is gabbro as are many of the boulders below.

1100

path in bracken

1000

sheepfold ✗ against boulder

900

quarry

800

Carrock End Mine

path in Gill Sike

ROAD

Further Gill Sike

ROAD

MOSEDALE ½

Stone Ends (farm)

Apronful of Stones

CALEBRECK 1¼
HESKET
NEWMARKET 3½

This is the shortest way to the top from a motor road, and the most straightforward. It affords intimate views of the crags, passing through them by a simple grass gully. This route, 'Rake Trod', is the one used and recommended by local people.

ASCENT FROM CALEBRECK
1300 feet of ascent : 3½ miles

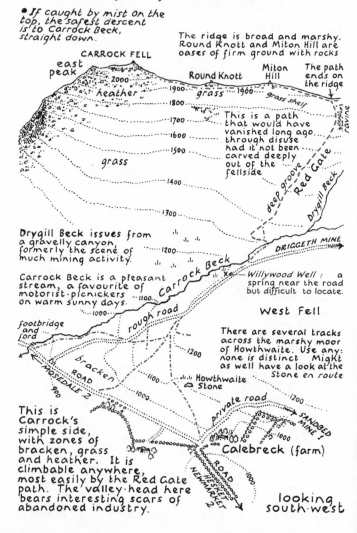

● If caught by mist on the top, the safest descent is to Carrock Beck, straight down.

The ridge is broad and marshy. Round Knott and Miton Hill are oases of firm ground with rocks

CARROCK FELL

east peak

2000

heather

Round Knott

Miton Hill

The path ends on the ridge

1900   grass   1900   grass shelf

1800

1700

1600

1500

This is a path that would have vanished long ago through disuse had it not been carved deeply out of the fellside

grass

1400

1300

deep groove

Red Gate

Drygill Beck

ravine

Drygill Beck issues from a gravelly canyon, formerly the scene of much mining activity.

1200

DRIGGETH MINE

Carrock Beck is a pleasant stream, a favourite of motorist-picnickers on warm sunny days.

Carrock Beck

Willywood Well : a spring near the road but difficult to locate.

1100

rough road

West Fell

1000

footbridge and ford

There are several tracks across the marshy moor of Howthwaite. Use any; none is distinct. Might as well have a look at the Stone en route

1200

MOSEDALE 2

ROAD

bracken

1100

Howthwaite Stone

900

1000

1200

SANDBED MINE 1

This is Carrock's simple side, with zones of bracken, grass and heather. It is climbable anywhere, most easily by the Red Gate path. The valley-head here bears interesting scars of abandoned industry.

private road

1000

Calebreck (farm)

ROAD

HESKET NEWMARKET 2

1000

looking south-west

THE SUMMIT

The top of the fell is elliptical in plan, with a cairn on low rocks at each extremity. Draped like a necklace around the western top (the higher) is a broad band of stones, the ruined wall of the ancient fort: a continuous link except for four breaches corresponding to the main points of the compass and serving as gateways. Within this wall is a heap of stones, possibly a tumulus, now hollowed out as a shelter. There is no obvious trace of buildings, and visitors should not be deceived by an enclosure on the south side, this being only a sheepfold built from the stones of the wall. New bilberry shoots impart a bright sheen to the top in early summer.

best fragment of
original masonry

QUARTER·MILE

N

best fragment of ···
original masonry
2100 ···   2000
tumulus
wall   east
of fort   peak
sheepfold

PLAN OF SUMMIT

The collapsed walls of
the fort, at the
south gateway

continued

THE SUMMIT

continued

DESCENTS. Descent on the east and south flanks is tricky, the few breaches in the impassable slope of crags and boulders at the edge of the plateau being difficult to locate, even in clear weather. The simplest plan is to follow the natural fall of land to the dry gully into which Further Gill Sike enters on the right and go down to Stone Ends by way of Rake Trod. A route to Mosedale direct may be attempted if it has been used observantly for the ascent.

In mist, the safest plan is to go down the easy north slope to Carrock Beck and follow the stream to the road.

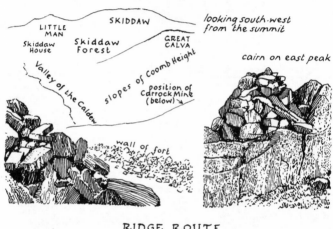

LITTLE MAN — SKIDDAW

Skiddaw House — Skiddaw Forest — GREAT CALVA

Valley of the Caldew

slopes of Coomb Height

position of Carrock Mine (below)

looking south-west from the summit

cairn on east peak

wall of fort

RIDGE ROUTE

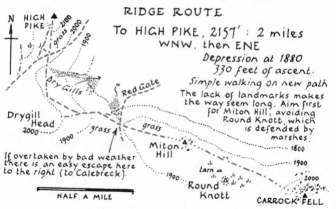

N — HIGH PIKE ▲ 2100

grass 2000

1900

Dry Gills

Red Gate

Drygill Head 2000

1900 — grass

grass

Miton Hill ▲ 1800

1900

tarn

Round Knott

1900

2000

CARROCK FELL ▲

If overtaken by bad weather there is an easy escape here to the right (to Calebreck).

HALF A MILE

To HIGH PIKE, 2157': 2 miles
WNW, then ENE
Depression at 1880
330 feet of ascent.
Simple walking on new path
The lack of landmarks makes the way seem long. Aim first for Miton Hill, avoiding Round Knott, which is defended by marshes.

THE VIEW

The best section of the view is eastwards, not towards Lakeland but away from it, across the wide and fertile valley of the Eden to the Pennines beyond: an extensive yet detailed scene better observed from the east peak.

The neighbouring heights do not show to advantage, but there is a good prospect of the fells around Ullswater, and Great Gable, Pillar & Co. fill in the notch of the Glenderaterra valley quite neatly. The upper Caldew valley features well.

The Solway Firth appears in the north-west, with Criffell prominent just to the right of the summit of High Pike.

Principal Fells

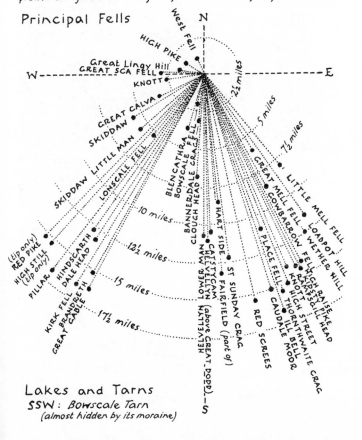

Lakes and Tarns

SSW: *Bowscale Tarn*
(almost hidden by its moraine)

Dodd

1647'

also variously known
as Skiddaw Dodd
and Little Dodd
and named Dodd Fell
on Bartholomews maps

from Longside Wood

from Millbeck road end

- ● Bassenthwaite
- ▲ SKIDDAW
- ▲ CARL SIDE
- ▲ ● DODD
- ● Dancing Gate
- ● Millbeck

Little
Crosthwaite

Keswick ●

MILES

0   1   2   3

NATURAL FEATURES

Dodd, like Latrigg, can be described as a whelp of Skiddaw crouched at the feet of his parent. But Dodd has latterly shown nothing of the family characteristics and the old man must today regard his offspring with surprise and growing doubt, and feel like denying his paternity and disowning the little wretch.

Skiddaw is a high, bare, rangy mountain, open to the winds of heaven; Dodd is stunted, and (apart from a few areas that have recently been cleared) is clothed from tip to toe in a growth of trees so luxurious that scarcely any part of the original appearance of the fell remains in view. Skiddaw is Lakeland through and through, one of the respected dignitaries of the district, absolutely true blue; Dodd would seem more in place in the dense and steaming jungles of the Amazon.

But Dodd is really an innocent party in this matter, the great change being none of his seeking but having been thrust upon him. In years gone by Dodd sported a few small woodlands, like a young man his first moustaches, with such success and evidence of fertility as to attract the attention of the Forestry Commission, then developing the Thornthwaite Forest just across Bassenthwaite Lake. Since 1920 the Commission have been rampant here, and, except for a single field at Little Crosthwaite, they have covered the fell thickly with growing timber.

The work has been tackled with imagination, and with due regard to amenity. Nobody is likely to complain much about the results of this enterprise. There might be a little regret that the regimentation and segregation of species is still persisted in, giving an unnatural patchwork effect, but, in general, Dodd has come through the transformation fairly well. The older deciduous trees fringing the base of the fell have been retained as a screen, and, where they occur elsewhere, have been left to develop; many of the matured pines and firs in the early plantations, growing singly, are excellent specimens, and there has been a fair mixing of species in the new plantations, with larch, spruce, pine and fir in variety. Admirable roads have been made, to give access to all parts of the forest, and it requires only a walk along them to appreciate the extent of the work involved in the maintenance of a great industry of this sort, and the skill and resource of those responsible for the enterprise. Dodd has not been spoiled, but given a new look; and it is a more

Scots pine

Larch

continued

NATURAL FEATURES

continued

interesting, and certainly a more fascinating, place than ever it was in the past. Skiddaw's frown betrays an old prejudice; true, Skiddaw has long had his own Forest but *that* is fine rolling upland country not desecrated by fancy trees .....*foreign* trees, moreover! If there *must* be trees on Dodd, aren't Lakeland trees good enough? Bah! says Skiddaw.

Douglas fir

As far as walkers are concerned, they may walk along the forest roads — *but not as of right*, and the courtesy thus extended is one that ought to be fully respected, please.

Only if it is desired to visit the summit of the fell is it necessary to leave the roads, and that objective can be reached, without causing damage to trees, using the path laid out in 2002 to the summit from the south-east. There is no excuse at all for barging through the plantations and crippling young trees.

Sitka spruce

The Forestry Commission refer to their plantations in this area by the title of Dodd Wood, and, because for many years the fell was completely covered, Dodd and Dodd Wood are often used as synonymous names; not always correctly, for the adjoining plantations on Long Side and north to Ravenstone are also part of the official Dodd Wood.

Geographically, Dodd is the first of the three great steps of Skiddaw rising from the head of Bassenthwaite Lake. The second step, Carl Side, is joined at mid-height: the link is a distinctive *col* from which flow the boundary streams, Skill Beck and Scale Beck. A feature is the pronounced northwest ridge; a less conspicuous ridge descends southeast from the summit. These ridges used to be followed by a wide fire-break amongst the dense plantations, resembling, from a distance, a centre parting in a head of hair. Today, in any view in which it can be seen, Dodd is readily identifiable by the dark covering of conifers on its slopes and its bare summit.

In 2001 the Forestry Commission laid out a series of circular walks all starting and finishing at the Old Sawmill Tearoom:
1. The Sandbed Gill Trail (marked by yellow-topped posts)
2. The Skill Beck Trail (marked by red-topped posts)
3. The Douglas Fir Trail (marked by blue-topped posts)
4. The Dodd Summit Trail (marked by green-topped posts)
The length varies from 1 mile to 3 miles; a leaflet is available at the tea room.

MAP

When the map on this page was prepared in 1962 it was the best available to the public at the time. It was the result of an amateur survey, using jigsaw tactics in lieu of precise instruments, but was quite reliable. Now that the map has been revised using satellite technology it is possible that it is still the best available. The prominent zig-zag path that approaches the summit from the south-east is not shown on Harvey's map of 2006, and on the 2008 edition of the 2½" Ordnance Survey map it is shown but the wrong shape.

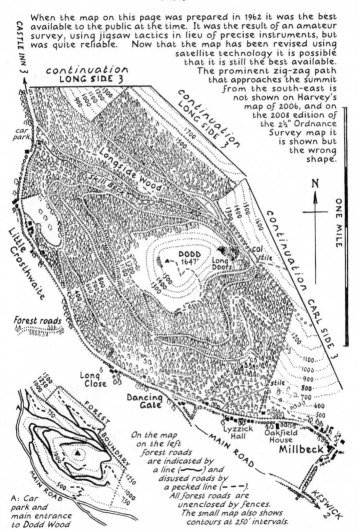

CASTLE INN 3

continuation LONG SIDE 3

continuation LONG SIDE 3

continuation CARL SIDE 3

ONE MILE

N

car park

Longside Wood

Skill Beck

Little Crosthwaite

DODD 1647'

Long Doors

col stile

Forest roads

Long Close

Dancing Gate

FOREST BOUNDARY

MAIN ROAD

stile

Scalebeck Gill

1200
1100
1000
900
800
700
600
500

Lyzzick Hall

Oakfield House

Millbeck

MAIN ROAD

KESWICK 2

On the map on the left forest roads are indicated by a line (———) and disused roads by a pecked line (— —). All forest roads are unenclosed by fences. The small map also shows contours at 250' intervals.

A: Car park and main entrance to Dodd Wood

Dodd Wood

The wide variety of tree species in Dodd Wood, unusual in coniferous plantations, adds an interest for observant visitors. The deciduous trees are old favourites, generally well-known; but there is difficulty to the untrained eye in identifying the softwood timber trees, which are of the same habit of growth and similar in appearance. All are evergreen, except the larch, and grow straight and tall from a main stem.

Of the species planted most extensively, the pines and the larches are distinctive enough to be recognised at sight, but there is much doubt about the firs and the spruces.

Douglas Fir and Norway Spruce (the latter being the 'Christmas Tree') look very much alike, but can be identified with certainty by their cones, which litter the ground beneath the older trees. The cone of the Douglas Fir (next page) has peculiar three-pronged bracts issuing between the scales, but the cone of the Norway Spruce is smooth, the scales overlapping closely and appearing to be made of brown paper. Sitka Spruce is easier to distinguish by reason of its sturdy and vigorous growth, prickly needles and blue-green colour.

Scots Pine

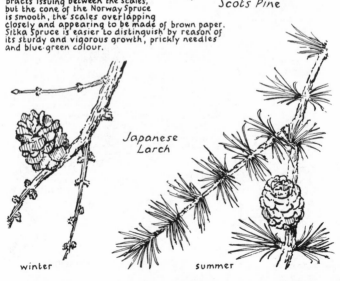

Japanese
Larch

winter   summer

Dodd Wood

The Forestry Commission's publication "Thornthwaite"* mentions the following species as in cultivation on Dodd (apart from deciduous trees):

Scots pine
Lodgepole pine
Mountain pine
Norway spruce
Sitka spruce
Japanese larch
European larch
Douglas fir
Noble fir
Western hemlock
Lawson's cypress
Western red cedar

The four last-named are not much in evidence. Douglas Fir is extensive up to 1000'; larch occurs in big 'stands' at middle height, 800'-1200'; the spruces thrive, Sitka especially, up to 1500', and the pines at all elevations.

*now out of print

Douglas Fir

Norway Spruce

Sitka Spruce

ASCENTS

The climbing of Dodd is not to be achieved merely by repeating the process of putting one foot before and higher than the other, as in the case of most ascents. On Dodd the Forestry Commission and a million or so allies in a massed formation — spruces, firs and larch (to say nothing of *Pinus mugo*) — must be outwitted, and some crafty manœuvring is required to reach the summit. Forcing a way ever upwards through the trees is not playing the game, and is out of the question anyway because the depths of the forest are quite impassable. Recourse must therefore be had to (a) the forest roads and (b) the forest paths.

THE FOREST ROADS:

The forest workers know not only how to grow trees but how to plan roads too, and they have made a really excellent job of laying passages for their vehicles. Considering the steepness

Forest road

of the fell the roads are wonderfully well graded, reaching to all parts of the forest without ever exceeding the gentlest of slopes, and they are well culverted, providing dry surfaces for walking even on the wettest days. Roughly metalled, they are not hard to the feet but are generally shaly, rather loose and soft. In long spirals and zigzags the roads climb as high as 1400 feet; some other means of access must be used, therefore, in later stages of the ascent to the summit, 200' higher.

Dodd is a small fell, yet there are already nearly five miles of 10' roads hidden amongst the plantations. In the contiguous Longside Wood (under the same management) are several more miles of forest roads, similarly concealed from the sight of travellers on the busy Keswick-Carlisle highway running along the base of the plantations.

At two places, forest roads effect junctions with the main road. These may be used by walkers to enter the forest, but it is more usual to use the entrance by the Old Sawmill Tearoom, where there is a bus stop and car park. (From April to October the tea room car park is currently also used by visitors to Mirehouse, the historic home of the Spedding family, on the occasions when it is open to the public.   Mirehouse is where Alfred Lord Tennyson was staying when he wrote *Morte d'Arthur*.)

ASCENTS

continued

THE FOREST PATHS :

Before the forest roads were cut the workers in the new plantations made use of a network of footpaths between the growing trees. Many of these old paths have gone out of

Forest path

commission or been superseded by the roads; others can still be traced although now heavily overshadowed; a few remain in regular use. Since Dodd Wood became part of the Whinlatter Forest Park new paths have been constructed for the benefit of visitors. Consequently there is now a surfaced route all the way from the car park to the summit; if you want to climb a mountain but left your boots at home this is the place to come. According to O.S. maps many of the forest paths form part of long distance walks, particularly the Allerdale Ramble, which runs from Borrowdale to the coast.

THE FOREST RIDES (FIRE-BREAKS) :

The fire-breaks were strips of rough fellside that were left unplanted to stop a fire spreading from one part of the forest to another. In 2006 no trace of any of them could be found.

THE DISUSED FOREST ROADS :

These are shown on the small map on page 4. They become overgrown with moss, heather and, eventually, young trees.

Fire-break (north-west ridge)

THE FELLED AREAS :

Except in the area around the summit these are not shown on the maps. Felling is going on all the time, and if you look closely at felled areas you will often find that young trees have been planted or have naturally regenerated.

THE OSPREY VIEWING POINT :

This is shown on the diagram on page 9. It is open only from April to August because the birds migrate to Africa for the winter. Telescopes are provided for watching a nest on the far side of the lake. There are only two osprey breeding sites in England, the other being in Rutland. In 2008 the birds moved to Dodd Wood, and another viewing point was set up farther up the hill.

ASCENT FROM THE OLD SAWMILL TEAROOM
1300 feet of ascent : 2½ miles

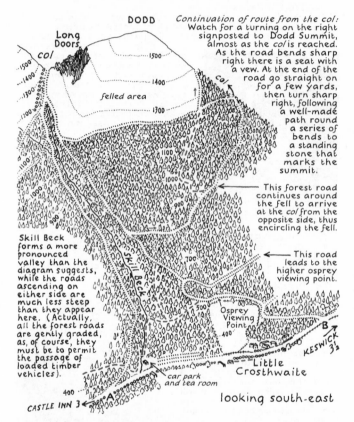

DODD

Long Doors

col

felled area

Continuation of route from the col:
Watch for a turning on the right signposted to Dodd Summit, almost as the col is reached. As the road bends sharp right there is a seat with a view. At the end of the road go straight on for a few yards, then turn sharp right, following a well-made path round a series of bends to a standing stone that marks the summit.

This forest road continues around the fell to arrive at the col from the opposite side, thus encircling the fell.

Skill Beck forms a more pronounced valley than the diagram suggests, while the roads ascending on either side are much less steep than they appear here. (Actually, all the forest roads are gently graded, as, of course, they must be to permit the passage of loaded timber vehicles).

This road leads to the higher osprey viewing point.

Skill Beck

Osprey Viewing Point

car park and tea room

KESWICK 3½

Little Crosthwaite

CASTLE INN 3

looking south-east

A and B are the two points where forest roads come down to the public highway. Both roads lead directly to the Long Doors col: in fact, they converge below it. The col is an interesting place, with unexpected cliffs.

The route from the col onwards lies on the far side of the fell and is not shown in the diagram (see note at top of page). An alternative route, not visiting the col, and about the same length, follows the south side of Skill Beck from the tea room and is marked throughout its length by posts with a green band round them. It is indicated by arrows on the diagram. Both routes are thoroughly recommended.

ASCENT FROM DANCING GATE
1320 feet of ascent : 1½ miles

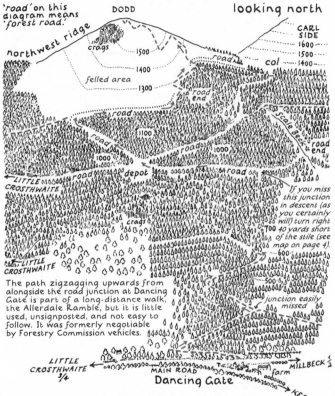

'road' on this diagram means 'forest road.'

DODD

looking north

northwest ridge

crags

1500

1400

felled area

1300

CARL SIDE
1600
1500
col 1400

road

road end

road

road

1100

road

road

1000

road

road end

1000

Scale Beck

road

depot

road

←— LITTLE CROSTHWAITE

If you miss this junction in descent (as you certainly will) turn right too 40 yards short of the stile (see map on page 4).

crags

LITTLE CROSTHWAITE

600

500

junction easily missed

The path zigzagging upwards from alongside the road junction at Dancing Gate is part of a long-distance walk, the Allerdale Ramble, but it is little used, unsignposted, and not easy to follow. It was formerly negotiable by Forestry Commission vehicles.

LITTLE CROSTHWAITE ←—
¾

MAIN ROAD
Dancing Gate

MILLBECK ½

farm

KESWICK 2½

As in other plantations of conifers, a deathly silence pervades the forest. Birds are evidently suspicious of the unnatural arrangement and ghostly twilight of the 'foreign' trees (although wood-pigeons find a safe haven here) and prefer the friendlier atmosphere of deciduous woodlands, where the sun can reach them and they can be happy and sing.

This is more a game than a walk. Snakes-and-ladders enthusiasts will find the route absorbing. Apart from the felled areas near the summit Dodd is a labyrinth of forest roads and paths. These are all the more confusing because the dense screen of trees makes it impossible to view the way ahead or to take bearings. Follow the arrows.

ASCENT FROM MILLBECK
1250 feet of ascent : 2 miles

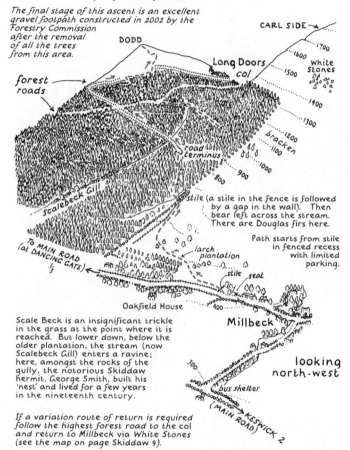

The final stage of this ascent is an excellent gravel footpath constructed in 2002 by the Forestry Commission after the removal of all the trees from this area.

CARL SIDE →

DODD

Long Doors col

WHITE STONES

1700
1600
1500
1400
1300
1200
1100
1000
900
800

forest roads

bracken

road terminus

Scalebeck Gill

stile (a stile in the fence is followed by a gap in the wall). Then bear left across the stream. There are Douglas firs here.

Path starts from stile in fenced recess with limited parking.

TO MAIN ROAD (AT DANCING GATE) ⅓

larch plantation

stile   seat

Oakfield House   400

Millbeck

looking north-west

300

Scale Beck is an insignificant trickle in the grass at the point where it is reached. But lower down, below the older plantation, the stream (now Scalebeck Gill) enters a ravine; here, amongst the rocks of the gully, the notorious Skiddaw hermit, George Smith, built his 'nest' and lived for a few years in the nineteenth century.

bus shelter

(MAIN ROAD) KESWICK 2

If a variation route of return is required follow the highest forest road to the col and return to Millbeck via White Stones (see the map on page Skiddaw 9).

Millbeck is conveniently placed for an ascent of Dodd, yet this is not a popular climb, and nobody will be encountered (except on the final stage) on 360 days in the year. The route up Scalebeck Gill is impracticable, and the forest is a maze, but follow the arrows and the top will be reached in due course.

THE SUMMIT

Anyone visiting the summit today would not recognise the drawing above: all the trees have gone, and the cairn has been replaced by a standing stone which bears the inscription 'Dodd Summit 1612 feet'. Presumably the stone was erected before the altitude was reassessed by the Ordnance Survey as 502 metres or 1647 feet. On the reverse of the stone are memorials to John Lole and Ian Sandelands of the first Seaton Scout Group, and to Malcolm McDougall. The trees were mountain pines, *Pinus mugo*. They covered the top completely, except for a tiny clearing which was left in deference to the cairn. Fifty years ago it was noted that the planting did not appear to be successful. Few trees were then flourishing: the majority looked unhealthy or even diseased and dying. The trees have not completely disappeared, for their stumps still remain, and the ground is littered with dead branches, which make walking difficult.

The path to the summit from the east was built in 2002.

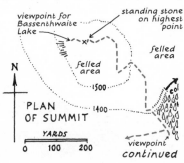

PLAN OF SUMMIT

N

viewpoint for Bassenthwaite Lake

standing stone on highest point

felled area

felled area

1500

1400

col

viewpoint continued

YARDS
0   100   200

:::::::: *forest road*
- - - - *path leading to forest road*

THE SUMMIT

continued

DESCENTS : The path to the west (towards Bassenthwaite Lake) soon comes to an end, and all descents start along the path to the east. When you come to a forest road there is a choice of routes. For the tea room stay on the road to the *col* and follow the valley of Skill Beck, or go left and immediately right at the start of the forest road and follow the green-topped posts. For Millbeck go left and immediately right at the start of the forest road, following the ridge. Then take a path on the right, which later becomes a forest road and bends sharp left. When you get to the main forest road turn right and immediately left onto a lesser road. After crossing Scalebeck Gill this becomes a path, which eventually leads to Millbeck. For Dancing Gate use the Millbeck route and turn right forty yards before leaving the plantation. The zigzag path to Dancing Gate is impossible to find from above.

RIDGE ROUTE

To CARL SIDE, 2447': 1½ miles :
SE, then NE and N
Depression at 1355'
1075 feet of ascent
An interesting traverse.

Follow the path down to the forest road and turn left to the *col.* Turn right for a hundred yards, and then left, crossing the forest fence by a stile. From the stile a path rises obliquely through the heather and comes out at the south ridge of Carl Side just above the main rash of White Stones. The ridge is then followed up.

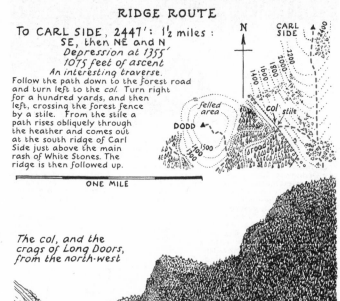

ONE MILE

The col, and the crags of Long Doors, from the north-west

THE VIEW

When trees covered the summit one could not see all the fells indicated on the diagram below without standing on tiptoes, craning the neck, leaping in the air and miscellaneous gyrations of the body not normally indulged in by people in their right senses. The felling has transformed the prospect. Only parts of Bassenthwaite Lake can be seen from the summit, but the whole of the lake can be seen by continuing beyond the summit to the end of the gravel path. In 1993 the area around the lake became a National Nature Reserve.

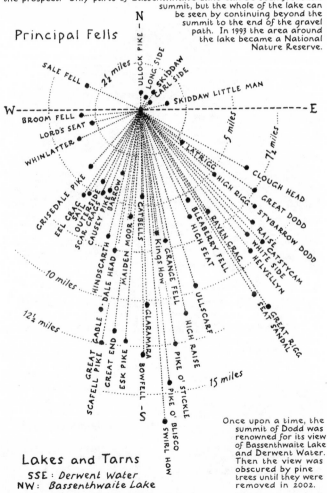

Principal Fells

Lakes and Tarns
SSE: Derwent Water
NW: Bassenthwaite Lake

Once upon a time, the summit of Dodd was renowned for its view of Bassenthwaite Lake and Derwent Water. Then the view was obscured by pine trees until they were removed in 2002.

Great Calva

2265'

from the path to
Skiddaw House

from Burn Tod

Orthwaite •   ▲ KNOTT
                         Mosedale •
              ▲ GREAT CALVA
BAKESTALL
    ▲   BOWSCALE
SKIDDAW   FELL
    ▲   • Skiddaw House

MILES

0   1   2   3   4

NATURAL FEATURES

Most regular visitors to Lakeland will be familiar with the outline of Great Calva even though they may never in their wanderings have been within miles of it, because its symmetrical pyramid neatly fills in the head of the valley opening south between the Skiddaw and Blencathra massifs and is conspicuously seen from many points on the busy road approaching Keswick from Grasmere.

It occupies a splendid position overlooking the broad depression of Skiddaw Forest, with which it seems to be inseparably associated, more so even than Skiddaw itself. Calva dominates the Forest, rising from it in a strange patchwork of colours indicative of areas of heather, its principal covering, that have been burnt off, are newly shooting up or are long established, giving odd contrasts in appearance.

The actual top, which is stony, is a fine belvedere, but behind is an extensive plateau without an irrigation system and so forming a morass across which one can step gingerly to the solid ground of Little Calva, a place of little interest; and, beyond, the fell drops away steeply in a series of spiky aretes to the magnificent Dash Falls. This is Calva's best aspect; nevertheless the fell's appeal is more likely to depend upon its unique function as the watchtower of Skiddaw Forest.

Bridge on the road to Skiddaw House, above Dash Falls

MAP

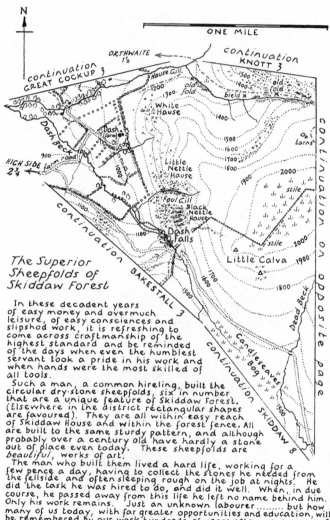

N

ONE MILE

ORTHWAITE 1½

continuation KNOTT 3

continuation GREAT COCKUP 3

Hause Gill

old fold

old fold

bield ×

White House

1200
1300
1500
1400
1400

Dash (farm)

Dash Beck

1500
1600
1700
1800

tarns

Little Nettle House

HIGH SIDE 2¾

900

farm road

1000

1100

Foul Gill

Black Nettle House

1900
2000

stile

Dash Falls

1100

continuation BAKESTALL 3

Little Calva

1700
1600
1500

1800
1900

stile
2000

continuation on opposite page

continuation SKIDDAW 8

Candleseaves Bog

Dead Beck

1500

The Superior Sheepfolds of Skiddaw Forest

In these decadent years of easy money and overmuch leisure, of easy consciences and slipshod work, it is refreshing to come across craftmanship of the highest standard and be reminded of the days when even the humblest servant took a pride in his work and when hands were the most skilled of all tools.

Such a man, a common hireling, built the circular dry-stone sheepfolds, six in number, that are a unique feature of Skiddaw Forest. (Elsewhere in the district rectangular shapes are favoured). They are all within easy reach of Skiddaw House and within the forest fence. All are built to the same sturdy pattern, and although probably over a century old have hardly a stone out of place even today. These sheepfolds are beautiful works of art.

The man who built them lived a hard life, working for a few pence a day, having to collect the stones he needed from the fellside and often sleeping rough on the job at nights. He did the task he was hired to do, and did it well. When, in due course, he passed away from this life he left no name behind him. Only his work remains. Just an unknown labourer........ but how many of us today, with far greater opportunities and education, will be remembered by our work hundreds of years after we are gone? Few indeed! Idleness builds no monuments.

MAP

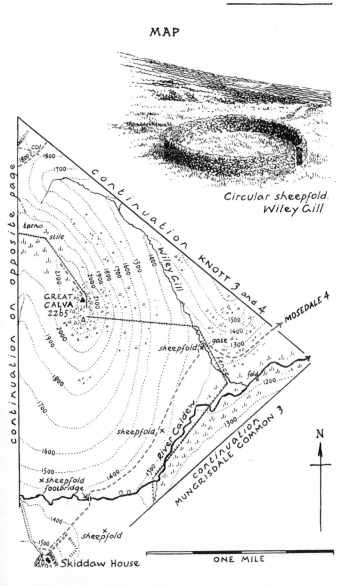

Circular sheepfold.
Wiley Gill

continuation on opposite page

col

1800

1800

1700

continuation KNOTT 3 and 4

tarns

stile

Wiley Gill

GREAT
CALVA
2265

sheepfold ×

gate

MOSEDALE 4

fold

sheepfold ×

River Caldew

sheepfold
footbridge

sheepfold ×

continuation MUNGRISDALE COMMON 3

N

Skiddaw House

ONE MILE

ASCENT FROM ORTHWAITE
1500 feet of ascent : 3¾ miles

GREAT CALVA

The col is grassy, but, unlike most green hollows between two hills, is narrow and well defined. Turn sharp right here to reach the fence, which goes directly to the top (left).

The summit comes into view at the col for the first time during the walk.

KNOTT

col

heather

2100

Little Calva

Stile

Stony ravine

fence

cotton grass

two tarns

2000

1900

1800

1900

Burn Tod
heather and stones

1700
1600
1500

sheepfold (ruin)

landslip

bield

The upper reaches of Hause Gill are very wild and stony. Keep to the bed of the stream, emerging where the ravine bends left, and continue up the valley to the col. (The col may be avoided by a short cut on the right.)

bracken

1300

grass

Hause Gill

1400

bield

Fox Gill

sheepfold. Note the difference between a sheepfold and a bield. A fold is an enclosure of stone walls to contain sheep; a bield is an open shelter of stone walls to protect sheep from bad weather. Thus a fold acts as a bield also, but a bield never serves as a fold.

bield

The fell rising on the left throughout the walk thus far is GREAT COCKUP

bracken

B

boulder

Path A is an old bridleway and easy to follow. Path B, keeping just above the wall, is harder to follow and is not much used nowadays. Path A has superior views; the feature of Path B is Brockle Crag, remarkable for its many pure white (quartz) stones.

B

DASH FARM

An easy walk in interesting territory above the pleasant Dash valley, but the last mile (beyond the col) is tedious.

1300

A Brockle Crag

1200

bracken

A

800

Brocklecrag

1100

1000

bracken

900

Hall

Cottage

Farm

Orthwaite

gate sandpit

700

Mirkholme (farm)

pastures

HIGH SIDE 2

Horsemoor Hills (farm)

Cassbeck Bridge

ROAD

looking south-east

Orthwaite Hall is a very beautiful house built in 1675 with stone-mullioned windows.

600

BASSENTHWAITE VILLAGE 1½

ASCENT FROM SKIDDAW HOUSE
900 feet of ascent : 2 miles

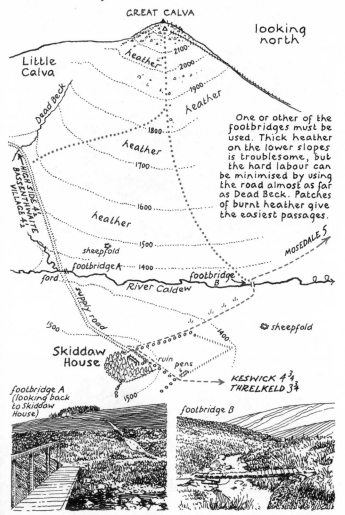

GREAT CALVA

looking north

Little Calva

heather 2100

2000

1900

heather

heather

1800

1700

heather

1600

heather

1500

sheepfold

footbridge A 1400

ford

River Caldew

footbridge B

Dead Beck

HIGH SIDE 4¼
BASSENTHWAITE
VILLAGE 4½

MOSEDALE 5

One or other of the
footbridges must be
used. Thick heather
on the lower slopes
is troublesome, but
the hard labour can
be minimised by using
the road almost as far
as Dead Beck. Patches
of burnt heather give
the easiest passages.

1500

supply road

Skiddaw House

ruin   pens

1500

1400

sheepfold

KESWICK 4¾
THRELKELD 3¾

footbridge A
(looking back
to Skiddaw
House)

footbridge B

THE SUMMIT

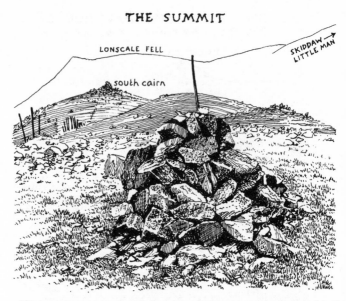

LONSCALE FELL

SKIDDAW LITTLE MAN →

south cairn

What appears to be the obvious top of the symmetrical pyramid of Great Calva, as seen on the climb up from Skiddaw Forest, is found on investigation not to be the true summit at all, and the prominent cairn overlooking this approach is succeeded by one at a greater elevation 130 yards further along a gentle incline. The top of the fell is made interesting by a scattering of stones and is given added distinction by a wire fence, which is ineffectual because of a gap of fifty yards near the summit. *In mist*, note that the *right*-angle in the fence occurs at the lower (south) cairn.

DESCENTS : The fence is a guide to the Caldew Valley, descending east from the south cairn; and, starting north-west from the top cairn, it leads safely down, after many changes of direction and a traverse of Little Calva, to the Skiddaw House road just above Dash Falls. For Threlkeld or Keswick, via Skiddaw House, go straight down the south slope but incline to the right when the steepness and stoniness have subsided, gaining the Skiddaw House road at the footbridge. (A beeline might be halted by the River Caldew, which, although only a mile and a half from its source, is already lusty.)

LONSCALE FELL

Skiddaw House

The south cairn

THE SUMMIT

continued

There is no need to sit shivering
in the lee of the cairn. A few
yards down the east slope,
across the fence, is a
splendidly·constructed
windproof shelter.

*summit
shelter*

RIDGE ROUTE

To KNOTT, 2329′ : 1½ miles : NW, then NE

Depression at 1810′
550 feet of ascent

Walkers whose boots let
water in will soon be
cognisant of the fact.

It matters not
which side of the
fence is taken; it is
slightly easier to avoid
the bogs on the east side.
Proceed to the accompaniment
of loud squelches as far as the
angle of the fence, where swing
down to the col, which is neat and
narrow. The pull up on to Knott is
steep initially, becoming easy.

To SKIDDAW there is no
convenient ridge, a descent to
the Skiddaw House road being
necessary whichever route is
taken. The best plan is to go up
to Skiddaw House and ascend
from there (see Skiddaw page 21).
(As a point of interest, it may
be mentioned that the fence,
if followed closely and starting
northwest, will lead almost to
the top of Skiddaw, after many
changes of direction).

grass   ▲ KNOTT
2330

2200
2100
2000
ORTHWAITE
1900
1800   *col*   1800
tarns   1700

N
ONE MILE
1900
2000

tarn
stile
LITTLE
CALVA
2100

GREAT CALVA ▲

THE VIEW

An observation of particular interest is mentioned on the next page following.

From the lower cairn there is the best of all prospects of Skiddaw Forest — a strange, silent wilderness irrigated by the infant Caldew. The neighbouring fells are not well presented, but there is a distant view of the Solway Firth bisected by the Sandale television mast, which isn't a very inspiring sight either.

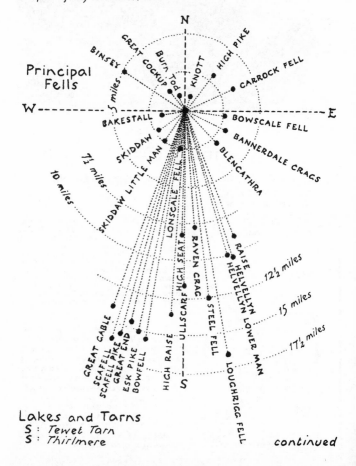

Principal Fells

Lakes and Tarns
S: Tewet Tarn
S: Thirlmere

continued

THE VIEW

continued

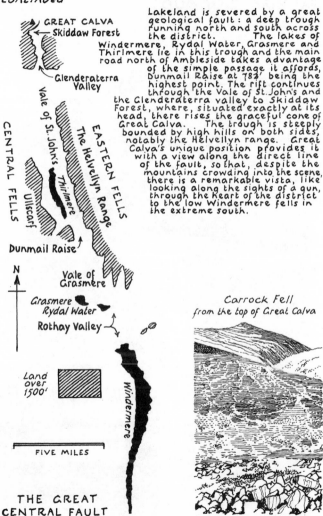

GREAT CALVA
Skiddaw Forest

Glenderaterra
Valley

Vale of St. John's

CENTRAL FELLS

EASTERN FELLS
The Helvellyn Range

Thirlmere

Ullscarf

Dunmail Raise

N

Vale of
Grasmere

Grasmere
Rydal Water
Rothay Valley

Land
over
1500'

Windermere

FIVE MILES

THE GREAT
CENTRAL FAULT

Lakeland is severed by a great geological fault: a deep trough running north and south across the district. The lakes of Windermere, Rydal Water, Grasmere and Thirlmere lie in this trough and the main road north of Ambleside takes advantage of the simple passage it affords, Dunmail Raise at 782' being the highest point. The rift continues through the Vale of St. John's and the Glenderaterra valley to Skiddaw Forest, where, situated exactly at its head, there rises the graceful cone of Great Calva. The trough is steeply bounded by high hills on both sides, notably the Helvellyn range. Great Calva's unique position provides it with a view along the direct line of the fault, so that, despite the mountains crowding into the scene, there is a remarkable vista, like looking along the sights of a gun, through the heart of the district to the low Windermere fells in the extreme south.

Carrock Fell
from the top of Great Calva

Great Cockup

1726'

from Longlands

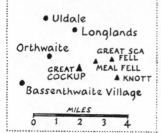

- Uldale
- Longlands

Orthwaite

GREAT SCA ▲ FELL

GREAT ▲ COCKUP ▲ MEAL FELL

▲ KNOTT

Bassenthwaite Village

MILES

0   1   2   3   4

Orthwaite Hall

NATURAL FEATURES

Viewed from a distance, Great Cockup appears as a modest but extensive eminence with no obvious summit and nothing calling for closer inspection. First impressions are confirmed by a tour of exploration, the fell underfoot proving no more attractive than the fell at a distance. Bracken is rampant on the lower slopes, much burning of heather has resulted in a dark and patchy appearance higher up, and the skyline never bestirs itself from placid curves to produce even the slightest excitement. Although not ornamental, however, Great Cockup is strongly functional, which perhaps matters more: its long spine, rising steeply from Orthwaite, divides the waters of the River Ellen from those of tributaries of the Derwent. The fell terminates abruptly in the deep cut of Trusmadoor; beyond, a ridge continues the height of land over Meal Fell to the major summit of the Uldale group, Great Sca Fell.

A feature of the south flank of Great Cockup and always conspicuous on a bright day is the white-streaked *Brockle Crag*. This is disappointing on close inspection, being no more than an untidy fall of quartzite rocks.

The Boulder
(Burn Tod behind)

Brockle Crag

The Boulder. On the Ordnance map of scale 6" = 1 mile there is inscribed the word 'Boulder' at a point alongside the old bridleway crossing the south flank of Great Cockup — a distinction so rare that a walker of an enquiring turn of mind must needs go in search of this natural wonder. Finding it is easy - it stands in isolation — but its dimensions are rather a disappointment, none exceeding a few feet. There are thousands of bigger specimens within a mile of Sty Head. This recording of an ordinary stone illustrates the dearth of features on the fell.

The boulder may be the debris of a now-vanished crag but its situation suggests that it is more probably an erratic left by a retreating glacier.

MAP

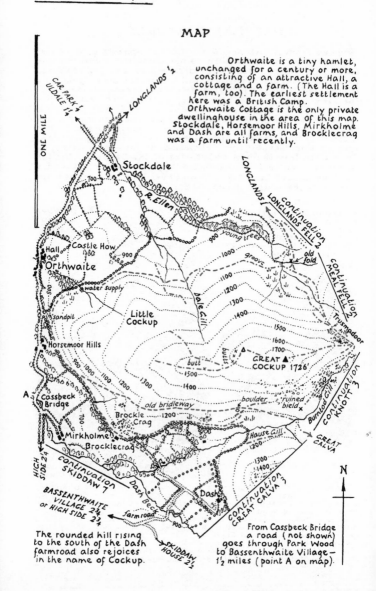

Orthwaite is a tiny hamlet, unchanged for a century or more, consisting of an attractive Hall, a cottage and a farm. (The Hall is a farm, too). The earliest settlement here was a British Camp.
Orthwaite Cottage is the only private dwellinghouse in the area of this map. Stockdale, Horsemoor Hills, Mirkholme and Dash are all farms, and Brocklecrag was a farm until recently.

CAR PARK ¾
ULDALE 1¼

LONGLANDS ½

ONE MILE

Stockdale

R. Ellen

700

LONGLANDS

CONTINUATION
LONGLANDS FELL 2

Young trees

900

CONTINUATION
MEAL FELL 2

Castle How
Hall
Orthwaite

900

1000

groove

old
fold

1100

water supply

800

1200

Trusmadoor

Little Cockup

1300

Dale Gill

1400

1500

CONTINUATION
KNOTT 3

sandpit

1600
1700

GREAT
COCKUP 1726'

Horsemoor Hills

800
900
1000
1100

butt

1500

1400

Strny Gill

Cassbeck
Bridge

old bridleway

boulder
ruined bield

Burnt Gill

GREAT
CALVA

A

Brockle
Crag

1200

Mirkholme
Brocklecrag

House Gill

1200

1300

N

HIGH
SIDE 2¾

CONTINUATION
SKIDDAW 7

Dash Beck

1400

CONTINUATION
GREAT CALVA 3

BASSENTHWAITE
VILLAGE 2¾
or HIGH SIDE 2¾

farmroad

Dash

900

SKIDDAW
HOUSE 2½

The rounded hill rising to the south of the Dash farmroad also rejoices in the name of Cockup.

From Cassbeck Bridge a road (not shown) goes through Park Wood to Bassenthwaite Village — 1½ miles (point A on map).

ASCENT FROM ORTHWAITE
950 feet of ascent : 2 miles

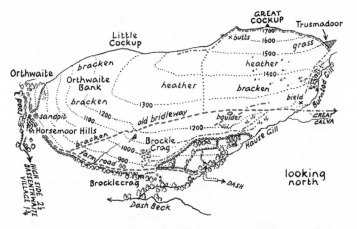

looking
north

The summit is easily reached from the highest part of the old bridleway, up a simple slope of grass and heather, the true summit being 300 yards beyond the cairned top first gained, just above the shooting butts. This route is better than a direct climb up Orthwaite Bank, where the bracken is dense and extensive. For a different route of return, go down the far slope to Trusmadoor and then use sheep-tracks alongside Burntod Gill; a further variation, crossing marshy ground, passes below Brockle Crag and joins the farm-road.

The Dash Valley

THE SUMMIT

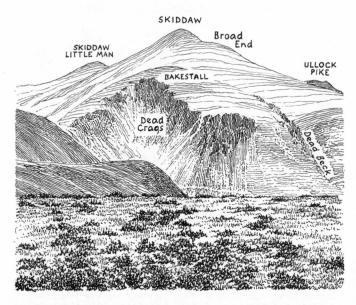

A small cairn marks the highest point, which is in the midst of an expanse of scanty, anaemic-looking heather on the crest of a gentle dome.   300 yards west there is a more definite top with a larger cairn, but this is quite obviously lower.   Nearer, to the north-east, there is a third summit without any cairn: this, too, is lower.   In 1962, when this page was originally prepared, the altitude of the highest point was estimated from the contours to be about 1720'. According to the 2005 edition of the Ordnance Survey 2½" map the correct altitude is 1726'.

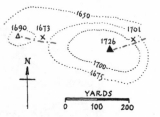

The surface levels of 1690, 1673 and 1701 shown in the diagram on this page are taken from an earlier 6" map.

DESCENTS may safely be made in any direction, a little care being necessary in bad weather in the neighbourhood of Trusmadoor, where there are small cliffs.

THE VIEW

Great Cockup is the most westerly of the Uldale Fells and thus has an unrestricted view across to the Solway Firth and Scotland, which deserves more attention than the rather unattractive mountain scene. Nevertheless the undisputed monarch in this picture is Skiddaw, rising magnificently nearby in the south.

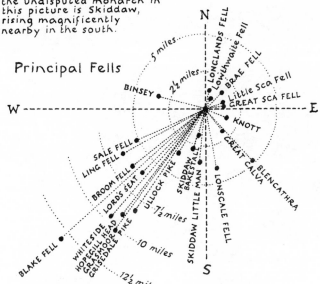

Principal Fells

Lakes and Tarns

WSW : Bassenthwaite Lake
Over Water (NW) cannot be seen
from the highest point, but is in
view from the other two tops.

RIDGE ROUTE

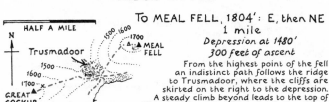

HALF A MILE

Trusmadoor

GREAT COCKUP

MEAL FELL

TO MEAL FELL, 1804': E, then NE
1 mile
Depression at 1480'
300 feet of ascent

From the highest point of the fell
an indistinct path follows the ridge
to Trusmadoor, where the cliffs are
skirted on the right to the depression.
A steady climb beyond leads to the top of
Meal Fell, the west cairn being first reached.

Great Sca Fell

2136'

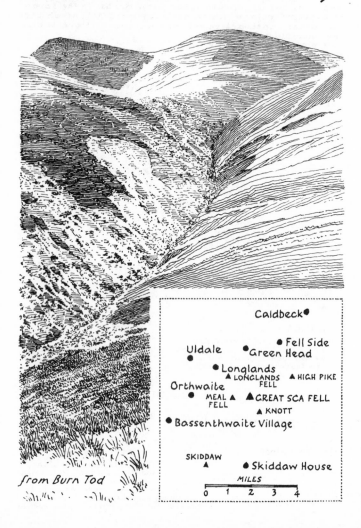

from Burn Tod

Caldbeck ●

● Fell Side

Uldale ● ● Green Head

● Longlands
▲ LONGLANDS ▲ HIGH PIKE
FELL

Orthwaite
● ▲ ▲ GREAT SCA FELL
MEAL
FELL ▲ KNOTT

● Bassenthwaite Village

SKIDDAW
▲ ● Skiddaw House

MILES

0   1   2   3   4

NATURAL FEATURES

The Uldale Fells rise in three ridges between west and north to merge in one common meeting-ground at the place of greatest altitude, this focal point being a smooth double-headed uplift of grassy fell, known to cartographers by the names of the twin summits, Great and Little Sca Fell, but to farmers and shepherds merely as Scafell. (No resemblance to any other

Scafell is intended, nor does it exist). All these ridges are gently-contoured and grassy, with bracken below 1500' and some patches of heather. They are excellent sheep-pastures, and it may be remarked that flocks can be watched with much greater facility on these smooth slopes than in rockier parts of the district: from any suitable vantage-point the movements of sheep can be observed over great distances. The watercourses, characteristic of the northern fells, are deeply cut and so steep-sided that vegetatious matter ekes a precarious existence between regular scourings by landslips.

Much the same pattern applies to the eastern side of the fell, which is intimately linked with Knott, the highest fell north of Skiddaw Forest, grass slopes and stony ravines predominating: here, however, the stony debris has been augmented by accumulations of waste from the extensive mining operations of past centuries. Nowadays Great Sca Fell is as it was before the miners came, a peaceful and undisturbed sheep pasture — and a quiet sanctuary in a world becoming discordant and noisy, where natural sanctuaries are shrinking fast yet were never in greater need.

Little Sca Fell (left) and Great Sca Fell, from the Longlands valley

MAP

Fellwalking is the healthiest and most satisfying of all outdoor exercises. Climbing the hills and tramping over rough country makes a man strong and keeps him fit (it cleans his mind and does his soul good, too). But many enthusiasts, the author one of them, are nevertheless quite happy to reach the tops with a minimum of expenditure of effort, short of being carried upwards on the backs of their wives or other companions, which is simply not in the best traditions of fellwalking. Easy paths are more to their liking than steep scrambles.

These seekers after simple routes should note with gratification the particular attractions of the maps of the Uldale and Caldbeck fells. The starting-points on the roads are considerably elevated, especially in the north, where climbing proper commences with a big advantage of close on 1000' already accounted for; the main summits lie well back at little more than 2000'; easy gradients are the rule. Walkers do not drop in their tracks here: they just go on and on........

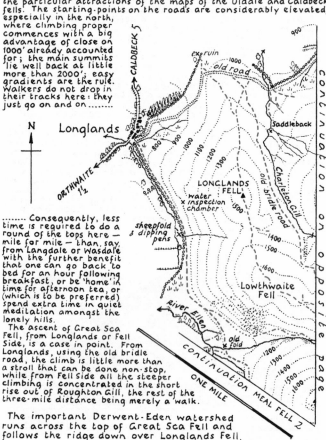

.... Consequently, less time is required to do a round of the tops here — than, say, from Langdale or Wasdale with the further benefit that one can go back to bed for an hour following breakfast, or be 'home' in time for afternoon tea, or (which is to be preferred) spend extra time in quiet meditation amongst the lonely hills.

The ascent of Great Sea Fell, from Longlands or Fell Side, is a case in point. From Longlands, using the old bridle road, the climb is little more than a stroll that can be done non-stop, while from Fell Side all the steeper climbing is concentrated in the short rise out of Roughton Gill, the rest of the three-mile distance being merely a walk.

The important Derwent-Eden watershed runs across the top of Great Sea Fell and follows the ridge down over Longlands Fell.

MAP

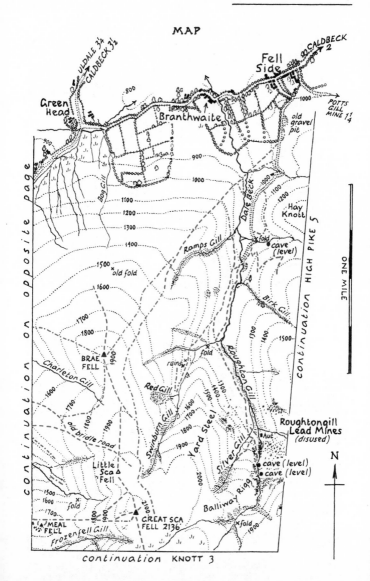

continuation on opposite page

continuation HIGH PIKE 5

continuation KNOTT 3

ULLDALE 3¼
CALDBECK 3½

∞ CALDBECK 2

Fell Side

POTTS GILL MINE 1¼

Green Head

Branthwaite

old gravel pit

Bog Gill

Dale Beck

Hay Knott

Ramps Gill

x fold
cave (level)

Birk Gill

x old fold

ONE MILE

BRAE FELL

ruins x
fold

Red Gill

Roughton Gill

Swinburn Gill

Yard Steel

Silver Gill

Roughtongill Lead Mines (disused)

x hut
cave (level)
cave (level)

Little Sca Fell

N

x fold

Balliway Rigg

MEAL FELL
Frozenfell Gill

CREAT SCA FELL 2136

x fold

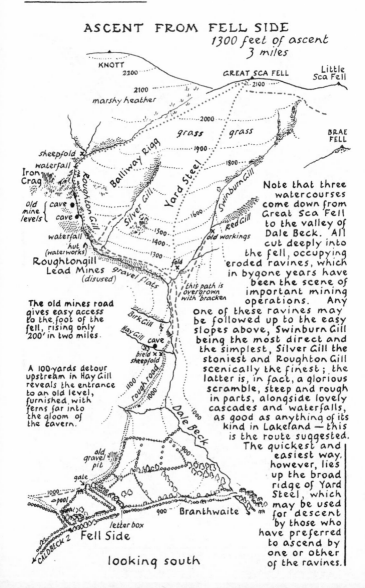

ASCENT FROM FELL SIDE
1300 feet of ascent
3 miles

KNOTT 2200

GREAT SCA FELL 2100

Little Sca Fell

marshy heather

2100

2000

grass grass

BRAE FELL

Ballway Rigg

1900

Yard Steel

1800

sheepfold ✗
waterfall

Iron Crag

Roughton Gill

Silver Gill

Swinburn Gill

1600

old mine levels

cave

cave

Red Gill

old workings

waterfall

1500

1400

hut (waterworks)

1300

fold ✗

Roughtongill Lead Mines (disused)

gravel flats

this path is overgrown with bracken

Note that three watercourses come down from Great Sca Fell to the valley of Dale Beck. All cut deeply into the fell, occupying eroded ravines, which in bygone years have been the scene of important mining operations. Any one of these ravines may be followed up to the easy slopes above, Swinburn Gill being the most direct and the simplest, Silver Gill the stoniest and Roughton Gill scenically the finest; the latter is, in fact, a glorious scramble, steep and rough in parts, alongside lovely cascades and waterfalls, as good as anything of its kind in Lakeland — this is the route suggested.

The old mines road gives easy access to the foot of the fell, rising only 200' in two miles.

Birk Gill

Hay Gill cave

A 100-yards detour upstream in Hay Gill reveals the entrance to an old level, furnished with ferns far into the gloom of the cavern.

bield ✗ sheepfold

rough road

1100

1000

Dale Beck

1000

old gravel pit

1000

gate

pool

900

Branthwaite

The quickest and easiest way, however, lies up the broad ridge of Yard Steel, which may be used for descent by those who have preferred to ascend by one or other of the ravines.

letter box

Fell Side

✗ CALDBECK 2

looking south

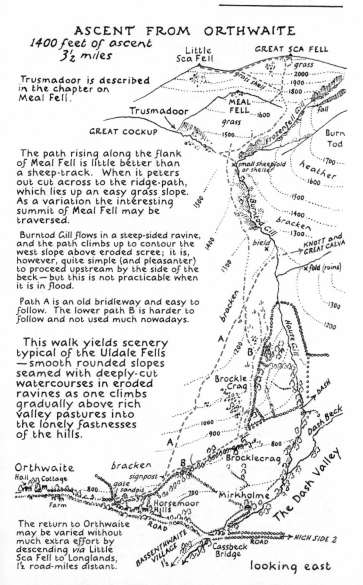

ASCENT FROM ORTHWAITE
1400 feet of ascent
3½ miles

Little Sca Fell

GREAT SCA FELL

grass

Great grass shelf

2000
1900
1800

Trusmadoor is described in the chapter on Meal Fell.

Trusmadoor

MEAL FELL

grass

1600

Frozenfell Gill

fall

GREAT COCKUP

1500

Burn Tod

The path rising along the flank of Meal Fell is little better than a sheep-track. When it peters out cut across to the ridge-path, which lies up an easy grass slope. As a variation the interesting summit of Meal Fell may be traversed.

small sheepfold or shelter

heather

1700

1600

1500

1400

bracken

1300

Burntod Gill

1500

Burntod Gill flows in a steep-sided ravine, and the path climbs up to contour the west slope above eroded scree; it is, however, quite simple (and pleasanter) to proceed upstream by the side of the beck — but this is not practicable when it is in flood.

1400

bield
x

KNOTT and GREAT CALVA

x fold (ruins)

1300

Path A is an old bridleway and easy to follow. The lower path B is harder to follow and not used much nowadays.

1300

1200

bracken

House Gill

A

1200

This walk yields scenery typical of the Uldale Fells — smooth rounded slopes seamed with deeply-cut watercourses in eroded ravines as one climbs gradually above rich valley pastures into the lonely fastnesses of the hills.

B

DASH

Brockle Crag

1000

900

Dash Beck

A

800

The Dash Valley

Brocklecrag

Orthwaite

bracken

signpost

B

Hall
Cottage

gate
sandpit

800

Mirkholme

Dash Beck

Farm

700

Horsemoor
Hills

ROAD

HIGH SIDE 2

The return to Orthwaite may be varied without much extra effort by descending *via* Little Sca Fell to Longlands, 1½ road-miles distant.

BASSENTHWAITE
VILLAGE

ROAD

1½

Cassbeck
Bridge

looking east

ASCENT FROM LONGLANDS
1550 feet of ascent : 2½ miles (3 via the bridle road)

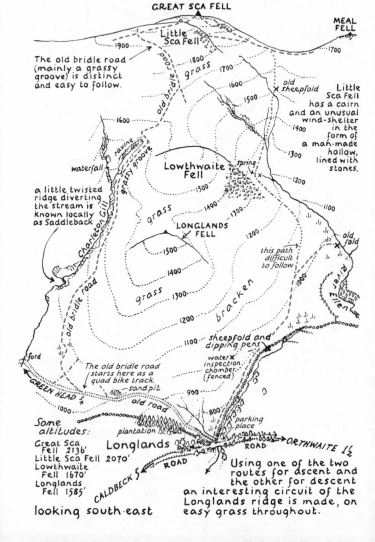

GREAT SCA FELL

MEAL FELL

Little Sca Fell

1900

1800

grass

1700

1700

The old bridle road (mainly a grassy groove) is distinct and easy to follow.

old bridle road

1600

1500

old × sheepfold

1400

1300

1200

Little Sca Fell has a cairn and an unusual wind-shelter in the form of a man-made hollow, lined with stones.

1600

ravine

grassy groove

waterfall

Charleton Gill

a little twisted ridge diverting the stream is known locally as Saddleback

Lowthwaite Fell

spring

×

1500

grass

1400

1300

1200

1100

LONGLANDS FELL

1500

1400

grass

1300

1200

this path difficult to follow

old fold

×

1000

River Ellen

bracken

old bridle road

1100

sheepfold and dipping pens

ford

The old bridle road starts here as a quad bike track. — sand pit

GREEN HEAD

1000

grass

1200

water × inspection chamber (fenced)

900

800

parking place

old road

plantation

Longlands

ROAD

ORTHWAITE 1½

CALDBECK 5

ROAD

Some altitudes:
Great Sca Fell 2136'
Little Sca Fell 2070'
Lowthwaite Fell 1670'
Longlands Fell 1585'

looking south-east

Using one of the two routes for ascent and the other for descent an interesting circuit of the Longlands ridge is made, on easy grass throughout.

THE SUMMIT

CARROCK FELL

The summit of Great Sca Fell

The top of the fell is as flat as a crown bowling green and several acres in extent. Despite the lack of stones in the area, a fine cairn sits precisely on the highest point, with paths radiating from it in all directions.

The lower summit, Little Sca Fell, is also crowned with a cairn and in addition has a peculiar depression around which a low wall has been built (stones being available nearby) to make it of service as a wind-shelter.

DESCENTS : The old bridle road is most easily picked up as it crosses the path to the north of Little Sca Fell. For Fell Side the ridge of Yard Steel is best: persevere to its extremity to join the mines path. Generally, whatever the destination, the grassy slopes are to be preferred to the ravines.

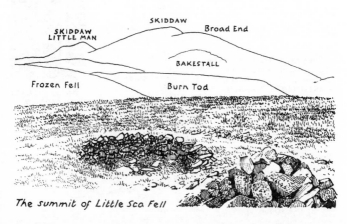

SKIDDAW LITTLE MAN   SKIDDAW   Broad End   BAKESTALL   Frozen Fell   Burn Tod

The summit of Little Sca Fell

THE VIEW

The scene is barren indeed, a sea of smooth unexciting hills, but fellwalkers who have deserted their favourite mountain haunts in Langdale or Borrowdale to come here on the recommendations of this book, and are regretting it, will note with nostalgic tears in their eyes an unexpected and faraway vista of the Bowfell group, today quite out of their reach. They must admit, however, albeit bitterly, that the view over the Cumbrian plain to and beyond the Solway Firth is one that not even Bowfell can surpass.

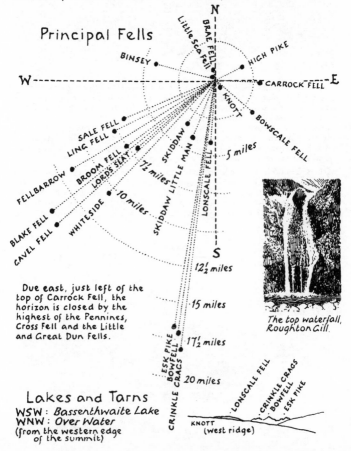

Principal Fells

N

W — — — — — — — E

S

LITTLE SCA FELL
BRAE FELL
HIGH PIKE
BINSEY
CARROCK FELL
KNOTT
BOWSCALE FELL
SALE FELL
LING FELL
BROOM FELL
LORD'S SEAT
SKIDDAW
SKIDDAW LITTLE MAN
LONSCALE FELL
FELLBARROW
BLAKE FELL
CAVEL FELL
WHITESIDE
ESK PIKE
BOWFELL
CRINKLE CRAGS

5 miles
7½ miles
10 miles
12½ miles
15 miles
17½ miles
20 miles

Due east, just left of the top of Carrock Fell, the horizon is closed by the highest of the Pennines, Cross Fell and the Little and Great Dun Fells.

The top waterfall, Roughton Gill

LONSCALE FELL
CRINKLE CRAGS
BOWFELL
ESK PIKE
KNOTT
(west ridge)

Lakes and Tarns

WSW : Bassenthwaite Lake
WNW : Over Water
(from the western edge of the summit)

RIDGE ROUTES

To KNOTT 2329′ : ¾ mile : S, then SE
Depression at 2085′ : 250 feet of ascent

Apart from an area of juicy peat-hags in the depression, where one must tread lightly, this is a simple walk on grass throughout. The path starts clearly but becomes intermittent.

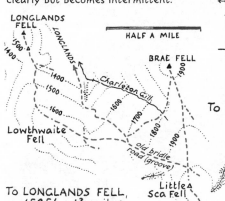

HALF A MILE

N

To BRAE FELL, 1920′
1 mile : N

Depressions at 2025′ and 1865′

75 feet of ascent

Except for a short distance on Little Sca Fell there is a clear path all the way. The second half of the route is easy going over a grass prairie with the cairn on Brae Fell directly in front.

To LONGLANDS FELL, 1585′ : 1¾ miles N, then NW
Depressions at 2025′, 1620′ and 1410′ 250 feet of ascent

Follow the path over Little Sca Fell and turn left onto the old bridle road. (To the right of this junction the bridle road has gone out of use, but the groove can still be followed for a short distance.) Leave the bridle road where it starts to slant down to Charleton Gill and keep on ahead over the grassy hump of Lowthwaite Fell. This is all easy going, and a grand way down from the tops on a summer's evening.

To MEAL FELL, 1804′ : ¾ mile : W
Depression at 1680′
100 feet of ascent

Take either of the paths to the west; there are two patches of scree high up, easily avoided, and the rest is grass until the stony and interesting top of Meal Fell is reached.

High Pike   2157'

from the west gate,
Carrock Hill Fort

Caldbeck

● Hesket
Newmarket

Fell Side ●

Calebreck ●

▲ BRAE
  FELL   ▲ HIGH PIKE

▲ GREAT   ▲ CARROCK
  SCA FELL   FELL

▲ KNOTT

● Mosedale

MILES

0   1   2   3   4   5

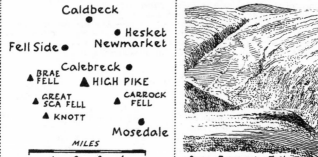

from Bowscale Fell

NATURAL FEATURES

All natives of Caldbeck and district have a deep-rooted respect for High Pike: it is a natural background to their lives, its name is a household word. This, not because the fell dominates the neighbourhood by a commanding presence — it is too flat and sprawling to catch the eye — but simply because it happens to be there, just over the treetops, and always has been there, playing a part in the development of the community.

In bygone days its rich mines provided a livelihood for the men, producing such a prolific variety of minerals that it used to be said, with much truth, *"Caldbeck Fells are worth all England else."* This former industry has now vanished (and so have five of the six public-houses in Caldbeck a century or more ago!) But High Pike is still, as ever, a grand sheep range and a fine territory for walking and leisurely pursuits, while the view from the summit, as an outlyer of Lakeland, is superb. Big events in history are celebrated here by the building and firing of a beacon. Carlisle knows when Caldbeck rejoices.

The fell is massive, occupying the north-east corner of the high country "back o' Skidda'," where it overlooks the Border and the valley of the Eden. There is volcanic rock underlying the higher parts but this is not greatly in evidence, the slopes being uniformly smooth and grassy except where broken by the eroded ravines that contain watercourses and are such a feature of the area. Beyond the summit is a hinterland of heathery moors, rarely visited and in a fair way to becoming a natural reserve for birds and animals.

High Pike from Knott

The Caldbeck Fell mines

All the mines in the Caldbeck Fells are located on the slopes of High Pike, along its boundaries or in proximity; and all are within the narrow belt of volcanic rock bounding the area of the Skiddaw slates.

All of the mines are now disused, most of them having been worked from a very early date (sixteenth century or before) and been productive of a great variety of valuable minerals.   The oldest and richest mine, Roughtongill, is reputed to have yielded 23 different ores and other minerals.

Caldbeck •

Fell Side •   Nether Row •

1   5   6

2   HIGH PIKE ▲   7

3   8
4

9
10

1: Hay Gill
2: Red Gill
3: Silver Gill
4: Roughton Gill
5: Potts Gill
6: Sandbed
7: Driggeth
8: Dry Gill
9: Brandy Gill
10: Carrock

Old level, Hay Gill

These places, for so long scenes of great activity, have today the sad desolation of death about them, but Nature is a great healer, given time, and traces of many former workings have disappeared except for the adits to the old levels.   The tunnels and shafts penetrated to great distances and depths in the fellside, forming a labyrinth of subterranean passages along the mineral veins, and when it is remembered that they were hewn with primitive tools and wedges long before gunpowder was known, imagination cannot start to comprehend the skill and industry of the miners of those days, and one is left merely wondering why the fortunate workers of today are prepared to debase their vocations and professions for greater personal rewards.   The Caldbeck miners had little schooling yet had nothing to learn about the dignity of labour or of loyalty in service.

Old level, Potts Gill (now gone)

Iron Crag
above Roughton Gill

Two mines were still in operation fifty years ago.   Sandbed was the main source of supply, Potts Gill the processing and despatching station, and the mineral then being won was *barytes* (pronounced *brytees*, locally *brytas*) a crystallised heavy stone with many commercial uses principally in the manufacture of glass and paint.   The most recent operators were McKechnie Brothers Limited.

Roughton Gill
pronounced
'Rowt'n Gill'

The lowest waterfall

Old mine-level (left)
and cascades

MAP

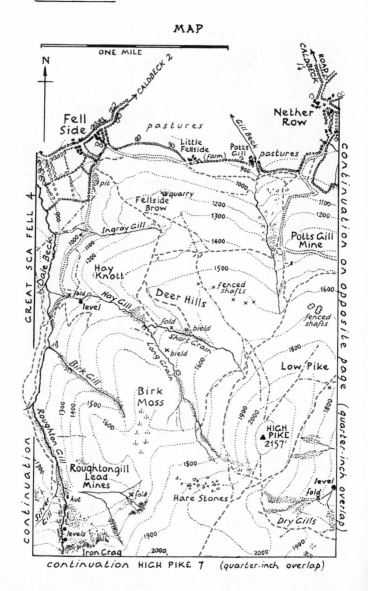

continuation HIGH PIKE 7 (quarter-inch overlap)

MAP

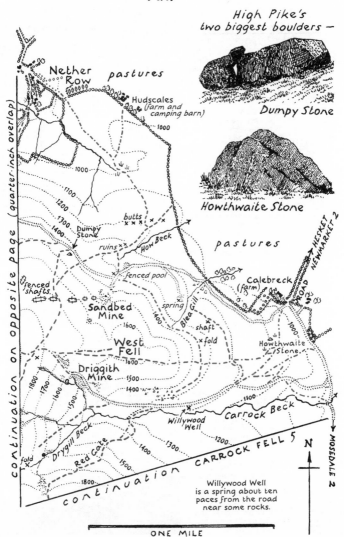

High Pike's
two biggest boulders —

Dumpy Stone

Howthwaite Stone

Nether Row

pastures

Hudscales
(farm and
camping barn)

1000

1000

1100

1200

1300

1400

Dumpy
Stone

butts

ruins

How Beck

fenced
shafts

fenced pool

Sandbed
Mine

spring

Blea Gill

shaft

fold

1600

pastures

Calebreck
(farm)

HESKET
NEWMARKET 2

ROAD

1000

Howthwaite
Stone

West
Fell

Driggith
Mine

1800

1700

1600

1500

1500

1400

1600

Willywood
Well

Carrock Beck

1100

fold

Drygill Beck

Red Gate

1400

1300

1200

1500

1800

continuation on opposite page (quarter-inch overlap)

continuation CARROCK FELL 5

MOSEDALE 2

N

Willywood Well
is a spring about ten
paces from the road
near some rocks.

ONE MILE

MAP

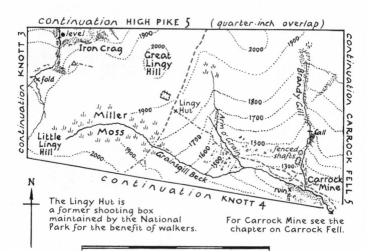

CONTINUATION HIGH PIKE 5 (quarter-inch overlap)

CONTINUATION KNOTT 3

CONTINUATION CARROCK FELL 5

• level

Iron Crag

Great Lingy Hill

× fold

Little Lingy Hill

Miller

Moss

Lingy × Hut

Brandy Gill

fall

fenced shafts

Grainsgill Beck

ruin ×

Carrock Mine

CONTINUATION KNOTT 4

N

The Lingy Hut is a former shooting box maintained by the National Park for the benefit of walkers.

For Carrock Mine see the chapter on Carrock Fell.

ONE MILE

Death of an Industry
Ruins, spoil-heaps and a scarred landscape mark the grave of the once-renowned Roughtongill Mine

ASCENT FROM FELL SIDE
1350 feet of ascent : 2½ miles

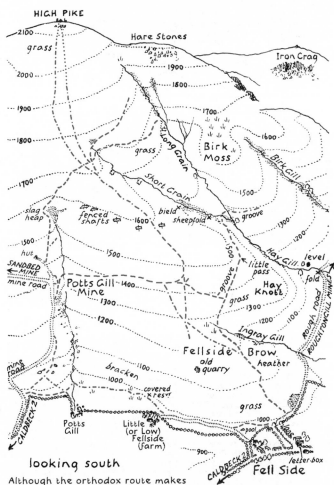

looking south

Although the orthodox route makes use of the Potts Gill Mine road and the path beyond, a more enjoyable plan is to use the paths going up from Fellside Brow. There are no walls to obstruct free wandering over these pleasant foothills. Life seems good here when the larks are rising and curlews wheeling overhead.

ASCENT FROM NETHER ROW
1300 feet of ascent : 2½ miles

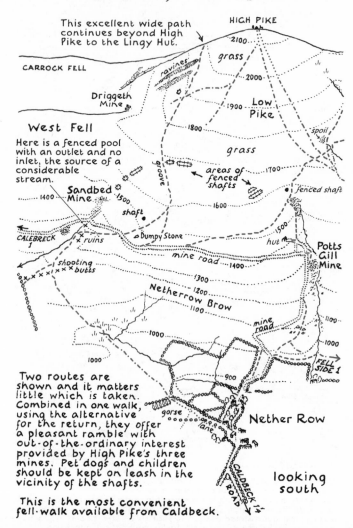

This excellent wide path continues beyond High Pike to the Lingy Hut.

HIGH PIKE

2100

grass

CARROCK FELL

ravines

2000

Driggeth Mine

1900   Low Pike

West Fell

1800

spoil

Here is a fenced pool with an outlet and no inlet, the source of a considerable stream.

grass

groove

1700

areas of fenced shafts

Sandbed Mine

1400   1500

fenced shaft

shaft

1600

CALEBRECK 1

ruins

Dumpy Stone

mine road

1500

hut

Potts Gill Mine

shooting butts

1400

1300

1200

Netherrow Brow

1100

mine road

1100

1000

1000

1000

900

FELL SIDE 1

Two routes are shown and it matters little which is taken. Combined in one walk, using the alternative for the return, they offer a pleasant ramble with out-of-the-ordinary interest provided by High Pike's three mines. Pet dogs and children should be kept on leash in the vicinity of the shafts.

This is the most convenient fell-walk available from Caldbeck.

gorse

lane

Nether Row

CALDBECK 1¼ ROAD

looking south

ASCENT FROM CALEBRECK
1300 feet of ascent · 2¼ miles

The main interest in this walk is concentrated in the naked ravines at the head of the valley. This is a happy hunting ground for students of geology.

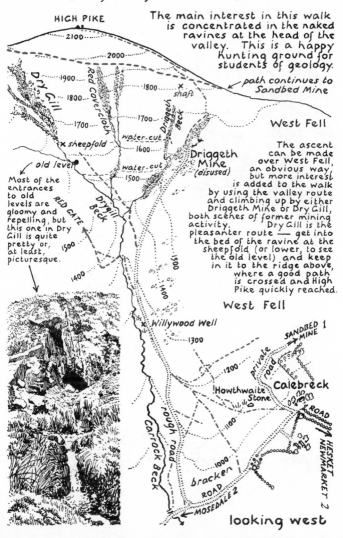

HIGH PIKE

2100

2000

Dry Gill

1900

1800

1700

x sheepfold

← old level

Most of the entrances to old levels are gloomy and repelling, but this one in Dry Gill is quite pretty or, at least, picturesque.

Red Coverdock

1800

1700

water-cut

1600

water-cut

1500

Driggeth Beck

x shaft

1800

path continues to Sandbed Mine

West Fell

Driggeth Mine *(disused)*

The ascent can be made over West Fell, an obvious way, but more interest is added to the walk by using the valley route and climbing up by either Driggeth Mine or Dry Gill, both scenes of former mining activity. Dry Gill is the pleasanter route — get into the bed of the ravine at the sheepfold (or lower, to see the old level) and keep in it to the ridge above, where a good path is crossed and High Pike quickly reached.

RED GATE

Drygill Beck

1500

1400

1500

1400

West Fell

x Willywood Well

1300

1200

SANDBED MINE

private road

Calebreck

!Howthwaite Stone

1100

ROAD

HESKET NEWMARKET 2

rough road

1000

bracken

ROAD

MOSEDALE 2

Carrock Beck

looking west

THE SUMMIT

BLENCATHRA

1960
looking
south

Apart from the mines
on the lower slopes,
High Pike is so deprived
of landmarks and other
distinguishing features that a
visitor is likely to approach the summit expecting only a
plain grassy top, perhaps even without a cairn since
stones are at a premium in the vegetatious prairies all
around. It is a surprise, therefore, to find a positive array
of objects of interest set out for inspection.

• The cairn is there all right, although the great sprawl of
  heaped stones hardly deserves the name. Obviously at some
  time in the past a good deal of hard labour has gone into the
  collection of these stones and their conveyance to the
  highest point of the fell. Hollowed out on the east side, away
  from the prevailing wind, this 'tumulus' is better described as
  a shelter.

More ••• on the next page →

1961
looking
south-east

CARROCK
FELL

THE SUMMIT

continued

- Some of the stones have been appropriated by the Ordnance Surveyors to provide material for a triangulation column nearby. On top of the column is a diagram, placed there in the year 2000, with radiating lines indicating the direction of various places. Some of these places, such as Carrock Fell, are obviously visible. Some, such as London, are obviously not visible. Some, such as Helvellyn, are not visible, but people not equipped with *The Northern Fells* might think that they were. This column is no longer in use, unlike the one on Binsey.

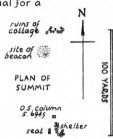

ruins of cottage

site of beacon

PLAN OF SUMMIT

N

100 YARDS

O.S. column 5.6945 ▫

seat ▪ ▫ shelter

- To the north of the column the turf is interrupted by a circular patch of stones and gravel: this is the site of the beacon, marked by a low cairn, and reserved for very special occasions.

- A few paces still further north is a commodious ruin, now used as a wind-shelter. Amazingly, this was originally a shepherd's cottage. A house with a view, indeed! Not even the most ardent fellwalker's ambition can have aspired to a residence on a mountain top.

- But, up to the end of 1960, the biggest surprise of all was a wrought-iron garden seat, a contraption of elaborate embellishments into the voluptuous curves of which tired limbs surrendered gratefully: no other fell top provided such luxurious comfort. Its very ornamentation proved its undoing, however, and it was removed and replaced late in 1960 with another seat — a structure of slate slabs, severely simple in design — after sheep had been found held captive by it, their horns entangled in the ironwork. Both seats, old and new, were placed on the summit as memorials to Mick Lewis, a youth of Nether Row, "who loved all these fells". Which is a nice thing to say of anybody.

DESCENTS : If it were not for the mine shafts, High Pike could be descended blindfold, so easy are its gradients. In clear weather, a way off may be found in any direction, but in mist preferably make for the Lingy Hut path 300 yards south-east and follow it left to gain the Potts Gill — Sandbed mine road near Dumpy Stone.

Great Lingy Hill
(looking to Blencathra)
Acres of dense fragrant heather (hence the name) make this the most delectable top in Lakeland for a summer day's siesta.

THE VIEW

Southwards, the high skyline of the Skiddaw-Blencathra mass permits only narrow vistas of distant Lakeland. As a viewpoint for looking out *from* Lakeland, and not *into* it, however, High Pike takes full advantage of its position on the perimeter and commands a magnificent prospect, all of it fair to look upon, ranging from the west Cumbrian coast and Solway Firth northwards to the Scottish hills and then, from the Border round to the east, the lofty Pennines rise beyond the wide Eden Valley.

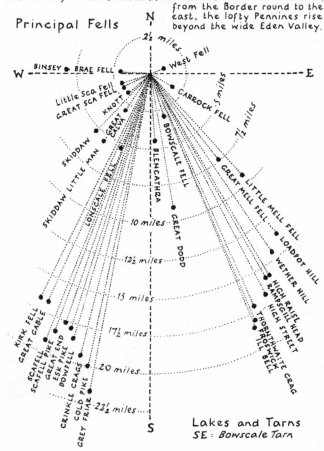

Principal Fells

Lakes and Tarns
SE : Bowscale Tarn

RIDGE ROUTES

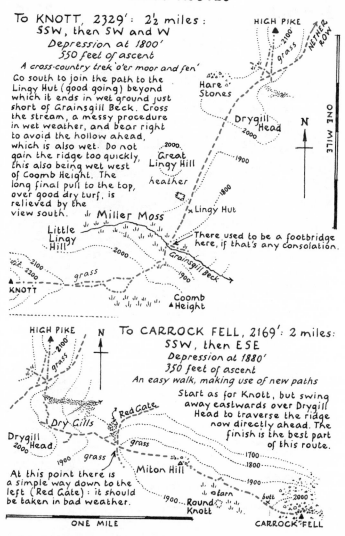

To KNOTT, 2329': 2½ miles:
SSW, then SW and W
Depression at 1800'
350 feet of ascent
A cross-country trek 'o'er moor and fen'

Go south to join the path to the Lingy Hut (good going) beyond which it ends in wet ground just short of Grainsgill Beck. Cross the stream, a messy procedure in wet weather, and bear right to avoid the hollow ahead, which is also wet. Do not gain the ridge too quickly, this also being wet west of Coomb Height. The long final pull to the top, over good dry turf, is relieved by the view south.

HIGH PIKE

2100

grass

NETHER ROW

ONE MILE

Hare Stones

N

Drygill Head

2000

2000 Great Lingy Hill

heather

1900

1800

Miller Moss

Little Lingy Hill

Lingy Hut

× There used to be a footbridge here, if that's any consolation.

2100 2200

grass

KNOTT

2000

Grainsgill Beck

1900

Coomb ▲ Height

HIGH PIKE

N

2100

grass

Dry Gills

Drygill Head
2000

Red Gate

1900

grass

grass

To CARROCK FELL, 2169': 2 miles:
SSW, then ESE
Depression at 1880'
350 feet of ascent
An easy walk, making use of new paths

Start as for Knott, but swing away eastwards over Drygill Head to traverse the ridge now directly ahead. The finish is the best part of this route.

At this point there is a simple way down to the left (Red Gate): it should be taken in bad weather.

Miton Hill

1700
1800

1900

1900

tarn

butt 2000

Round Knott

ONE MILE

CARROCK FELL

Knott   2329'

Fell Side
● Green Head
● Uldale
● Longlands   ▲ HIGH PIKE
● Orthwaite
          ▲ GREAT SCA FELL
          ▲ KNOTT   ▲ CARROCK
                            FELL
● Bassenthwaite   Mosedale
  Village   ▲ GREAT CALVA
                        ▲ BOWSCALE
    SKIDDAW   FELL
       ▲   ● Skiddaw House

MILES
0   1   2   3   4   5

from
Bowscale Fell

NATURAL FEATURES

Knott occupies a commanding position across the middle of the group of fells north of Skiddaw Forest, of which it is the highest.   Long and narrow, it is nearly four miles from end to end, the extremities being rough but the in-between a vast smooth sheep pasture — grand tramping country in spite of a lack of rocks, landmarks and features of interest. Side spurs run down from the main ridge to the Caldew, which takes away most of the fell's water. Other streams go west ultimately to join the Derwent at the foot of Bassenthwaite Lake; northwards, Roughton Gill is the sole agent of drainage. Like all the fells in this area, the watercourses have carved deep ravines, the sides of which are stripped of vegetation, leaving exposed a gravelly subsoil, often of such garish colour that the rifts are conspicuous from afar as bright yellow and red curtains draping the green slopes.

On the whole this is an easy, accommodating fell with no natural hazards, but it is the very absence of identifiable objects that makes the top especially confusing in mist, and in such conditions it is well to bear in mind that these innocuous pastures contain, near the extremity of the eastern shoulder, a very dangerous trap for walkers not familiar with the lie of the land.

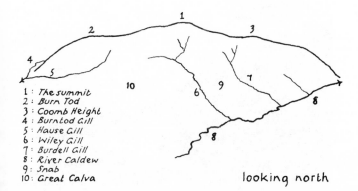

1 : The summit
2 : Burn Tod
3 : Coomb Height
4 : Burntod Gill
5 : Hause Gill
6 : Wiley Gill
7 : Burdell Gill
8 : River Caldew
9 : Snab
10 : Great Calva

looking north

MAP

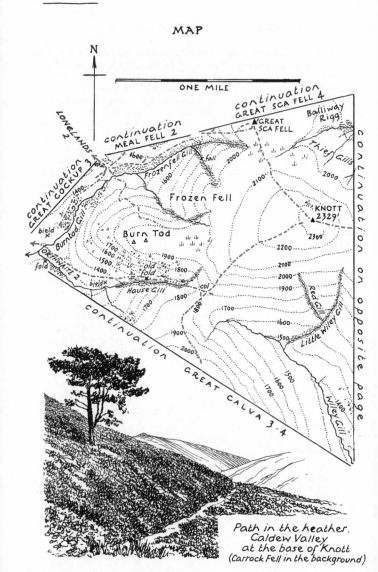

Path in the heather.
Caldew Valley
at the base of Knott
(Carrock Fell in the background)

MAP

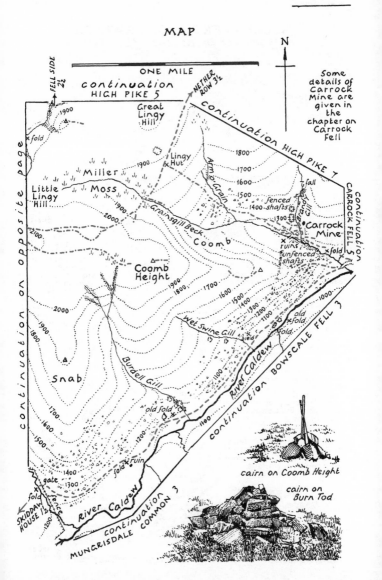

Some details of Carrock Mine are given in the chapter on Carrock Fell

ONE MILE

N

FELL SIDE 2½
continuation HIGH PIKE 5
NETHER ROW 3½
continuation HIGH PIKE 7
continuation CARROCK FELL 5
continuation on opposite page
continuation BOWSCALE FELL 3
continuation MUNGRISDALE COMMON 3
SKIDDAW HOUSE 1¾

Great Lingy Hill

Lingy Hut

Miller Moss

Little Lingy Hill

Grainsgill Beck

Coomb

Aiken Grain

fall

fenced shafts

Carrock Mine

ruins

unfenced shafts

fold

Coomb Height

Wet Swine Gill

Snab

Burdell Gill

old fold

fold

River Caldew

old fold

gate

fold

fence

ruin

River Caldew

cairn on Coomb Height

cairn on Burn Tod

ASCENT FROM ORTHWAITE
1500 feet of ascent : 3¾ miles

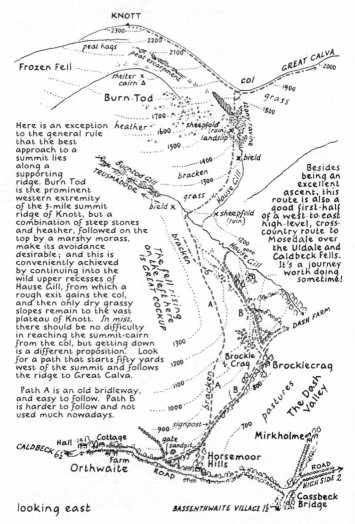

KNOTT

2300
2200
2100

peat hags

peat escarpment

Frozen Fell

GREAT CALVA

col

2000

shelter ×
cairn △

Burn Tod

grass

1900

1800

1700

heather

stony ravine

sheepfold (ruin)
landslip

1600

1500

1400

× bield

Burn Tod Gill

TRUSMADOOR

bracken

Hause Gill

1300

grass

bield ×

× sheepfold (ruin)

Hause Gill

1200

Hause Gill

Here is an exception to the general rule that the best approach to a summit lies along a supporting ridge. Burn Tod is the prominent western extremity of the 3-mile summit ridge of Knott, but a combination of steep stones and heather, followed on the top by a marshy morass, make its avoidance desirable; and this is conveniently achieved by continuing into the wild upper recesses of Hause Gill, from which a rough exit gains the col, and then only dry grassy slopes remain to the vast plateau of Knott. *In mist, there should be no difficulty in reaching the summit-cairn from the col, but getting down is a different proposition.* Look for a path that starts fifty yards west of the summit and follows the ridge to Great Calva.

Besides being an excellent ascent, this route is also a good first-half of a west-to-east high-level, cross-country route to Mosedale over the Uldale and Caldbeck Fells. It's a journey worth doing sometime!

The fell rising on the left here is GREAT COCKUP

bracken

A

B

DASH FARM

1300

1200

Brockle Crag

Brocklecrag

1100

A

B

800

The Dash Valley

Path A is an old bridleway, and easy to follow. Path B is harder to follow and not used much nowadays.

bracken

1000

pastures

900

signpost

700

Mirkholme

CALDBECK 6½

Hall

Cottage

gate
sandpit

Farm
Orthwaite

ROAD

Horsemoor Hills

ROAD

ROAD

HIGH SIDE 2

looking east

BASSENTHWAITE VILLAGE 1½

Cassbeck Bridge

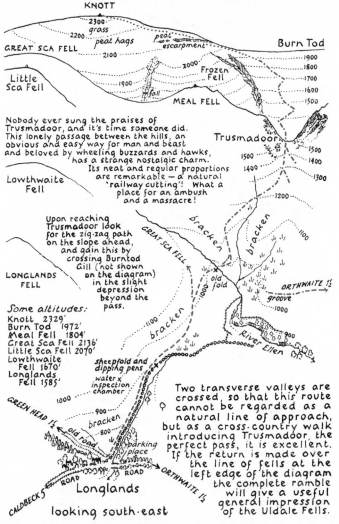

ASCENT FROM LONGLANDS
1700 feet of ascent : 3½ miles

KNOTT

2300
grass
2200   peat hags   peat
escarpment
GREAT SCA FELL   Burn Tod
2100   1900
                                                  1800
                    2000   Frozen   1700
Little   Fell   1600
Sca Fell   1900   1500
                    fall
                        MEAL FELL

Trusmadoor

Nobody ever sung the praises of
Trusmadoor, and it's time someone did.
This lonely passage between the hills, an
obvious and easy way for man and beast   1500   1500
and beloved by wheeling buzzards and hawks,   1400
has a strange nostalgic charm.   1400
            Its neat and regular proportions   1300
            are remarkable — a natural
Lowthwaite   'railway cutting'! What a
Fell   place for an ambush   1200
                and a massacre!

        Upon reaching   bracken   bracken
        Trusmadoor look   1100
        for the zig-zag path   GREAT SCA FELL
        on the slope ahead,
        and gain this by
        crossing Burntod
        Gill (not shown   old   ORTHWAITE 1½
LONGLANDS   on the diagram)   fold   groove
FELL   in the slight
            depression   1100   1000
            beyond the   bracken
            pass.   River Ellen   900

Some altitudes:
Knott   2329'
Burn Tod 1972'
Meal Fell 1804'   sheepfold and
Great Sca Fell 2136'   dipping pens
Little Sca Fell 2070'   water x
Lowthwaite   inspection
Fell 1670'   chamber
Longlands   Two transverse valleys are
Fell 1585'   crossed, so that this route
                                          cannot be regarded as a
GREEN HEAD 1½   1000   natural line of approach,
            old road   900   but as a cross-country walk
                        bracken   introducing Trusmadoor, the
                    800   perfect pass, it is excellent.
                            parking   If the return is made over
                            place   the line of fells at the
                        ROAD   left edge of the diagram
                    ROAD   the complete ramble
CALDBECK 5   ROAD   ORTHWAITE 1½   will give a useful
            Longlands   general impression
                                          of the Uldale Fells.
        looking south-east

ASCENT FROM FELL SIDE
1500 feet of ascent
3½ miles

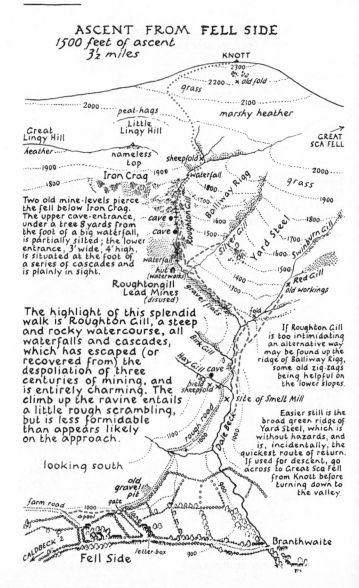

KNOTT

2300

old fold

2200

grass

2100

2000

peat·hags

Little
Lingy Hill

marshy heather

Great
Lingy Hill

GREAT
SCA FELL

heather

nameless
top

sheepfold

1900

Iron Crag   1900

waterfall

Balliway Rigg

grass

2000

1800

1800

1900

Two old mine·levels pierce
the fell below Iron Crag.
The upper cave-entrance,
under a tree 8 yards from
the foot of a big waterfall,
is partially silted; the lower
entrance, 3' wide, 4' high,
is situated at the foot of
a series of cascades and
is plainly in sight.

cave

cave

1700

1600

Silver Gill

Yard Steel

1500

1800

1700

Swinburn Gill

1600

waterfall

hut
(waterworks)

1400

1300

Red Gill
old workings

Roughtongill Lead Mines
(disused)

Gravel falls

fold

The highlight of this splendid
walk is Roughton Gill, a steep
and rocky watercourse, all
waterfalls and cascades,
which has escaped (or
recovered from) the
despoliation of three
centuries of mining, and
is entirely charming. The
climb up the ravine entails
a little rough scrambling,
but is less formidable
than appears likely
on the approach.

If Roughton Gill
is too intimidating
an alternative way
may be found up the
ridge of Balliway Rigg,
some old zig-zags
being helpful on
the lower slopes.

Birk Gill

Hay Gill   cave

field
sheepfold

site of Smelt Mill

rough road

Dale Beck

1100

1000

1000

Easier still is the
broad green ridge of
Yard Steel, which is
without hazards, and
is, incidentally, the
quickest route of return.
If used for descent, go
across to Great Sca Fell
from Knott before
turning down to
the valley.

looking south

old
grave pit

farm road   1000

gate

pool

CALDECK 2

letter-box

Fell Side

900

Branthwaite

The valley of Dale Beck, leading to Roughton Gill
In the foreground are the ruins of the smelt mill (now gone).

ASCENT FROM MOSEDALE
1650 feet of ascent : 4½ miles

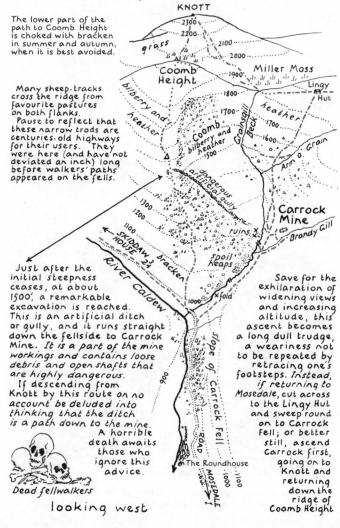

KNOTT

The lower part of the path to Coomb Height is choked with bracken in summer and autumn, when it is best avoided.

Many sheep-tracks cross the ridge from favourite pastures on both flanks.
Pause to reflect that these narrow trods are centuries-old highways for their users. They were here (and have not deviated an inch) long before walkers' paths appeared on the fells.

Coomb Height

Miller Moss

Lingy Hut

Grainsgill Beck

heather

bilberry and heather

Coomb bilberry and heather

Arm o' Grain

dangerous artificial gully

Carrock Mine

ruins

Brandy Gill

SKIDDAW HOUSE 3½

1300

1200

1100

bracken

spoil heaps

River Caldew

fold

Just after the initial steepness ceases, at about 1500', a remarkable excavation is reached. This is an artificial ditch or gully, and it runs straight down the fellside to Carrock Mine. It is a part of the mine workings and contains loose debris and open shafts that are highly dangerous.
If descending from Knott by this route on no account be deluded into thinking that the ditch is a path down to the mine.
A horrible death awaits those who ignore this advice.

Save for the exhilaration of widening views and increasing altitude, this ascent becomes a long dull trudge, a weariness not to be repeated by retracing one's footsteps. Instead, if returning to Mosedale, cut across to the Lingy Hut and sweep round on to Carrock Fell; or better still, ascend Carrock first, going on to Knott and returning down the ridge of Coomb Height

slope of Carrock Fell

The Roundhouse

MOSEDALE 1

Dead fellwalkers

looking west

THE SUMMIT

CARROCK FELL

BOWSCALE FELL

*looking east to
the gap of Mosedale*

If the party consists of more than one person, and if, further, a bat, ball and wickets can be found in the depths of somebody's rucksack, a cricket match can be played on turf that many a county ground might covet.   Apart from this, no suggestions can be made for whiling away the time (unless the party be a mixed one), the smooth top being completely without anything worth investigating. The solitary walker, unable to indulge in communal games or pastimes, will find himself wondering who carried up the stones to make the cairn, and whence they came: must have been another lonely soul with nobody to play with!

DESCENTS: Routes of ascent may be reversed (Roughton Gill requires care).   The territory is confusing in mist, due to the absence of landmarks. The most obvious route is east to Mosedale: if this way off is used keep strictly to the ridge down to the road, avoiding an artificial 'ditch' cutting across the crest: this is part of the Carrock Mine workings, NOT A PATH.

Note that the foot of this path is choked with bracken in summer and autumn, when it is best avoided.

*above
Mosedale from the
eastern shoulder*

In the foreground is an abandoned 'dig' (mine workings). It is near to the end of the 'ditch' or gully that goes steeply and dangerously (shafts) down to Carrock Mine

*left
The eastern shoulder
from Mosedale*

THE VIEW

This view hardly comes up to expectations: the highest of the Caldbeck Fells is rather disappointing in this respect. The scene is extensive enough in the northern arc, ranging across the Solway Firth to the Scottish hills and round to the Pennines in the east, there being nothing higher to obstruct, but this panorama is more pleasing from the neighbouring High Pike. To the south there is a restricted glimpse of the central peaks of Lakeland between the masses of Blencathra and Skiddaw.

The broad top of the fell permits no depth to the picture in any direction and its worth as a viewpoint suffers accordingly.

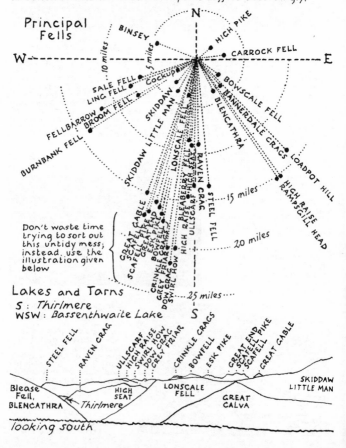

Principal Fells

N
BINSEY
HIGH PIKE
W — — — — — — — — — — — — E
CARROCK FELL
10 miles
5 miles
SALE FELL
LINE FELL
Cockup
BOWSCALE FELL
FELLBARROW
BROOM FELL
SKIDDAW
BANNERDALE CRAGS
BURNBANK FELL
SKIDDAW LITTLE MAN
LONSCALE FELL
BLENCATHRA
LOADPOT HILL
RAVEN CRAG
HIGH RAISE
RAMPSGILL HEAD
HIGH RAISEBERRY FELL
ULLSCARF FELL
STEEL FELL
15 miles

Don't waste time trying to sort out this untidy mess; instead, use the illustration given below

GREAT GABLE
SCAFELL
SCAFELL PIKE
GREAT END
ESK PIKE
BOWFELL
CRINKLE CRAGS
GREY FRIAR
DOW CRAG
SWIRL HOW
HIGH RAISE
SWIRL HOW
HIGH SEAT
ULLSCARF

20 miles

Lakes and Tarns

S : Thirlmere
WSW : Bassenthwaite Lake

25 miles
S

STEEL FELL
RAVEN CRAG
ULLSCARF
HIGH RAISE
SWIRL HOW
DOW CRAG
GREY FRIAR
CRINKLE CRAGS
BOWFELL
ESK PIKE
GREAT END
SCAFELL PIKE
SCAFELL
GREAT GABLE

Blease Fell, BLENCATHRA
Thirlmere
HIGH SEAT
LONSCALE FELL
GREAT CALVA
SKIDDAW LITTLE MAN

looking south

RIDGE ROUTES

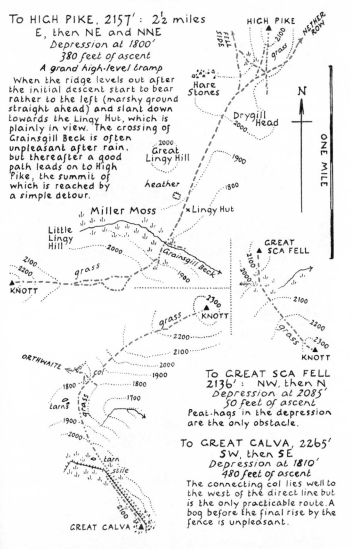

TO HIGH PIKE, 2157': 2½ miles
E, then NE and NNE
Depression at 1800'
380 feet of ascent
A grand high-level tramp

When the ridge levels out after the initial descent start to bear rather to the left (marshy ground straight ahead) and slant down towards the Lingy Hut, which is plainly in view. The crossing of Grainsgill Beck is often unpleasant after rain, but thereafter a good path leads on to High Pike, the summit of which is reached by a simple detour.

HIGH PIKE — NETHER ROW — FELL SIDE — 2100 — grass
Hare Stones
Drygill Head — 2000
Great Lingy Hill — 2000 — 1900
heather — 1800
Miller Moss — ×Lingy Hut
Little Lingy Hill — 2000 — Grainsgill Beck — 1900
2100 — 2200 — grass — KNOTT
GREAT SCA FELL — 2100 — 2000
2300 — KNOTT — 2100
grass — 2200 — 2200 — 2300 — KNOTT
ORTHWAITE — col — 2000 — 1900 — 1800 — 1700
1800 — tarns
1900
2000
tarn — stile
GREAT CALVA — 200

N

ONE MILE

TO GREAT SCA FELL 2136': NW, then N
Depression at 2085'
50 feet of ascent
Peat-hags in the depression are the only obstacle.

TO GREAT CALVA, 2265'
SW, then SE
Depression at 1810'
480 feet of ascent
The connecting col lies well to the west of the direct line but is the only practicable route. A bog before the final rise by the fence is unpleasant.

Latrigg

1203'

This is the Latrigg near Keswick
— there is another,
less well-known,
near Over Water.

from the Blencathra Centre
(showing the east ridge going
down to Brundholme Woods)

▲ SKIDDAW
▲ LITTLE MAN
▲ LONSCALE FELL
● Millbeck
Threlkeld ●
▲ LATRIGG
● Keswick

MILES
0 1 2 3 4

from the Orthwaite road

NATURAL FEATURES

Latrigg is to Keswick what Loughrigg is to Ambleside and Helm Crag to Grasmere : a small hill, an excellent viewpoint, a great favourite of local folk and visitors. Latrigg is pastoral and parkland in character, not rough fell, and the summit is the easiest of promenades, so that this is not a climb calling for old clothes and heavy boots : 'Sunday best' is quite appropriate dress. The woods, once a haven for courting couples and other wildlife, are privately owned, being part of the Mirehouse Estate, and in recent years they have been increasingly managed for the benefit of walkers. There are three information panels, and a circular walk has been created. It heads east from Spoony Green for two miles and returns at a lower level. A leaflet is available at the Tourist Information Centre in Keswick.

Latrigg has been well described as 'the cub of Skiddaw'. It crouches at the foot of the broad southern slopes of the parent, too small to be significant in the geography of the mass, although a long east ridge is reponsible for the formation of the short side-valley of Lonscale.   The River Greta flows along the southern base, occupying a wooded gorge of outstanding scenic beauty, appreciated best from the disused railway from Keswick to Threlkeld.

1 : The summit
2 : East ridge
3 : Brundholme Woods
4 : Slope of
        Skiddaw Little Man
5 : Slope of
        Lonscale Fell
6 : Glenderaterra Beck
7 : Lonscale Valley (below)
8 : River Greta
9 : Gale Gill

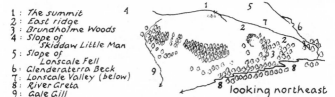

looking northeast

Latrigg's top is a smooth grassy pasture innocent of rock except for a few yards of outcrop at the summit where the native stone breaks through the turf.   This is seen to be slate. The wall across the top to the east is built of slate.

Not long ago, in fact since the turn of the 20th century, Latrigg's top was described as having a scattering of boulders of volcanic rock deposited there by a retreating glacier.   These boulders were identified as having their origin in the crags of Clough Head and it is therefore simple to reconstruct (but difficult to imagine) the scene here at the end of the Ice Age : the glacier tore from its moorings in the narrows of St. John's Vale, and, taking the route of the present St. John's Beck and River Greta and being joined by tributaries of ice from the Glenderamackin, the Glenderaterra and the Naddle Valleys, slowly withdrew from the hills, scouring the side of Lonscale Fell and Skiddaw and depositing the rubble collected on its journey as it disintegrated. The presence of Clough Head rocks on the top of Latrigg indicates that the surface of the glacier must have been higher than the present elevation of the fell.

These boulders have now gone, possibly removed with the trees to make a smooth sheepwalk. Just a few 'erratics' can still be found by diligent search, but the evidence of the movement of the glacier is more abundant lower down the fellside and about the bed of the Greta, where, to a trained eye, there are several manifestations of glacial action, much of it unearthed during the construction of the railway.

MAP

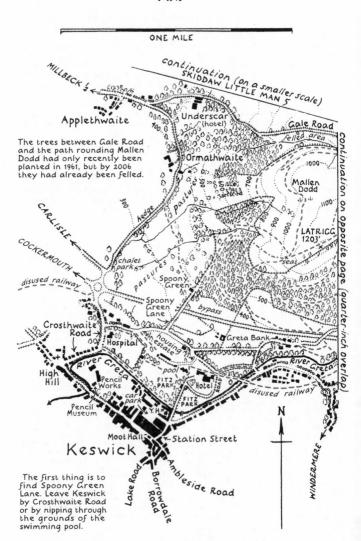

ONE MILE

MILLBECK ½

Applethwaite

The trees between Gale Road and the path rounding Mallen Dodd had only recently been planted in 1961, but by 2006 they had already been felled.

continuation (on a smaller scale) SKIDDAW LITTLE MAN 5

Underscar (hotel)

Gale Road
felled area

Ormathwaite

Mallen Dodd

continuation on opposite page (quarter-inch overlap)

CARLISLE

COCKERMOUTH

disused railway

hedge

pastures

300

400

700

800

900

1000

1100

LATRIGG 1203'

seat

chalet park

pastures

Spoony Green

Spoony Green Lane

bypass

500

400

Crosthwaite Road

Hospital

housing estate

Greta Bank

River Greta

River Greta

High Hill

River Greta

Pencil Works

pool

FITZ PARK

Hotel

disused railway

car park

Pencil Museum

FITZ PARK

Y.H.

N

Moot Hall ← Station Street

Keswick

The first thing is to find Spoony Green Lane. Leave Keswick by Crosthwaite Road or by nipping through the grounds of the swimming pool.

Lake Road

Borrowdale Road

Ambleside Road

WINDERMERE

MAP

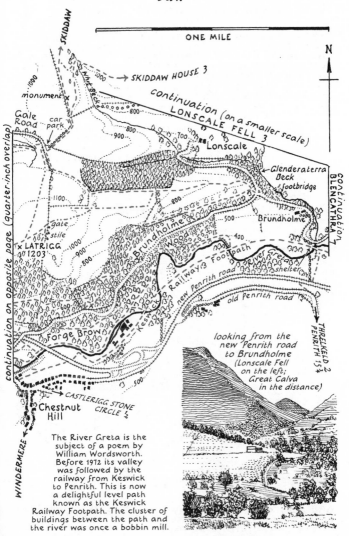

ONE MILE

N

SKIDDAW

→ SKIDDAW HOUSE 3

continuation (on a smaller scale)
LONSCALE FELL 3

monument ×

Gale Road

car park

Lonscale

Glenderaterra Beck footbridge

continuation BLENCATHRA 7

Brundholme

× LATRIGG 1203

gate
stile

Brundholme Wood

shelter

Keswick Railway Footpath

new Penrith road

old Penrith road

THRELKELD 2
PENRITH 15½

Forge Brow

looking from the
new Penrith road
to Brundholme
(Lonscale Fell
on the left;
Great Calva
in the distance)

CASTLERIGG STONE CIRCLE ½

Chestnut Hill

WINDERMERE

continuation on opposite page (quarter-inch overlap)

The River Greta is the
subject of a poem by
William Wordsworth.
Before 1972 its valley
was followed by the
railway from Keswick
to Penrith. This is now
a delightful level path
known as the Keswick
Railway Footpath. The cluster of
buildings between the path and
the river was once a bobbin mill.

ASCENT FROM KESWICK
950 feet of ascent: 2½ miles

The original path, rounding Mallen Dodd, is the easiest route to the top, but there are a number of short-cuts. The start of Route A is easily missed. It leaves the main path by a gate post at the end of a short stretch of fence. For Route B turn sharp right onto a forest road and then turn left after passing through a gate. This route is best avoided because of a difficult stretch just below the fence. Route C leaves the main path shortly after it crosses a stream. All these paths are provided with stiles where they cross the forest fence. At the time of writing this is a good place to see red squirrels, but in a few years they will probably all be gone.

Happily, the superb view from the summit is available also to non-climbers, and the old and infirm, with the assistance of a car, can enjoy it by a simple stroll from the road end.

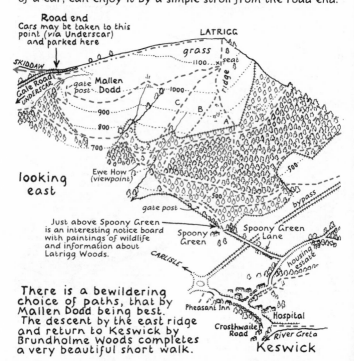

Road end
Cars may be taken to this point (via Underscar) and parked here

LATRIGG

SKIDDAW

Gate Road
UNDERSCAR

grass

1100 — x seat

ridge

gate post   Mallen Dodd

1000

C   B

900

A

800

700

500

Ewe How (viewpoint)

looking east

500   bypass

gate post

Just above Spoony Green is an interesting notice board with paintings of wildlife and information about Latrigg Woods.

500

Spoony Green

Spoony Green Lane

housing estate

CARLISLE

There is a bewildering choice of paths, that by Mallen Dodd being best. The descent by the east ridge and return to Keswick by Brundholme Woods completes a very beautiful short walk.

Pheasant Inn

Crosthwaite Road

Hospital

River Greta

Keswick

ASCENT FROM THRELKELD
900 feet of ascent : 3 miles

This simple climb by the east ridge can be made with
equal facility from Keswick. Take the road behind the
swimming pool signposted "Windebrowe & Brundholme"
— this degenerates into a lane but improves in scenery
as it enters and passes through the woods: a delightful
walk with interesting glimpses of the River Greta below.

From Threlkeld, the bridge over
Glenderaterra Beck is reached
along the road signposted
"Wescoe & Derwent Folds",
turning down a lane
to the left at Wescoe.
This bridge can also
be reached from
Keswick by the
Keswick Railway
Footpath, turning
left just before
the shelter.

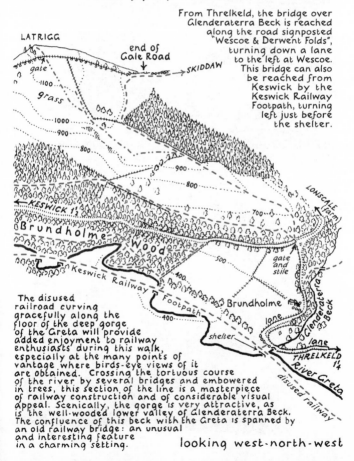

The disused
railroad curving
gracefully along the
floor of the deep gorge
of the Greta will provide
added enjoyment to railway
enthusiasts during this walk,
especially at the many points of
vantage where birds-eye views of it
are obtained. Crossing the tortuous course
of the river by several bridges and embowered
in trees, this section of the line is a masterpiece
of railway construction and of considerable visual
appeal. Scenically, the gorge is very attractive, as
is the well-wooded lower valley of Glenderaterra Beck.
The confluence of this beck with the Greta is spanned by
an old railway bridge: an unusual
and interesting feature
in a charming setting.

looking west-north-west

Underskiddaw, looking to Bassenthwaite Lake

.... Two views from Latrigg.................
Blease Fell, Blencathra, from the east ridge

THE SUMMIT

The top of Latrigg is a green sward, crossed by an excellent gravel path that runs along the top of a causeway. 150 yards west of the summit the path passes almost over the top of a little rocky knoll where there are good views of Keswick and Derwent Water. 100 yards farther west is a seat in a commanding position bearing the inscription 'a 90th birthday tribute to Ronald Lupton of Keswick 23/1/91'. The area was once covered in trees, but now only a pine and two larches remain; even the stumps have gone.

The top of Latrigg is a grand place, especially for fellwalkers on the retired list: here they can recline for hours, recalling joyful days when they had energy enough to climb to the tops of all the mountains in view. Strange how all the best days of memory are to do with summit-cairns....... Will there be mountains like these in heaven...... or is *this* heaven, before death, and will there never again be hills to climb? Is Latrigg the last of all? But no, it needn't be — there's still Orrest Head, even easier...... Funny, that's where we came in ......

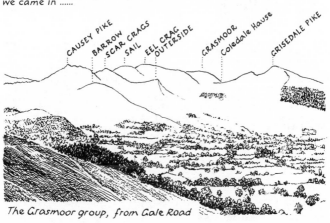

The Grasmoor group, from Gale Road

THE VIEW

There is complete contrast between the northern and southern halves of the view. The northern, consisting of featureless slopes sweeping up to a high skyline, will hardly get a second glance unless the ling is in bloom, but to the south is a panorama of crowded detail, all of it of great beauty: indeed, this scene is one of the gems of the district. The roofs of Keswick are below, Derwent Water is set out just beyond, in its lovely entirety, and in the distance Borrowdale and the Newlands Valley are seen winding deeply amongst the sombre mountains. The far horizon is a jumbled upheaval of peaks, with many dear old friends standing up proudly: Helvellyn, Bowfell, the Scafells, Great Gable, Pillar, the Buttermere fells, and, much nearer, the striking outline of the Grasmoor group. There is enough of interest in this charming picture to engage the attention for many hours, and Latrigg is a place to visit time and time again, for the scene is never quite the same but always fresh and exciting. The view is so much the best reason for climbing Latrigg that it is almost a pity to make the ascent on a day of poor visibility.

Principal Fells

Principal Fells (panorama diagram with radiating compass lines labelled N, W, S and distances in MILES 1–17)

SKIDDAW LITTLE MAN
SKIDDAW (summit not seen)
CARL SIDE
DODD
BARF
LORD'S SEAT
WHINLATTER
GRISEDALE PIKE
OUTERSIDE
GRASMOOR
EEL CRAG
SAIL   BARROW
CAUSEY PIKE
RED PIKE
HIGH STILE   ROBINSON
PILLAR   HINDSCARTH
DALE HEAD
CATBELLS
KING'S HOW
GRANGE FELL
GREAT CRAG
WALLA CRAG
GREAT GABLE
LINGMELL
SCAFELL   BASE BROWN
SCAFELL PIKE   GREAT END
ESK PIKE
BOWFELL
GLARAMARA
CRINKLE CRAGS
COLD PIKE
GREY FRIAR
DOW CRAG

Lakes and Tarns

ESE: *Tewet Tarn*
SSW: *Derwent Water*
NW: *Bassenthwaite Lake*

THE VIEW

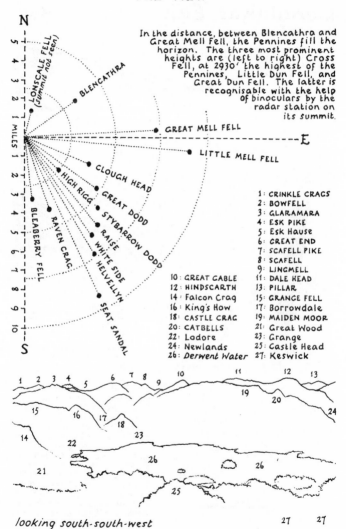

In the distance, between Blencathra and Great Mell Fell, the Pennines fill the horizon. The three most prominent heights are (left to right) Cross Fell, at 2930' the highest of the Pennines, Little Dun Fell, and Great Dun Fell. The latter is recognisable with the help of binoculars by the radar station on its summit.

1: CRINKLE CRAGS
2: BOWFELL
3: GLARAMARA
4: ESK PIKE
5: Esk Hause
6: GREAT END
7: SCAFELL PIKE
8: SCAFELL
9: LINGMELL
10: GREAT GABLE
11: DALE HEAD
12: HINDSCARTH
13: PILLAR
14: Falcon Crag
15: GRANGE FELL
16: King's How
17: Borrowdale
18: CASTLE CRAG
19: MAIDEN MOOR
20: CATBELLS
21: Great Wood
22: Ladore
23: Grange
24: Newlands
25: Castle Head
26: *Derwent Water*
27: Keswick

looking south-south-west

Longlands Fell

1585'

from the north-west

Fell Side
Uldale
Green Head
Longlands
LONGLANDS ▲
FELL   ▲ BRAE FELL
Orthwaite
▲ GREAT
SCA FELL
Bassenthwaite

MILES
0   1   2   3   4

The simple, uncomplicated pyramid of Longlands Fell terminates the northwest ridge of Great Sca Fell. It marks the end of Lakeland in this direction: beyond is a pleasant countryside extending to the Solway Firth. It is a neat little hill, conspicuous in many views although overtopped by bulkier masses behind. The waters of the Ellen and the Eden catchments divide along its crest.

MAP

North of Longlands Fell is a stretch of
moorland crossed by the unenclosed
road linking Uldale and Caldbeck,
this being joined by the road from
Longlands on the slope of a low hill,
Aughertree Fell, a place of ancient
history described on page 6. Rising
beyond is Sandale Fell ('Barren Fell'
is the lesser-known correct name)
with a prominent television mast
disgracing the skyline.
Then follows the great
North Cumbrian plain
extending to Carlisle
and the Border.

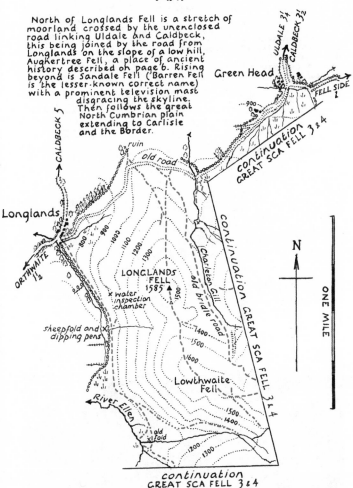

The ridge of Longlands Fell is the watershed between the River
Ellen (west) and the Eden catchment (east). This is worthy of
comment, the fell being the lowest and smallest of three ridges
jutting northwards from a central mass; the others are Brae
Fell and High Pike.

ASCENT FROM LONGLANDS
900 feet of ascent : 1¼ miles

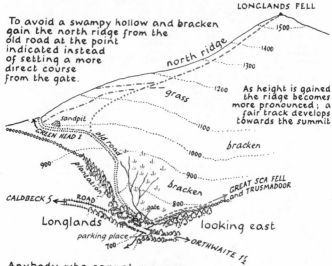

To avoid a swampy hollow and bracken gain the north ridge from the old road at the point indicated instead of setting a more direct course from the gate.

LONGLANDS FELL

north ridge

grass

As height is gained the ridge becomes more pronounced; a fair track develops towards the summit

sandpit

GREEN HEAD 1

old road

bracken

bracken

900

CALDBECK 5   ROAD   plantation

gate

GREAT SCA FELL and TRUSMADOOR

Longlands

looking east

parking place   700   ORTHWAITE 1½

Anybody who cannot manage this short and simple climb is advised to give up the idea of becoming a fellwalker.

Longlands

THE SUMMIT

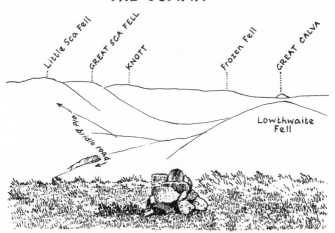

The grassy top of the fell is small and neat, and crowned by a small cairn.   It has merit both as a viewpoint and a place for a siesta, but no features of interest.

DESCENTS: A fair track leaves the summit, aiming north for the highest point of the old road between Longlands and Green Head, and this route is usually followed. Some swampy ground would be met by taking a more direct line for Longlands. But the grassy slopes may be descended with ease anywhere —— indeed, if nobody is watching, rapid progression by roly-poly may be indulged in by the young in heart; but *mind that swamp!*

RIDGE ROUTE : For a diagram, see Great Sca Fell 10.

Longlands Fell, from Over Water

THE VIEW

As befits its position as the northern outpost of Lakeland Longlands Fell commands an excellent view over declining foothills to the Solway Firth and Scotland, the prospect in this direction being in fact more satisfactory than that to the south, where higher fells obstruct the distant scene; but the Grasmoor fells display an exciting skyline to the west of Skiddaw.

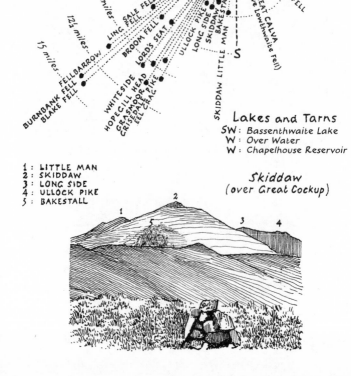

Principal Fells

N
W --- BINSEY --- E
BRAE FELL
Little Sca Fell
GREAT SCA FELL
KNOTT
GREAT CALVA (above Lowthwaite fell)
5 miles
7½ miles
10 miles
12½ miles
15 miles
LING FELL
SALE FELL
BROOM FELL
LORD'S SEAT
FELLBARROW
BURNBANK FELL
BLAKE FELL
WHITESIDE
HOPEGILL HEAD
GRASMOOR
GRISEDALE PIKE
EEL CRAG
ULLOCK PIKE
LONG SIDE
SKIDDAW
BAKESTALL
SKIDDAW LITTLE MAN
S

Lakes and Tarns

SW : Bassenthwaite Lake
W : Over Water
W : Chapelhouse Reservoir

1 : LITTLE MAN
2 : SKIDDAW
3 : LONG SIDE
4 : ULLOCK PIKE
5 : BAKESTALL

Skiddaw
(over Great Cockup)

Aughertree Fell

Let's get the name right first. It is pronounced *Affertree*.
This low hill, a continuation of the moorland running from
Longlands Fell in a north-westerly direction, is really outside
the area covered by this book, but is worthy of mention.
There is not enough of it to occupy more than a half-hour's
walking, but it has a special interest for the student of past
civilisations. On the gentle northern slope are traces of three
ancient enclosures and a tumulus. The enclosures are circular,
about 70 yards in diameter, and although now overgrown the
parapets and ditches are still plain to see.   There is no good
point of vantage for surveying the encampment as a whole (an
aerial view would reveal the arrangement better) and in fact
some searching of the wide breast of the fell is necessary to
locate the various earthworks. The site has been excavated on
several occasions and yielded many of its secrets.

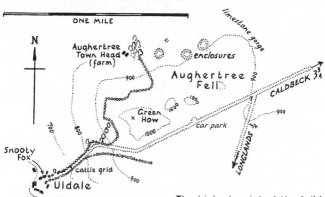

The highest point of the fell is
Green How, about 1060', only a
few minutes' easy climbing from
the unenclosed motor road above
Uldale, which gives convenient access, the whole fell being an open
sheep pasture. The northern slope descends to a dry gorge, where
limestone is in evidence: the fell lies within the continuous strata
of limestone (very narrow just here) that extends from Egremont to
Shap along the western and northern perimeter of Lakeland. There
are good formations at Caldbeck. A horrible object on the nearby
skyline (Sandale Television Mast) contrasts oddly with the ancient
earthworks of Aughertree Fell.

Long Side

2405'

Bassenthwaite
High Side
Ravenstone
ULLOCK ▲ SKIDDAW
PIKE ▲ ▲ LONG SIDE
▲ CARL SIDE
▲ DODD
Millbeck
Little
Crosthwaite
Keswick ●

MILES
0 1 2 3

from Carlside col

NATURAL FEATURES

The highest point on the lofty, steep-sided ridge rising between Bassenthwaite Lake and the 'hidden' valley of Southerndale is a small and shapely pyramid delicately poised above a rough, shadowed declivity facing into the massive breast of Skiddaw. The ridge leading up over Ullock Pike from the north, Longside Edge, is neat and interesting — a splendid high-level way for walkers — but beyond the highest point soon loses itself in the wide plateau of Carl Side.

The summit is strictly nameless, Long Side proper being the broad heathery flank overlooking Bassenthwaite Lake. Below 1500' this slope is planted with massed regiments of conifers and forms a part of the Forestry Commission's Dodd Wood.

Longside Edge, looking from Ullock Pike

MAP

N

This map is on a larger scale than the 'continuing' map of Skiddaw

continuation ULLOCK PIKE 3

CASTLE INN 2¾

continuation SKIDDAW 9

▲ ULLOCK PIKE

× fold

Longside Edge

LONG SIDE 2405

SKIDDAW

car park

Longside Wood

Skill Beck

continuation DODD 4

continuation CARL SIDE 3

Little Crosthwaite

Gable Gill

KESWICK 3¼

LITTLE CROSTHWAITE (forest road)

ONE MILE

The forest fences have a twofold purpose — to mark the boundaries of the forest and to keep out sheep and other grazing animals. They fail in the latter object.

Both the forest and the fellside above it are areas of public access, and the only likely reason that no stile has been provided in the fence at 1600' is that it was thought that nobody would want one. The fence can be crossed 40 yards to the right of the top left-hand corner, but it is better to leave the forest where Gable Gill comes in from the open fell and follow this watercourse up to the ridge, a stony scramble.

The highest of the forest roads have gone out of use and are being reclaimed by nature.

ASCENT FROM LITTLE CROSTHWAITE
2050 feet of ascent : 2½ miles

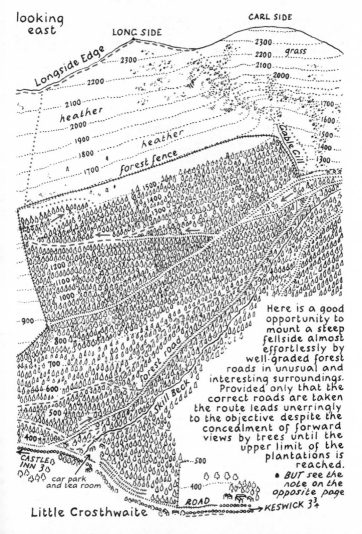

looking east

LONG SIDE

CARL SIDE

Longside Edge

2300

grass

2300
2200
2100
2000

heather

2200
2100
2000

1700
1600
1500
1400
1300

heather

1900
1800
1700

forest fence

Gable Gill

1500
1400
1300

1200

1100

1000

900

800
700
600
500
400

forest road

Skill Beck

CASTLE INN 3
car park and tea room

500

400

ROAD

KESWICK 3¾

Little Crosthwaite

Here is a good opportunity to mount a steep fellside almost effortlessly by well-graded forest roads in unusual and interesting surroundings. Provided only that the correct roads are taken the route leads unerringly to the objective despite the concealment of forward views by trees until the upper limit of the plantations is reached.

• BUT see the note on the opposite page

ASCENT FROM RAVENSTONE
2150 feet of ascent : 2¼ miles

Neither The Edge nor Longside Edge can be compared with Striding Edge on Helvellyn or Sharp Edge on Blencathra, for there is no rock to handle and nothing steep enough to carry a risk of accident; nevertheless they provide fine walking on a ridge narrow enough in places to give startling glimpses downwards and heathery enough to supply springy couches for better enjoyment of the delectable views. This is a good route and it should be noted as a line of approach to Skiddaw more interesting than others preferred by the crowds

SKIDDAW

CARL SIDE   LONG SIDE   Longside Edge   ULLOCK PIKE

Carlside col

fold

heather

On gaining the ridge, Skiddaw is massively in sight across the valley of Southerndale —an aspect of Skiddaw not generally known.

Southerndale

Southerndale Beck

grass

The Edge

Kiln Pots

BARKBETH

Watch for green path inclining right at brow of hill

The track on The Edge is distinct all the way along, with contrasting views to left and right. The pyramid of Ullock Pike is a glorious object rising ahead.

Raven Crag

Start up the steep path, between fences, from a gate on the roadside at the end of the grounds of the hotel.

gate

feet road

gate

This delightful climb deserves a high, even urgent, priority from fellwalkers who know it not. The undulating Edge, of firm dry turf, is an inspiring ladder to the eminently desirable Ullock Pike, the ridge beyond is fine and the views are excellent.

looking south-east

Ravenstone Hotel

KESWICK 5

layby

sign (DODD WOOD)

Main road
(Buses No. 554 and X4)

HIGH SIDE ½
CASTLE INN 2½

THE SUMMIT

The hills of Galloway · Criffel

Solway Firth

West Cumbrian plain

ULLOCK PIKE

Bassenthwaite Lake

Its furnishings of fragrant vegetation — small soft carpets of dry mosses, bilberry and short heather; its quietness, airy elevation and glorious views make this one of the choicest of summits. It is a place fashioned by heaven for the repose and recuperation of tired limbs — or designed by the devil for the abandonment of all further effort. Before composing oneself to slumber, however, it is well to reflect that the edge of a profound abyss is only a short roll distant.

DESCENTS : Best way off is provided by the Edge, but if aiming for the Keswick area the south ridge of Carl Side is more convenient. In mist, Gable Gill is a safe but rough route to Dodd Wood and the road.

RIDGE ROUTES

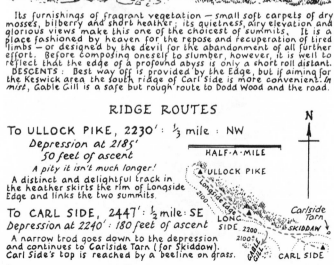

To ULLOCK PIKE, 2230' : ⅓ mile : NW

Depression at 2185'
50 feet of ascent
A pity it isn't much longer!

A distinct and delightful track in the heather skirts the rim of Longside Edge and links the two summits.

N

HALF·A·MILE

▲ULLOCK PIKE

Longside Edge 2100

LONG SIDE 2200

2100'

GABLE GILL

Carlside Tarn

SKIDDAW

▲ CARL SIDE

To CARL SIDE, 2447' : ½ mile : SE

Depression at 2240' : 180 feet of ascent

A narrow trod goes down to the depression and continues to Carlside Tarn (for Skiddaw). Carl Side's top is reached by a beeline on grass.

THE VIEW

Each of the summits buttressing Skiddaw to the south commands a magnificent prospect of distant ranges from Helvellyn round to Grasmoor; Long Side's view, in addition, includes the wide plain north-westwards to the Cumbrian coast, and, across the Solway, Criffell and the hills of Galloway.

Principal Fells

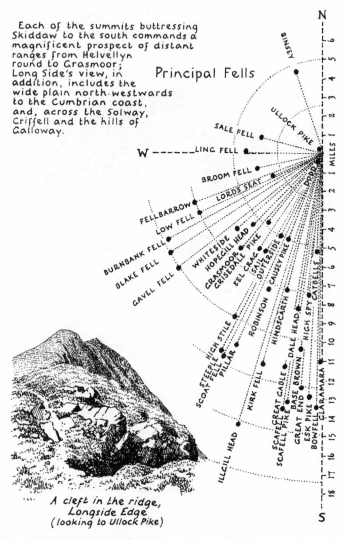

A cleft in the ridge,
Longside Edge
(looking to Ullock Pike)

THE VIEW

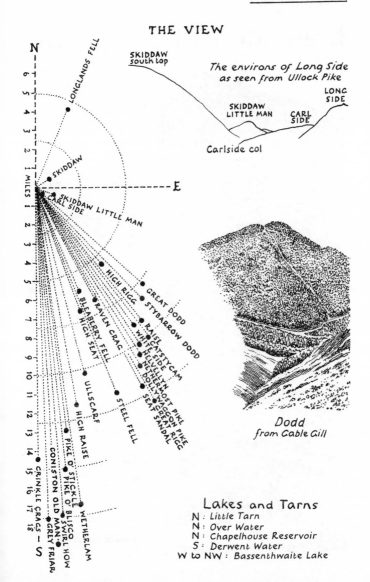

N

6
5
4
3
2
1

MILES

E

LONGLANDS FELL

SKIDDAW

CARL SIDE

SKIDDAW LITTLE MAN

HIGH RIGG

GREAT DODD

STYBARROW DODD

RAVEN CRAG

RAISE

WATSON'S DODD

WHITESIDE

BLEABERRY FELL

HIGH SEAT

WHITESIDE

HELVELLYN LOWER MAN

HELVELLYN

NETHERMOST PIKE

DOLLYWAGGON PIKE

HIGH RAGGEN PIKE

SEAT SANDAL

ULLSCARF

STEEL FELL

HIGH RAISE

PIKE O' STICKLE

PIKE O' BLISCO

HARRISON STICKLE

ESK PIKE

SWIRL HOW

GREY FRIAR

WETHERLAM

CRINKLE CRAGS

CONISTON OLD MAN

6
7
8
9
10
11
12
13
14
15
16
17
18

S

The environs of Long Side as seen from Ullock Pike

SKIDDAW south top

SKIDDAW LITTLE MAN

CARL SIDE

LONG SIDE

Carlside col

Dodd
from Cable Gill

Lakes and Tarns
N : Little Tarn
N : Over Water
N : Chapelhouse Reservoir
S : Derwent Water
W to NW : Bassenthwaite Lake

Lonscale Fell

2344'

from Roughten Gill

SKIDDAW ▲   **Skiddaw**
● House

  BLENCATHRA ▲

▲   ▲ **LONSCALE**
SKIDDAW   FELL
LITTLE
MAN

Threlkeld ●
▲ LATRIGG

● **Keswick**

MILES

0   1   2   3

NATURAL FEATURES

From the summit-ridge of Skiddaw the main watershed eastwards switchbacks over Little Man and Jenkin Hill to Lonscale Fell, this being the familiar outline so conspicuously in view on the southern approaches to Keswick. Lonscale Fell, a graceful and gentle curve against the sky, ends very abruptly in a sharp peak (which also features prominently in most views of the range) whence the ground falls away steeply to the deep narrow valley of Glenderaterra Beck; beyond rises Blencathra.

It is interesting to note that the watershed, between Derwent (south) and Caldew (north), does not persist along the highest ground of Lonscale Fell and the function is taken over by a low ridge that runs away north-east just short of the summit and continues as a wide marshy upland separating the headwaters of the Glenderaterra from the basin of the upper Caldew.

All the interest of Lonscale Fell lies in its east face, a mile-long rough declivity out of character with the general structure of the fell and unusual in an area where smooth grass slopes predominate.

Nowadays exclusively used for sheep-rearing, there was a time when minerals were won from the fell and the old mine-workings are still in evidence on the floor of the Glenderaterra valley.

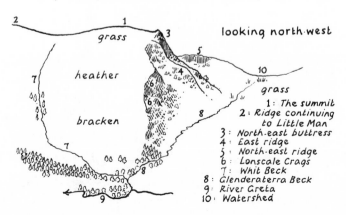

looking north-west

grass

heather

bracken

1: The summit
2: Ridge continuing to Little Man
3: North-east buttress
4: East ridge
5: North-east ridge
6: Lonscale Crags
7: Whit Beck
8: Glenderaterra Beck
9: River Greta
10: Watershed

Lonscale Fell 3

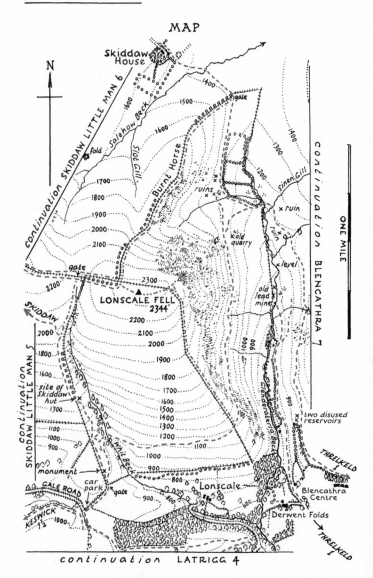

ASCENT FROM KESWICK
2150 feet of ascent : 3¾ - 4¼ miles

LONSCALE FELL

east peak

remains of sheep pen

gate

path behind fence

grass

SKIDDAW HOUSE

A

heather

heather

Lonscale Crags

C

site of former refreshment hut

× falls

heather

B

gate

bracken

wide footpath

bracken

bracken

Whit Beck has fine scenery but is too rough to use as a way up.

monument †

bracken

Whit Beck

gate

Lonscale

car park

gate

CALE ROAD

→ BRUNDHOLME

KESWICK

LATRIGG

looking north

For a diagram of the route from Keswick to the end of Gale Road see Skiddaw 11

Three routes are suggested:

A makes partial use of the tourist path to Skiddaw but leaves it to follow the fence to the source of Whit Beck.

B leaves the Skiddaw House path and heads straight up through the bracken and heather. There is no path, and this route is best avoided in summer and autumn when the bracken is high. Note that the crossing of Whit Beck is difficult after rain.

C has an interest the other routes lack: it climbs along the rising rim of Lonscale Crags with splendid views down into the Glenderaterra Valley.

Lonscale is a farm in a wonderfully secluded position overlooked by the popular path to Skiddaw House.

ASCENT FROM THE GLENDERATERRA VALLEY
(DIRECT to the EAST PEAK)

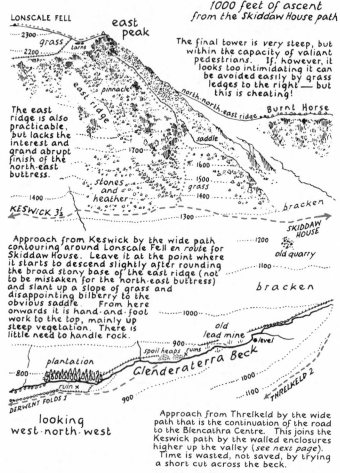

1000 feet of ascent
from the Skiddaw House path

LONSCALE FELL

east peak

2300
2200
grass   tarns

east ridge

pinnacle

The final tower is very steep, but within the capacity of valiant pedestrians. If, however, it looks too intimidating it can be avoided easily by grass ledges to the right — but this is cheating!

north-north-east ridge

Burnt Horse

The east ridge is also practicable, but lacks the interest and grand abrupt finish of the north-east buttress.

saddle

1700
1600
1500
1400

KESWICK 3½

1400

stones and heather

grass

1300

bracken

SKIDDAW HOUSE

1200

old quarry

1100

bracken

Approach from Keswick by the wide path contouring around Lonscale Fell en route for Skiddaw House. Leave it at the point where it starts to descend slightly after rounding the broad stony base of the east ridge (not to be mistaken for the north-east buttress) and slant up a slope of grass and disappointing bilberry to the obvious saddle. From here onwards it is hand-and-foot work to the top, mainly up steep vegetation. There is little need to handle rock.

1000

old lead mine

•level

900
spoil heaps ruins

plantation

Glenderaterra Beck

800
ruin

1000

THRELKELD 2

1100

DERWENT FOLDS 1

900

looking west-north-west

Approach from Threlkeld by the wide path that is the continuation of the road to the Blencathra Centre. This joins the Keswick path by the walled enclosures higher up the valley (*see next page*).
Time is wasted, not saved, by trying a short cut across the beck.

For scramblers only. From some viewpoints the north-east buttress looks excessively steep, almost precipitous, but it is much easier than appearances suggest. *Nevertheless this is not a route for descent.*

ASCENT FROM THE GLENDERATERRA VALLEY
(via the BURNT HORSE RIDGE)
1000 feet of ascent from the watershed.

east peak

LONSCALE FELL

Gate gives access to a path going down to Keswick

SKIDDAW

east ridge

2300

north east buttress

2200

grass

grass

2100

saddle

2000

1900

1800

1700

Burnt Horse

Continue up the valley to the watershed (here Skiddaw House comes into view ahead) and ascend by the fence rising on the left: this is a sure guide (even in mist) to the top of the fell.

1500

KESWICK

bracken

1400

bracken

1600

1500

old quarry

1200

× × ruins
× ×

SKIDDAW HOUSE

1100

bracken

1000

fold

1400

1300

gate

1100

THRELKELD

1200

1300

DERWENT ← WATERSHED → EDEN

looking south-south-west

This is an interesting 'face-saver' for people who have set forth to climb the north-east buttress — and wish they hadn't when they see it. The route is simple, and quite good above the Burnt Horse crags, the dominating feature being the east peak, which soars up grandly (but somewhat reproachfully) ahead.

The Burnt Horse ridge, looking north

RIDGE ROUTE

To SKIDDAW LITTLE MAN, 2837': 1½ miles: WNW
Depression at 2180': 675 feet of ascent.
Easy, straightforward walking

This route, a bee-line, is on grass throughout, following a wall and a fence most of the way. On Jenkin Hill the much-frequented tourist path to Skiddaw is crossed.

Lonscale Crags, from the path to Skiddaw House

At the point illustrated, the path from Keswick swings sharply to the north, being here roughly hewn out of the living rock, and contours at 1250' along the side of Glenderaterra Valley.

THE SUMMIT

LITTLE MAN

SKIDDAW

Jenkin Hill

old wall

The cairn that stands on the highest point and the smaller cairn to the south owe their existence to the enviable energy of some person or persons unknown, who have carried stones from the old wall to make them. Do not omit the short walk to the East Peak — a magnificent belvedere.

The summit tower, East Peak

THE VIEW

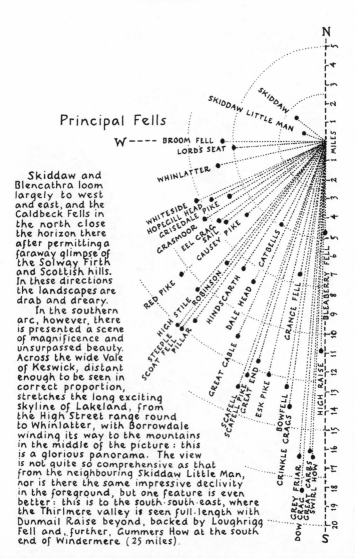

Principal Fells

Skiddaw and
Blencathra loom
largely to west
and east, and the
Caldbeck Fells in
the north close
the horizon there
after permitting a
faraway glimpse of
the Solway Firth
and Scottish hills.
In these directions
the landscapes are
drab and dreary.

In the southern
arc, however, there
is presented a scene
of magnificence and
unsurpassed beauty.
Across the wide Vale
of Keswick, distant
enough to be seen in
correct proportion,
stretches the long exciting
skyline of Lakeland, from
the High Street range round
to Whinlatter, with Borrowdale
winding its way to the mountains
in the middle of the picture: this
is a glorious panorama. The view
is not quite so comprehensive as that
from the neighbouring Skiddaw Little Man,
nor is there the same impressive declivity
in the foreground, but one feature is even
better: this is to the south-south-east, where
the Thirlmere valley is seen full-length with
Dunmail Raise beyond, backed by Loughrigg
Fell and, further, Gummers How at the south
end of Windermere (25 miles).

THE VIEW

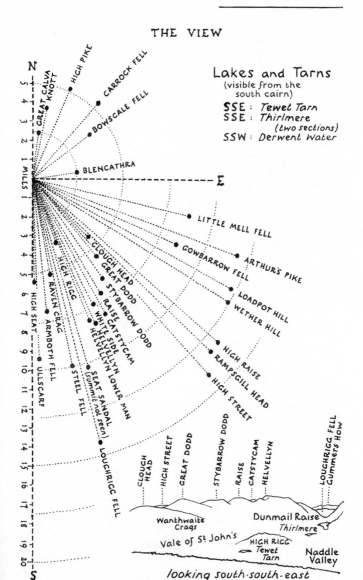

Lakes and Tarns
(visible from the south cairn)
SSE : *Tewet Tarn*
SSE : *Thirlmere*
     (*two sections*)
SSW : *Derwent Water*

N
5
4
3
2
1
MILES
1
2
3
4
5
6
7
8
9
10
11
12
13
14
15
16
17
18
19
20
S

E

HIGH PIKE
GREAT CALVA
KNOTT
CARROCK FELL
BOWSCALE FELL
BLENCATHRA
LITTLE MELL FELL
GOWBARROW FELL
ARTHUR'S PIKE
CLOUGH HEAD
HIGH RIGG
GREAT DODD
STYBARROW DODD
RAISE
CATSTYCAM
WHITE SIDE
HELVELLYN LOWER MAN
RAVEN CRAG
HIGH SEAT
ARMBOTH FELL
ULLSCARF
SEAT SANDAL (summit not seen)
STEEL FELL
LOUGHRIGG FELL
LOADPOT HILL
WETHER HILL
HIGH RAISE
RAMPSGILL HEAD
HIGH STREET

CLOUGH HEAD
HIGH STREET
GREAT DODD
STYBARROW DODD
RAISE
CATSTYCAM
HELVELLYN
LOUGHRIGG FELL
Gummers How
Wanthwaite Crags
Dunmail Raise
Thirlmere
Vale of St John's
HIGH RIGG
Tewet Tarn
Naddle Valley

looking south-south-east

Meal Fell

1804'

Uldale
Longlands
Orthwaite
MEAL ▲
FELL
▲ GREAT
SCA FELL
▲ KNOTT
Bassenthwaite Village

MILES
0   1   2   3   4

from Burntod Gill

NATURAL FEATURES

Thrusting out from the smooth western declivity of Great Sca Fell is a long ridge that swells into two subsidiary fells before coming down sharply to the little hamlet of Orthwaite. The first of these, that nearer Sca Fell, takes the form of a pyramid, its summit appearing from certain viewpoints as a shapely peak. Although of small and slender proportions, this fell is distinctive and its summit is unusual, yet until recently it was without a name on 1" Ordnance Survey maps, the information being vouchsafed only on sheets of 2½" scale and upwards, as Meal Fell. The smooth grassy slopes, badly eroded where they drop steeply into the bounding ravines, have little of interest, the one remarkable feature being the great cleft of Trusmadoor, which conclusively marks the boundary between the fell and the second elevation on the ridge, Great Cockup.

MAP

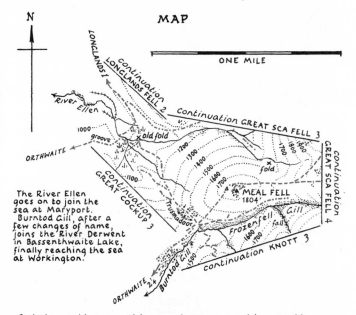

N

ONE MILE

Longlands
continuation LONGLANDS FELL 2

River Ellen

Continuation GREAT SCA FELL 3

1000

groove

old fold

ORTHWAITE

continuation GREAT COCKUP 3

1100

1200
1300
1400
1500
1600
1700

1700
1600

fold

continuation GREAT SCA FELL 4

MEAL FELL
1804

Trusmadoor

Frozenfell Gill

falls

1600
1700

continuation KNOTT 3

Burntod Gill

1500

ORTHWAITE 2¾

The River Ellen goes on to join the sea at Maryport. Burntod Gill, after a few changes of name, joins the River Derwent in Bassenthwaite Lake, finally reaching the sea at Workington.

Strictly speaking, a *path* is a *made* way, a *track* is a *trodden* way. The only *path* on this map is the one between the old sheepfold and Longlands; the others are *tracks*, the ways used by sheep over the centuries, narrow trods that never deviate, though many of them are quite distinct and well-trodden. Nevertheless, when the majority of writers use the word 'track', they mean a rough unmetalled road, and this is the meaning that is intended whenever the word occurs on Ordnance Survey maps.

ASCENT FROM ORTHWAITE
1050 feet of ascent : 3 miles

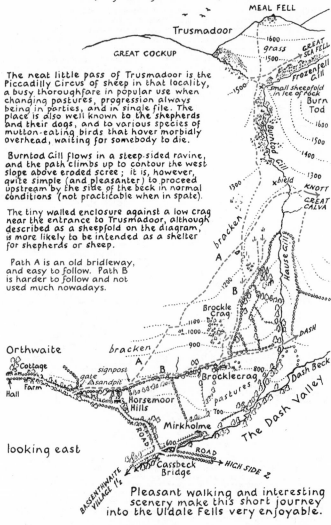

MEAL FELL

Trusmadoor

GREAT COCKUP

1600 grass
1500
GREAT
SEA FELL
Frozenfell Gill
1500
small sheepfold in lee of rock
Burn Tod
1600
1500
1400
Burntod Gill
1300
x bield
KNOTT
GREAT CALVA
1300
Hause Gill
1200
bracken
A
B
Brockle Crag
1100
1000
DASH
900
bracken
A
B
800
Brocklecrag
Dash Beck
pastures
The neat little pass of Trusmadoor is the Piccadilly Circus of sheep in that locality, a busy thoroughfare in popular use when changing pastures, progression always being in parties, and in single file. The place is also well known to the shepherds and their dogs, and to various species of mutton-eating birds that hover morbidly overhead, waiting for somebody to die.

Burntod Gill flows in a steep-sided ravine, and the path climbs up to contour the west slope above eroded scree; it is, however, quite simple (and pleasanter) to proceed upstream by the side of the beck in normal conditions (not practicable in spate).

The tiny walled enclosure against a low crag near the entrance to Trusmadoor, although described as a sheepfold on the diagram, is more likely to be intended as a shelter for shepherds or sheep.

Path A is an old bridleway, and easy to follow. Path B is harder to follow and not used much nowadays.

Orthwaite

Cottage
Farm
Hall
gate
signpost
sandpit
Horsemoor Hills
A
B
700
Mirkholme
The Dash Valley
600
ROAD
ROAD
HIGH SIDE 2
BASSENTHWAITE VILLAGE 1½
Cassbeck Bridge

looking east

Pleasant walking and interesting scenery make this short journey into the Uldale Fells very enjoyable.

ASCENT FROM LONGLANDS
1100 feet of ascent : 2¼ miles

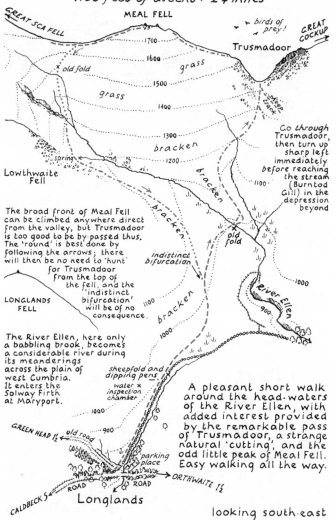

GREAT SCA FELL

MEAL FELL

birds of prey!

GREAT COCKUP

Trusmadoor

old fold

grass

grass

bracken

1700
1600
1500
1400
1300
1200
1100

spring ×

Lowthwaite Fell

Go through Trusmadoor, then turn up sharp left immediately before reaching the stream (Burntod Gill) in the depression beyond

bracken

1100

bracken

old fold

The broad front of Meal Fell can be climbed anywhere direct from the valley, but Trusmadoor is too good to be by-passed thus. The 'round' is best done by following the arrows; there will then be no need to 'hunt' for Trusmadoor from the top of the fell, and the 'indistinct bifurcation' will be of no consequence.

indistinct bifurcation

bracken

River Ellen

1000

900

LONGLANDS FELL

1100

1000

The River Ellen, here only a babbling brook, becomes a considerable river during its meanderings across the plain of west Cumbria. It enters the Solway Firth at Maryport.

sheepfold and dipping pens

water × inspection chamber

1000

GREEN HEAD 1½

old road

900

A pleasant short walk around the head-waters of the River Ellen, with added interest provided by the remarkable pass of Trusmadoor, a strange natural 'cutting', and the odd little peak of Meal Fell. Easy walking all the way.

parking place

ROAD

ROAD

CALDBECK 5

ROAD

ORTHWAITE 1½

Longlands

looking south-east

THE SUMMIT

SKIDDAW

A surprise awaits the visitor, for the summit-cairn turns out to be not a cairn at all but a circular wall-shelter, like a shooting-butt, a ring of loose stones having been superimposed on outcropping rocks at the highest point.   The top of the fell is a plateau, with a cairn on the western edge and ponds in a slight depression. Some rashes of scree make this the one stony top in the Uldale Fells.   Descents are simple, on grass, in any direction.

from the west

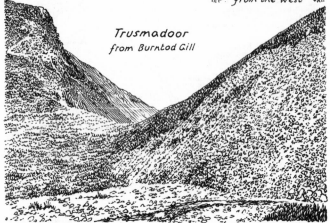

Trusmadoor
from Burntod Gill

THE VIEW

As from all the Uldale Fells the prospect seawards will appeal more than the view inland, which, from Meal Fell, consists only of the featureless grass slopes of higher fells close at hand.

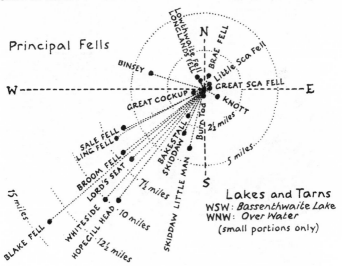

Principal Fells

Lakes and Tarns
WSW: Bassenthwaite Lake
WNW: Over Water
(small portions only)

RIDGE ROUTES

TO GREAT SCA FELL, 2136': ¾ mile : E
Depression at 1680'
460 feet of ascent

A grass shelf sloping up to the col between Little and Great Sca Fell is seen from afar and may be aimed for, but there is no difficulty in going straight up.

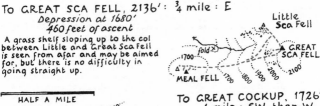

TO GREAT COCKUP, 1726':
1 mile : SW, then W
Depression at 1480'
250 feet of ascent

Trusmadoor lies across a direct course, and is best skirted on the south side, just above Burntod Gill. A steep climb follows up the edge, then becomes easy.

Mungrisdale Common 2077'

Mungrisdale is pronounced
Mun-grize-dl, with the
emphasis on *grize*

from Skiddaw

GREAT ▲ CALVA   BOWSCALE
                        FELL

SKIDDAW

▲   ●   ▲ MUNGRISDALE
   Skiddaw   COMMON
   House

     ▲   BLENCATHRA
  LONSCALE
    FELL

        ● Threlkeld

MILES

0   1   2   3   4

To add to its other failings,
Mungrisdale Common does
not lend itself to illustration.
Most fells have at least one
good aspect, but the Common,
from whatever side it is seen,
has no more pretension to
elegance than a pudding
that has been sat on.
  In the drawing above, the
skyline is formed by Bowscale
Fell and Blencathra. Below,
appearing as a flat-topped
dome, is the Common, rising
beyond Skiddaw Forest.

NATURAL FEATURES

Mungrisdale Common's natural attractions are of a type that appeals only to sheep: it is more an upland prairie than a hill. There is little on these extensive grass slopes to provide even a passing interest for an ordinary walker, and nothing at all to encourage a visit. Sinen Gill, however, has long been known to geologists, the shy Skiddaw granite here, in the heart of slate country, revealing itself as a surface rock.

The Common, which is actually across the watershed from Mungrisdale and therefore rather oddly named, is bounded on three sides by the Caldew and its tributaries, and rises to Blencathra gently in the south, with Roughten Gill providing a useful line of demarcation. In point of fact the Common is properly the further northern slope of Blencathra, a dreary appendage to a fine mountain.

The Eden-Derwent catchment boundary traverses the height of land from the Stake, but is not well defined.

Waterfall, Sinen Gill

MAP

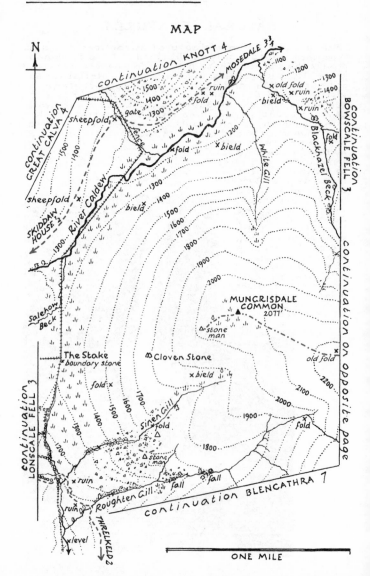

N

continuation KNOTT 4

MOSEDALE 3³

continuation GREAT CALVA 4

SKIDDAW HOUSE 2

River Caldew

sheepfold

sheepfold

gate

fence

fold

ruin

old fold

ruin

bield

ruin

fold

Blackhazel Beck

continuation BOWSCALE FELL 3

fold

bield

White Gill

bield

MUNGRISDALE COMMON 2077

stone man

old fold

continuation on opposite page

Salehow Beck

The Stake
boundary stone

Cloven Stone

bield

fold

Sinen Gill

fold

stone man

continuation LONSCALE FELL 3

fold

ruin

ruin

Roughten Gill

fall

fall

fold

level

THRELKELD 2

continuation BLENCATHRA 7

ONE MILE

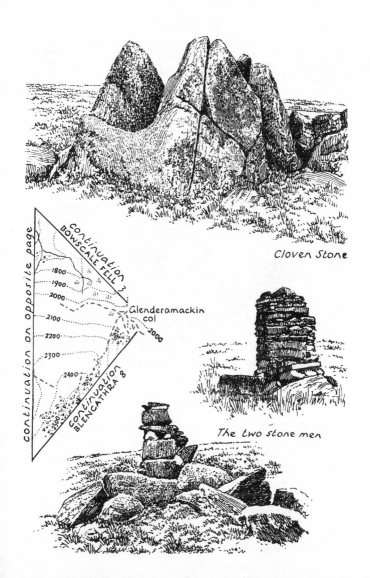

Cloven Stone

continuation on opposite page

continuation BOWSCALE FELL 3

1800
1900
2000
2100
2200
2300
2400

Glenderamackin col

2000

continuation BLENCATHRA 8

The two stone men

ASCENTS

There is little point in providing diagrams of ascent that will never be used. Only shepherds are likely to wander across the top of the Common, and they know the way to it well enough already. It is a place best left to them and the sheep. Precious holiday hours should not be wasted here.

The ascent (for people who won't be told) is accomplished with ease either from the Glenderamackin col (a dull walk) or from the Glenderaterra valley (which, combined with an inspection of Sinen Gill and having a good view in the rear, has rather more purpose to it). Purists who prefer to follow watersheds must start from The Stake, passing Cloven Stone. But, if the top is to be visited at all, it can most conveniently be done, and with least sacrifice of time, as an unorthodox route of descent from Blencathra, sweeping in a wide arc round to the Glenderaterra for Threlkeld: all easy going.

Granite slabs in the bed of the Caldew   The Stake

THE SUMMIT

Since Mungrisdale Common was given the status of a separate fell in *The Northern Fells* it has acquired some of the attributes of a fell, with a cairn on the highest point and faint paths radiating from it. A thousand tufts of tough bent and cotton-grass crown the plateau forming the summit, yet not one can be comfortably reclined upon, this being a summit that holds indefinitely all the water that falls upon it.

Strictly this is not a top that could be accepted by standards of mountaineering as a separate summit: it forfeits this proud qualification because on one side (that linking with Blencathra) the loss of altitude to the connecting depression (peat-hags and ponds here) is barely perceptible — perhaps 15 feet at most.

Descents are simple in all directions, but it is as well to note that the Caldew, along the northern base, cannot be forded.

THE VIEW

The view is redeemed from mediocrity only by a striking grouping southwest, above the valley of the Glenderaterra. In other directions, apart from a distant glimpse of the Solway, there is little of interest.

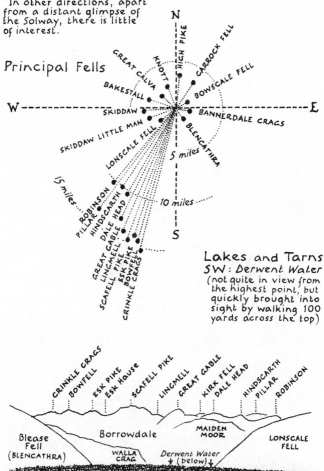

Principal Fells

N

GREAT CALVA
KNOTT
HIGH PIKE
CARROCK FELL
BAKESTALL
BOWSCALE FELL

W

SKIDDAW
BANNERDALE CRAGS

E

SKIDDAW LITTLE MAN
LONSCALE FELL
BLENCATHRA

5 miles

15 miles

ROBINSON
PILLAR
HINDSCARTH
DALE HEAD

10 miles

GREAT GABLE
LINGMELL
SCAFELL PIKE
ESK PIKE
BOWFELL
CRINKLE CRAGS

S

Lakes and Tarns

SW: Derwent Water (not quite in view from the highest point, but quickly brought into sight by walking 100 yards across the top)

CRINKLE CRAGS
BOWFELL
ESK PIKE
ESK HOUSE
SCAFELL PIKE
LINGMELL
GREAT GABLE
KIRK FELL
DALE HEAD
HINDSCARTH
PILLAR
ROBINSON

Blease Fell (BLENCATHRA)

Borrowdale

WALLA CRAG

MAIDEN MOOR

Derwent Water (below)

LONSCALE FELL

looking south-west

Skiddaw

3053'

from Burntod Gill

NATURAL FEATURES

Make no mistake about Skiddaw.

Heed not the disparaging criticisms that have been written from time to time, often by learned men who ought to have known better, about this grand old mountain.   It is an easy climb, yes; its slopes are smooth and grassy, yes; it has no frightful precipices, no rugged outcrops, agreed; it offers nothing of interest or entertainment to rock-gymnasts, agreed. If these are failings, they must be conceded. But are they not quite minor failings ?   Are they failings at all ?

Skiddaw is the fourth highest peak in Lakeland and but little lower than the highest, Scafell Pike. It is the oldest mountain in the district, according to the evidence of its rocks, definitely not the most impressive in appearance but certainly one of the noblest.   The summit is buttressed magnificently by a circle of lesser heights, all of them members of the proud Skiddaw family, the whole forming a splendid and complete example of the structure of mountains, especially well seen from all directions because of its isolation. Its lines are smooth, its curves graceful; but because the slopes are steep everywhere, the quick build-up of the *massif* from valley levels to central summit is appreciated at a glance — and it should be an appreciative glance, for such massive strength and such beauty of outline rarely go together.......
Here, on Skiddaw, they do.

• Orthwaite

Bassenthwaite
•

• Dash

▲ BAKESTALL

High Side

SKIDDAW

ULLOCK PIKE ▲   ▲   • Skiddaw
LONG SIDE ▲   House
CARL SIDE ▲   ▲ SKIDDAW LITTLE MAN
Little • Crosthwaite
▲ DODD   ▲ LONSCALE
                        FELL

• Millbeck
• Applethwaite

LATRIGG ▲   Threlkeld
•

MILES

0   1   2   3   • Keswick

continued

NATURAL FEATURES

continued

Geographically, too, the mountain is of great importance, its main ridge forming the watershed between the Derwent and the Eden. This feature emphasises Skiddaw's supremacy over the rest of the northern fells, for, although situated in the south-west corner of the group, the waters from its eastern slopes cut through the middle of this outlying barrier to augment the drainage from the Pennines — and not even the neighbouring Blencathra, much more handily placed to the east, has been able to accomplish this feat. Engineers have noted this enterprise on the part of Skiddaw and once planned to impound its eastern flow in a reservoir at Caldew Head, but this was never done.

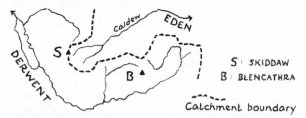

S : SKIDDAW
B : BLENCATHRA

Catchment boundary

Skiddaw has special interests for geologists. It is apparent, even to unobservant walkers, that the stones covering the summit and exposed in eroded gullies and valleys are very different in character from those seen in the central parts of the district: the latter are of volcanic origin, those on Skiddaw are marine deposits and consist in the main of soft shale or slate which splits readily into thin wafers and soon decays and crumbles when exposed to the atmosphere; hence it has no commercial value.

Skiddaw was formed long before the volcanoes of central Lakeland became active; later it overlooked a vast glacier system, a world of ice. Some volcanic boulders are found along the lower southern slopes of the Skiddaw group: these rocks have been identified with those of the cliffs enclosing St. John's-in-the-Vale, having been carried along and deposited here when the glaciers retreated and scoured the flanks of Skiddaw on their passage to the frozen sea.

continued

NATURAL FEATURES

continued

Skiddaw displays a quite different appearance to each of the four points of the compass. The southern aspect is a very familiar sight to visitors, being in unrestricted view from Derwent Water, the Borrowdale fells and most of the higher summits of Lakeland. There is a classical quality about this view from the south. Skiddaw and its outliers rise magnificently across the wide Vale of Keswick in a beautifully symmetrical arrangement, as if posed for a family photograph. The old man himself is the central figure at the back of the group, with his five older children in a line before him (the favourite son, Little Man, being placed nearest) and the two younger children at the front. (Finicky readers who dispute this analogy because no mother to the brood is included in the picture (this is admitted, all the characters being masculine except sweet little Latrigg) are proferred the explanation that Skiddaw is a widower, the old lady having perished in the Ice Age — she couldn't stand the cold).

from the south

SKIDDAW
ULLOCK PIKE · LONG SIDE · CARL SIDE · LITTLE MAN · Jenkin Hill · LONSCALE FELL
DODD · Underskiddaw · LATRIGG

The western aspect is best known to Bassenthwaite folk, who enjoy a secret delight few others have discovered — the glorious sunset colourings of the mountain, winter and summer alike: a beauty that brings people to their doors in rapt admiration. There is little beauty of outline, though, Skiddaw here appearing at its most massive, a great arc high in the sky, and the only shapeliness in the scene from the west is provided by the graceful cone of Ullock Pike and the curving ridge beyond. Two deep valleys, long shadowy recesses in the mountain, are conspicuous features.

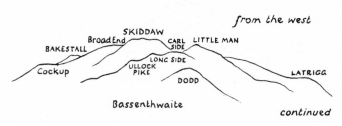

from the west

SKIDDAW
BAKESTALL · Broad End · CARL SIDE · LITTLE MAN
Cockup · ULLOCK PIKE · LONG SIDE · DODD · LATRIGG
Bassenthwaite

continued

NATURAL FEATURES

continued

Skiddaw, northwards, faces the unfrequented Uldale Fells, and not many regular visitors to Lakeland would recognise it in an uncaptioned photograph taken from this side. The northern aspect is truly impressive nonetheless; not quite so overpowering as when viewed from Bassenthwaite to the west but having now a greater majesty and dignity. The summit-ridge is seen end-on and appears as a neat pyramid overtopping the sprawling mass of Broad End, below which is the remarkable combe of Dead Crags. All waters coming down this side of Skiddaw, as those on the south and west, in due course reach the Derwent.

from the north

The east slopes of the mountain, collectively known as Skiddaw Forest, dominate the vast upland basin of Caldew Head, a scene more suggestive of a Scottish glen than of Lakeland, a place incredibly wild and desolate and bare, its loneliness accentuated by the solitary building of Skiddaw House, yet strongly appealing and, in certain lights, often strangely beautiful. In this great hollow the waters unite to form the River Caldew, an important feeder of the Eden. Skiddaw is least impressive from the east because there is much less fall on this side. The scene is in view, although not intimately, from Blencathra.

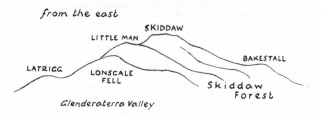

from the east

continued

NATURAL FEATURES

continued

This, then, is Skiddaw, a giant in stature. But an affable and friendly giant.

And a benevolent one. Keswick people have an inborn affection for Skiddaw, and it is well earned. The mountain makes a great contribution to the scenic beauty of this most attractively-situated town, shelters it from northerly gales, supplies it with pure water, feeds its sheep, and provides a recreation ground for its visitors. Throughout the centuries Skiddaw's beacon has warned of the town's troubles and alarms — "the red glare on Skiddaw roused the burghers of Carlisle" — and today shares in its rejoicings.

Skiddaw's critics have passed on, or will soon pass on. Their span of life is short. Skiddaw has stood there in supreme majesty, the sole witness to the creation of Lakeland, for millions of years and will be there to the end of time, continuing to give service and pleasure to insignificant and unimportant mortals.

Let us at least be grateful.

At the back o' beyond.....   *Skiddaw House*

MAP

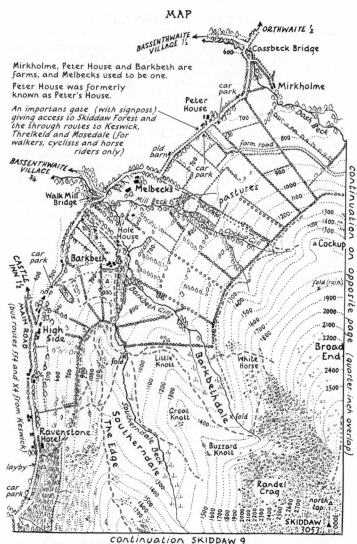

Mirkholme, Peter House and Barkbeth are farms, and Melbecks used to be one.

Peter House was formerly known as Peter's House.

An important gate (with signpost) giving access to Skiddaw Forest and the through routes to Keswick, Threlkeld and Mosedale (for walkers, cyclists and horse riders only)

BASSENTHWAITE VILLAGE 1½

Cassbeck Bridge

ORTHWAITE ½

Mirkholme

Dash Beck

car park

Peter House

old barn

car park

700

700

800

900

1000

1100

1200

1300

1400

1500

farm road

Pastures

Cockup Gill

△ Cockup

continuation on opposite page (quarter-inch overlap)

BASSENTHWAITE VILLAGE ¾

Walk Mill Bridge

Melbecks

Mill Beck

Hole House

Barkbeth

Barkbeth Gill

fold (ruin)

1900

2000

2100

2200

2400

2500

Broad End

CASTLE INN 1½

MAIN ROAD

(bus routes 554 and X4 from Keswick)

car park

High Side

fold

Little Knott

Barkbethdale

White Horse

fold

1500

1600

1700

1800

Ravenstone Hotel

layby

car park

The Edge

Southerndale

Southerndale Beck

Great Knott

1400

Buzzard Knott

1300

1400

1500

1600

1800

1500

1600

1700

1800

1900

2000

2100

2200

2300

2400

2500

2600

2700

Randel Crag

north top

SKIDDAW 3053

CONTINUATION SKIDDAW 9
(two-thirds inch overlap)

MAP

For ease of reference, the map of Skiddaw on this and the accompanying pages includes the whole *massif*, although the outlying summits (shown in CAPITALS) have separate chapters in the book.

The supply road to Skiddaw House is narrow and unenclosed, with a loose and gravelly surface. It is not good enough for cars (cheers) but is a very convenient means of access to the great wilderness of Skiddaw Forest for travellers on foot.

Skiddaw Forest is the general name of the vast heathery amphitheatre at the base of the eastern slopes of Skiddaw. It is a forest entirely without trees (except for a planted windbreak at Skiddaw House).

In the 1960s Skiddaw House was a row of cottages in partial occupation by shepherds. In the 1990s it was the remotest Youth Hostel in the Lake District. As the crow flies it is over 2 miles from the nearest habitation or public road (Black Sail being only 1½ miles from Gatesgarth).

In 2006, several years after the hostel closed down, it was found to be untouched, with books and games in the common room, and Marmite on the dining room table. In 2007 it reopened as a Y.H.A. bunkhouse. The shelter at the back of the house is open to all.

ONE MILE

N

continuation on opposite page (quarter-inch overlap)

DASH FARM
farm road
Dash Beck
Dash Falls (Whitewater Dash)
cave
Dead Beck
Dead Crags
BAKESTALL
fold
fold (ruin)
Tod Gill
north col
north top
SKIDDAW 3053'
supply road
Candleseaves Bog
fold
Hare Crag
butts
fold
River Caldew
Far Grain
GREAT CALVA
Dead Beck
Skiddaw Forest
Skiddaw House

continuation SKIDDAW 10 (two-thirds inch overlap)

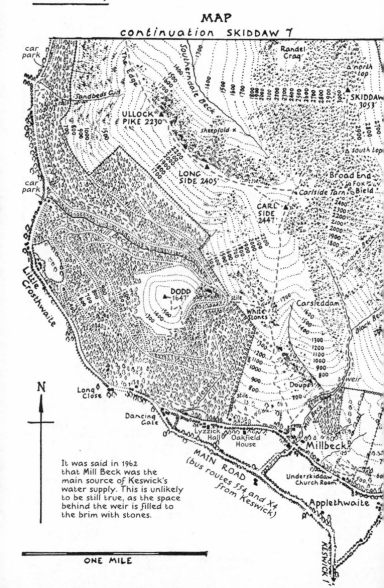

MAP
continuation SKIDDAW 7

car park

The Edge

Sandbeds Gill

ULLOCK PIKE 2230'

Southerndale Beck

sheepfold ×

LONG SIDE 2405'

Randel Crag

north slope

SKIDDAW 3053'

south slope

Broad End

Carlside Tarn

Fox Bield

CARL SIDE 2447'

car park

Little Crosthwaite

DODD 1647'

White Stones

Carlsiddam

Longside Beck

stile

Southerndale Beck

Tongues Beck

Black Beck

weir

Doups

stile

Long Close

Dancing Gate

Calvert Gill

Lyzzick Hall

Oakfield House

Millbeck

N

MAIN ROAD (bus routes 554 and X4 from Keswick)

Underskiddaw Church Room

Applethwaite

KESWICK

It was said in 1962 that Mill Beck was the main source of Keswick's water supply. This is unlikely to be still true, as the space behind the weir is filled to the brim with stones.

ONE MILE

MAP

continuation SKIDDAW 8

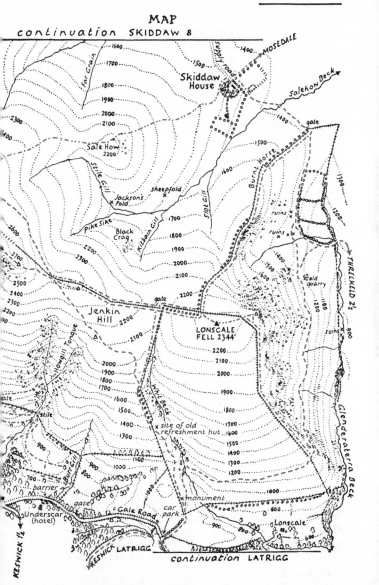

MOSEDALE

Skiddaw House

Salehow Beck

far Grain

Sale How 2200

gate

Stile Gill

sheepfold

Jackson's Fold

Pike Side

Black Crag

Kilbeck Gill

Sloi Gill

Burnt Horse

ruins

ruins

old quarry

THRELKELD 2½

ruins

Jenkin Hill

gate

LONSCALE FELL 2344'

Longill Tongue

Whit Beck

Glenderaterra Beck

stile

site of old refreshment hut

barrier

Bull Gill

gate

Gale Road

monument

car park

Underscar (hotel)

Lonscale

KESWICK 1½

KESWICK LATRIGG

continuation LATRIGG

ASCENT FROM KESWICK
2850 feet of ascent : 5½ miles

see next page

looking north-east

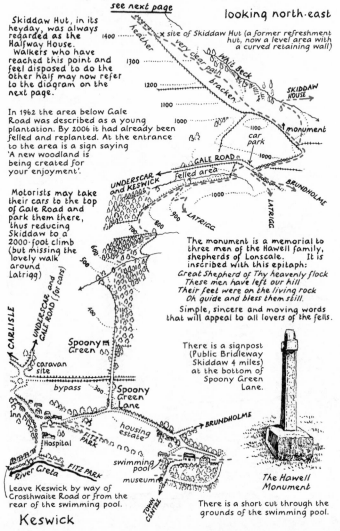

Skiddaw Hut, in its heyday, was always regarded as the Halfway House. Walkers who have reached this point and feel disposed to do the other half may now refer to the diagram on the next page.

In 1962 the area below Gale Road was described as a young plantation. By 2006 it had already been felled and replanted. At the entrance to the area is a sign saying 'A new woodland is being created for your enjoyment'.

Motorists may take their cars to the top of Gale Road and park them there, thus reducing Skiddaw to a 2000-foot climb (but missing the lovely walk around Latrigg)

x site of Skiddaw Hut (a former refreshment hut, now a level area with a curved retaining wall)

SKIDDAW HOUSE

monument

car park

GALE ROAD

UNDERSCAR and KESWICK   felled area

BRUNDHOLME

LATRIGG

LATRIGG

CARLISLE

UNDERSCAR and GALE ROAD (for cars)

Spoony Green

caravan site

bypass

Spoony Green Lane

Inn

FITZ PARK

Hospital

housing estate

BRUNDHOLME

swimming pool

museum

River Greta   FITZ PARK

TOWN CENTRE

Leave Keswick by way of Crosthwaite Road or from the rear of the swimming pool.

Keswick

The monument is a memorial to three men of the Hawell family, shepherds of Lonscale. It is inscribed with this epitaph:

Great Shepherd of Thy heavenly flock
These men have left our hill
Their feet were on the living rock
Oh guide and bless them still.

Simple, sincere and moving words that will appeal to all lovers of the fells.

There is a signpost (Public Bridleway Skiddaw 4 miles) at the bottom of Spoony Green Lane.

The Hawell Monument

There is a short cut through the grounds of the swimming pool.

ASCENT FROM KESWICK

continued

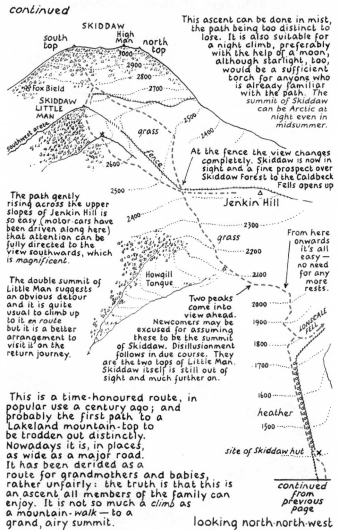

This ascent can be done in mist, the path being too distinct to lose. It is also suitable for a night climb, preferably with the help of a moon, although starlight, too, would be a sufficient torch for anyone who is already familiar with the path. The summit of Skiddaw can be Arctic at night even in midsummer.

SKIDDAW
High Man
south top
north top
3000
2900
2800
2700
Fox Bield
SKIDDAW LITTLE MAN
2600
2500
2400
grass
fence
southwest arête

At the fence the view changes completely. Skiddaw is now in sight and a fine prospect over Skiddaw Forest to the Caldbeck Fells opens up

2500

Jenkin Hill

The path gently rising across the upper slopes of Jenkin Hill is so easy (motor-cars have been driven along here) that attention can be fully directed to the view southwards, which is *magnificent*.

2400
grass
2300
2200
2100

From here onwards it's all easy — no need for any more rests.

The double summit of Little Man suggests an obvious detour and it is quite usual to climb up to it *en route* but it is a better arrangement to visit it on the return journey.

Howgill Tongue

Two peaks come into view ahead. Newcomers may be excused for assuming these to be the summit of Skiddaw. Disillusionment follows in due course. They are the two tops of Little Man. Skiddaw itself is still out of sight and much further on.

2000
1900
1800
1700
1600

LONSCALE FELL

This is a time-honoured route, in popular use a century ago; and probably the first path to a Lakeland mountain-top to be trodden out distinctly. Nowadays it is, in places, as wide as a major road. It has been derided as a route for grandmothers and babies, rather unfairly: the truth is that this is an ascent all members of the family can enjoy. It is not so much a *climb* as a mountain-*walk* — to a grand, airy summit.

heather
1500

site of Skiddaw hut ✕

continued from previous page

looking north·north·west

ASCENT FROM MILLBECK
2750 feet of ascent : 2¾ miles

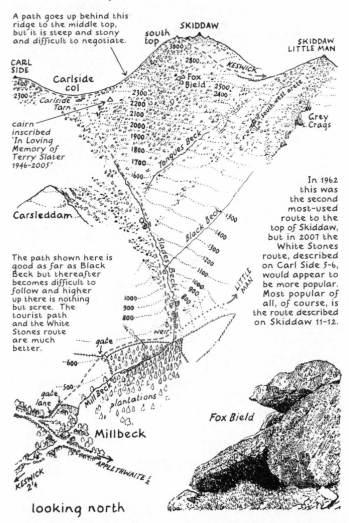

A path goes up behind this ridge to the middle top, but it is steep and stony and difficult to negotiate.

SKIDDAW

south top

SKIDDAW LITTLE MAN

CARL SIDE

Carlside col

KESWICK

2400
2300

Carlside Tarn

cairn inscribed 'In Loving Memory of Terry Slater 1946-2005'

3000
2800
Fox Bield
2500
2400
2300
2200
2100
2000
1900
1800
1700
1600

south west area

Grey Craqs

Tongues Beck

Carsleddam

In 1962 this was the second most-used route to the top of Skiddaw, but in 2007 the White Stones route, described on Carl Side 5-6, would appear to be more popular. Most popular of all, of course, is the route described on Skiddaw 11-12.

Black Beck

1500
1400
1300
1200
1100
1000
900

LITTLE MAN

The path shown here is good as far as Black Beck but thereafter becomes difficult to follow and higher up there is nothing but scree. The tourist path and the White Stones route are much better.

Slades Beck

1000
900
800

weir

gate

600

gate lane

500

Millbeck

Millbeck Lane

plantations

Fox Bield

APPLETHWAITE ½

KESWICK 2¼

looking north

ASCENT FROM APPLETHWAITE
2700 feet of ascent : 3 miles

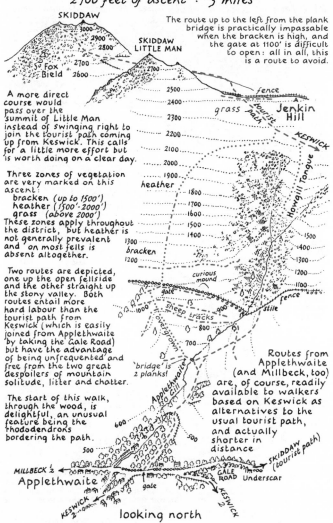

The route up to the left from the plank bridge is practically impassable when the bracken is high, and the gate at 1100' is difficult to open: all in all, this is a route to avoid.

A more direct course would pass over the summit of Little Man instead of swinging right to join the tourist path coming up from Keswick. This calls for a little more effort but is worth doing on a clear day.

Three zones of vegetation are very marked on this ascent:
bracken (up to 1500')
heather (1500'-2000')
grass (above 2000')
These zones apply throughout the district, but heather is not generally prevalent and on most fells is absent altogether.

Two routes are depicted, one up the open fellside and the other straight up the stony valley. Both routes entail more hard labour than the tourist path from Keswick (which is easily joined from Applethwaite by taking the Gale Road) but have the advantage of being unfrequented and free from the two great despoilers of mountain solitude, litter and chatter.

The start of this walk, through the wood, is delightful, an unusual feature being the rhododendrons bordering the path.

Routes from Applethwaite (and Millbeck, too) are, of course, readily available to walkers based on Keswick as alternatives to the usual tourist path, and actually shorter in distance

Map labels

SKIDDAW
3000
2900
2800
2700
2600
Fox Bield

SKIDDAW LITTLE MAN
2700
2500
2400
2300
2200
2100
2000
1900
heather
1800
1700
1600
1500
1400
1300
bracken
1200

fence
grass
tourist path
Jenkin Hill
KESWICK
Howgill Tongue
1500
1400
1300
1100

curious mound
gate
stile
fence
Sheep tracks
1000
900
overgrown
800
700
'bridge' is 2 planks!
Applethwaite Gill
600
500
500
SKIDDAW (tourist path)
MILLBECK ½
Applethwaite
gate
KESWICK 2
GALE ROAD Underscar
KESWICK 2

looking north

ASCENTS FROM BASSENTHWAITE VILLAGE AND HIGH SIDE

2800 feet of ascent : 4 - 4½ miles (from Bassenthwaite Village)

2700 feet 3¼ · 3¾ miles (from High Side)

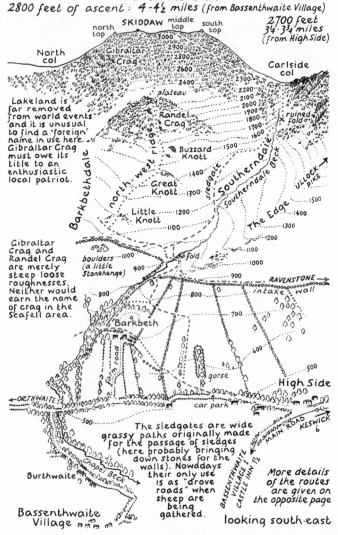

SKIDDAW

north top · middle top · south top

North col

Gibraltar Crag

Carlside col

3000
2900
2800
2600
2400
2300
2200
2100
2000
1900
1800
1700
1600
1500
1400
1300
1200
1100
1000
900
800
700
600
500

plateau

Randel Crag

ruined fold ×

Barkbethdale

north west

Buzzard Knott

Great Knott

Little Knott

sledgate

Southerndale

Southerndale Beck

The Edge

ULLOCK PIKE

Lakeland is far removed from world events and it is unusual to find a 'foreign' name in use here. Gibraltar Crag must owe its title to an enthusiastic local patriot.

Gibraltar Crag and Randel Crag are merely steep loose roughnesses. Neither would earn the name of crag in the Scafell area.

boulders (a little Stonehenge)

fold

RAVENSTONE →

intake wall

Barkbeth

gorse

High Side

← ORTHWAITE

tom road

car park

MAIN ROAD

KESWICK 6

Chapel Beck

Burthwaite

The sledgates are wide grassy paths originally made for the passage of sledges (here probably bringing down stones for the walls). Nowadays their only use is as "drove roads" when sheep are being gathered.

BASSENTHWAITE VILLAGE 1½ · CASTLE INN 1¾

Bassenthwaite Village

More details of the routes are given on the opposite page

looking south-east

ASCENTS FROM BASSENTHWAITE VILLAGE
AND HIGH SIDE
continued

THE NORTH-WEST RIDGE: Ask a Barkbeth sheep what the north-west ridge of Skiddaw is like and it will reply without hesitation "C'est magnifique" (if it is French, which is unlikely) — which just shows how tastes differ, for most walkers, less easily satisfied, will consider it disappointing. Its one attribute is its peace and quietness. There is no path along it, no line of cairns, no litter, nothing to show that others may have passed this way.   It is a low, gentle hump, entirely grassy (hence the enthusiastic rejoinder quoted above), rising between Southerndale and Barkbethdale and not too well-defined until the ground steepens into Randel Crag; a few easy rocks here may be scrambled up or circumvented to give access to a grassy shelf, where the ridge proper ends. A tiny tarn here is shaped like a W. Rising ahead is the scree-slope falling from Skiddaw's top: this is vaster than it appears to be and much longer, but not unpleasant to ascend, the scree being a soft, yielding shale. The only interest here derives from an attempt to score a bull's-eye by 'hitting' the summit-cairn direct (it is out of sight until the last minute).

SOUTHERNDALE, too, is quiet and unfrequented although a clear-cut valley and useful for quick and easy progress, the final climb up to Carlside col giving less trouble than the approach to it suggests.   A sledgate 'road' is a good help until it comes to an end by an old and scattered cairn. From the col a loose and stony path leads diagonally up to the middle top. Southerndale is dominated more by Long Side and Ullock Pike than by Skiddaw.

Neither of these routes, nor that via Barkbethdale, is to be compared as a way up Skiddaw from the north-west, in interest, views or grandeur, with the fine high-level traverse of Ullock Pike and Long Side; they are direct routes, however, and as such have a certain appeal.

Concave and convex slopes

Concave slopes are honest; convex slopes are deceitful.

concave

When ascending a concave slope the summit can be seen at all stages; on a convex slope it *seems* to be visible but what the climber sees is a skyline that recedes as he gains height.

convex

The final slope of Skiddaw above Randel Crag is an exasperating example of convexity

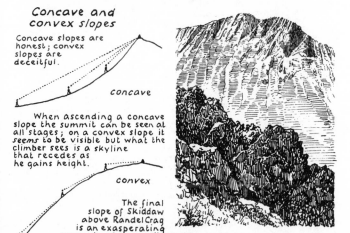

Ullock Pike, from Randel Crag

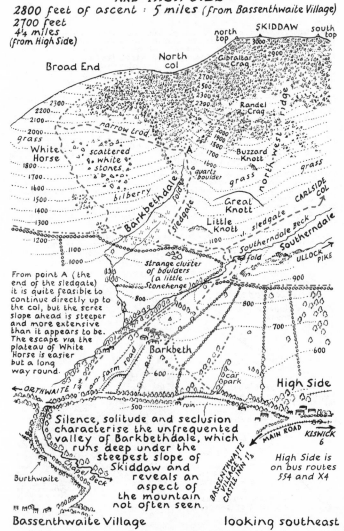

ASCENTS FROM BASSENTHWAITE VILLAGE
AND HIGH SIDE
2800 feet of ascent : 5 miles (from Bassenthwaite Village)
2700 feet
4¼ miles
(from High Side)

Broad End

North col

SKIDDAW

north top

south top

Gibraltar Crag

3000

2900

2700

2500

2300

2200

Randel Crag

Buzzard Knott

2100

2000

narrow trod

2000

grass

1900

1800

White Horse

scattered white stones

1700

quartz boulder

1600

grass

grass

1800

1700

1600

bilberry

1500

1400

1300

Barkbethdale

sledgate

Great Knott

CARLSIDE COL

Little Knott

sledgate

Southerndale

1100

Southerndale Beck

1200

1100

ULLOCK PIKE

1000

strange cluster of boulders (a little Stonehenge)

fold

900

800

From point A (the end of the sledgate) it is quite feasible to continue directly up to the col, but the scree slope ahead is steeper and more extensive than it appears to be. The escape via the plateau of White Horse is easier but a long way round.

800

700

600

Barkbeth

car park

←ORTHWAITE 1¼

farm road

600

500

High Side

ruin

←ORTHWAITE 1¼

MAIN ROAD

KESWICK 6

Silence, solitude and seclusion characterise the unfrequented valley of Barkbethdale, which runs deep under the steepest slope of Skiddaw and reveals an aspect of the mountain not often seen.

Chapel Beck

Burthwaite

BASSENTHWAITE VILLAGE 1½

CASTLE INN 1½

High Side is on bus routes 554 and X4

Bassenthwaite Village

looking southeast

Southerndale from the gate in the intake wall above Barkbeth. Carlside col, Long Side and Ullock Pike on skyline.

Barkbethdale from Little Knott on the north-west ridge. Looking to Skiddaw; Randel Crag below on right.

ASCENT FROM MELBECKS
2500 feet of ascent : 3 miles

This route is included only because of the insistence of the Ordnance Survey (repeated in various editions of their maps of 1" scale and upwards) in depicting a bridleway from the road-corner near Melbecks up to the intake wall — which might attract the attention of walkers and lure them in search of it.

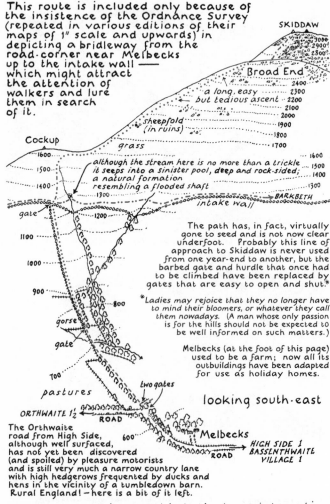

SKIDDAW

3000'
2900'
2800'

Broad End

2400
a long, easy 2300
but tedious ascent 2200
2100
2000
1900
1800

sheepfold
(in ruins)

Cockup

grass

1600
1600
1500
1500
1400
1400
1300

although the stream here is no more than a trickle it seeps into a sinister pool, deep and rock-sided; a natural formation resembling a flooded shaft

1300

BARKBETH

intake wall

gate

1200

1100

1000

900

800

gorse

gate

700

pastures

two gates

ORTHWAITE 1½
ROAD

The path has, in fact, virtually gone to seed and is not now clear underfoot. Probably this line of approach to Skiddaw is never used from one year-end to another, but the barbed gate and hurdle that once had to be climbed have been replaced by gates that are easy to open and shut.*

*Ladies may rejoice that they no longer have to mind their bloomers, or whatever they call them nowadays. (A man whose only passion is for the hills should not be expected to be well informed on such matters.)

Melbecks (at the foot of this page) used to be a farm; now all its outbuildings have been adapted for use as holiday homes.

looking south-east

The Orthwaite road from High Side, although well surfaced, has not yet been discovered (and spoiled) by pleasure motorists and is still very much a narrow country lane with high hedgerows frequented by ducks and hens in the vicinity of a tumbledown barn. Rural England! — here is a bit of it left.

600

Melbecks

HIGH SIDE 1
BASSENTHWAITE
VILLAGE 1

ROAD

Of all ways up Skiddaw this is the least interesting.

ASCENT FROM THE ROAD TO SKIDDAW HOUSE
1800 feet of ascent : 2 miles from Dash Falls

2750 feet : 6 miles from High Side or Bassenthwaite Village

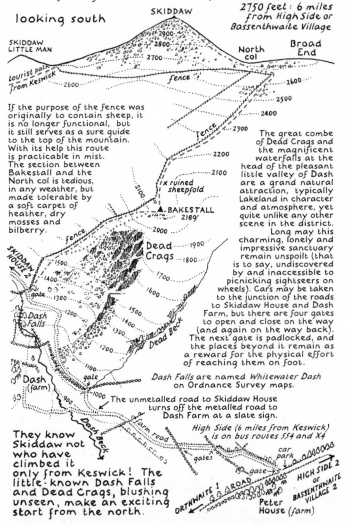

looking south

SKIDDAW

SKIDDAW LITTLE MAN

North col

Broad End

2900
2800
2700

tourist path from Keswick

2600

fence

2600

2500

2400

Fence   2300

2200

2100

2100

x ruined sheepfold

▲ BAKESTALL 2189'

2000

1900

1800

Dead Crags

1700

1600

1500

1400

1200

1300

Dead Beck

fence

SKIDDAW HOUSE 2

gate

1500
1400
1300
1200
1100

Dash Falls

1000

gate

Dash (farm)

900

Dash Beck

If the purpose of the fence was originally to contain sheep, it is no longer functional, but it still serves as a sure guide to the top of the mountain. With its help this route is practicable in mist. The section between Bakestall and the North col is tedious, in any weather, but made tolerable by a soft carpet of heather, dry mosses and bilberry.

The great combe of Dead Crags and the magnificent waterfalls at the head of the pleasant little valley of Dash are a grand natural attraction, typically Lakeland in character and atmosphere, yet quite unlike any other scene in the district. Long may this charming, lonely and impressive sanctuary remain unspoilt (that is to say, undiscovered by and inaccessible to picnicking sightseers on wheels). Cars may be taken to the junction of the roads to Skiddaw House and Dash Farm, but there are four gates to open and close on the way (and again on the way back). The next gate is padlocked, and the places beyond it remain as a reward for the physical effort of reaching them on foot.

Dash Falls are named Whitewater Dash on Ordnance Survey maps.

The unmetalled road to Skiddaw House turns off the metalled road to Dash Farm at a slate sign.

High Side (6 miles from Keswick) is on bus routes 554 and X4

farm road

car park

gates

gate

ORTHWAITE   B.B. ROAD

Peter House (farm)

HIGH SIDE 2 or BASSENTHWAITE VILLAGE 2

They know Skiddaw not who have climbed it only from Keswick! The little-known Dash Falls and Dead Crags, blushing unseen, make an exciting start from the north.

ASCENT FROM SKIDDAW HOUSE
1600 feet of ascent : 2½ miles (via Sale How); 1700 feet, 3 miles (via Hare Crag)

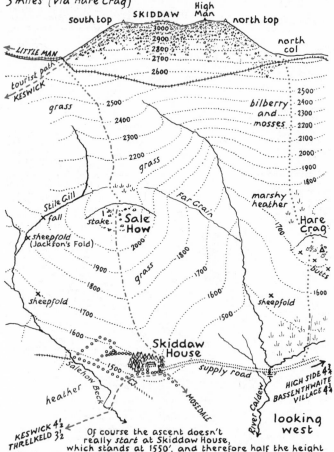

Of course the ascent doesn't really *start* at Skiddaw House, which stands at 1550', and therefore half the height of the mountain has been climbed by the time it is reached.

The eastern slopes of Skiddaw are gently inclined, and progress is smooth and simple. Two routes are given, alike in having an intermediate height; the more direct, by Sale How, is on dry grass; that by Hare Crag is rather more interesting but wet initially. The Hare Crag route follows the important Derwent-Eden watershed.

THE SUMMIT

looking south

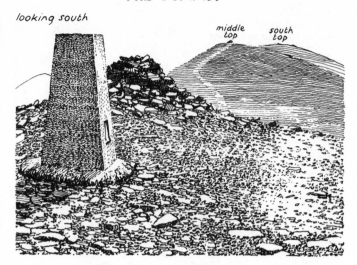

middle
top

south
top

Some walkers, but not many, will be disappointed by the ease with which the summit of Skiddaw can be gained, especially if they have used the tourist path from Keswick, but the top itself is rough enough and airy enough to suit all tastes. It takes the form of a stony, undulating ridge exceeding 3000' throughout its length of almost half a mile — a glorious promenade high in the sky, where one can enjoy a rare feeling of freedom and escape from a world far below, and, for a time, forgotten.

There is a south top and a north top, a middle top and a main top, all in a line and connected by a pavement of slaty stones. In mist it is not uncommon to assume the middle top to be the highest point, there being a descent immediately following (when approached from the south, as is usual) but a final halt should not be made until the Ordnance Survey's triangulation column (S 1543) is reached: this is the true, the indisputable, summit.

Close to the column is an indicator with grooves pointing at various features in the view. The inclusion of Borrowdale suggests that the person who produced it didn't bother to visit the summit or to consult *The Northern Fells*.

A feature of the ridge is a series of roughly-erected wind shelters of stones, crescent-shaped to make them snug (they fail lamentably in this object) — these are only partially effective against cruel gales and useless as a protection in rain. The summit is completely exposed to the north and its weather can be fierce.

Skiddaw is often described as 'merely a grassy hill'. But its summit is the summit of a mountain.

continued

THE SUMMIT

continued

DESCENTS

The few shaded areas ((|||)) are rough: these apart, the summit may be left safely in any direction. The only continuous path is that to Keswick.

All routes involve the descent of some preliminary slaty scree, extensive on the west and south slopes.

These routes include small ascents to subsidiary summits.

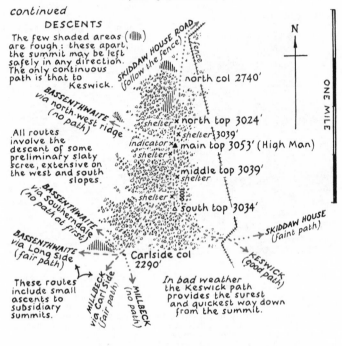

SKIDDAW HOUSE ROAD (follow the fence)

fence

north col 2740'

BASSENTHWAITE via north-west ridge (no path)

shelter × north top 3024'

× shelter 3039'

indicator ▲ main top 3053' (High Man)

× shelter

middle top 3039'

× shelter

shelter ×

△ south top 3034'

SKIDDAW HOUSE (faint path)

BASSENTHWAITE via Southerndale (no path at first)

BASSENTHWAITE via Long Side (fair path)

Carlside col 2290'

KESWICK (good path)

MILLBECK via Carl Side (fair path)

MILLBECK (no path)

In bad weather the Keswick path provides the surest and quickest way down from the summit.

N

ONE MILE

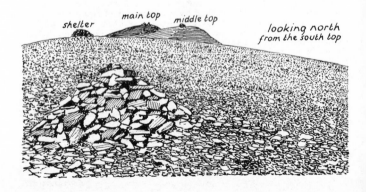

shelter   main top   middle top

looking north from the south top

RIDGE ROUTES

To SKIDDAW LITTLE MAN, 2837': 1 mile : S. then SSE
Depression at 2680'
190 feet of ascent

Use the Keswick path as far as the
first fence, and follow this to the right
across a grassy depression to the stony
cone now directly ahead.

To CARL SIDE, 2447':
1 mile : S. then SW
Depression at 2290'
160 feet of ascent
One unavoidable rough section

From the shelter on the middle
top go bravely down a loose
and stony path south-west to
the col. The flat plateau of Carl
Side rises directly beyond a small tarn. Before
the present path materialised, a route to the col
from the south top was often used, every passage
causing a fresh disturbance of the scree on the big
slope and obliterating the incipient paths that
would otherwise develop; it remains to be seen how
long the present path will survive.

To BAKESTALL, 2208': 1¼ miles : NNE
Depression at 2160' : 40 feet of ascent.
A good route, but only if aiming for the Skiddaw House road.

From the north top, go down to the col and across
to the fence, which leads unerringly but tediously
to the objective.

North top and Gibraltar Crag

THE VIEW

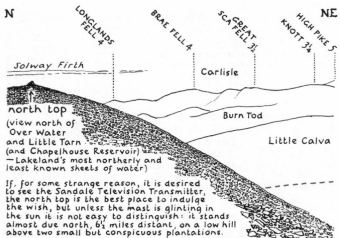

N   NE

LONGLANDS FELL 4   BRAE FELL 4   GREAT SCA FELL 3½   HIGH PIKE 5   KNOTT 3½

Solway Firth   Carlisle

↑
north top   Burn Tod
(view north of
Over Water   Little Calva
and Little Tarn
(and Chapelhouse Reservoir)
—Lakeland's most northerly and
least known sheets of water)

If, for some strange reason, it is desired
to see the Sandale Television Transmitter,
the north top is the best place to indulge
the wish, but unless the mast is glinting in
the sun it is not easy to distinguish: it stands
almost due north, 6½ miles distant, on a low hill
above two small but conspicuous plantations.

The figures accompanying the names of fells indicate distances in miles

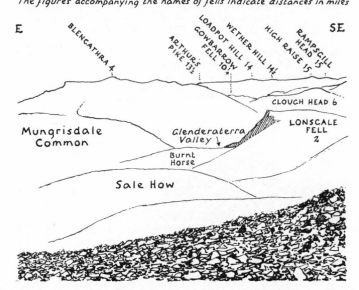

E   SE

BLENCATHRA 4   ARTHUR'S PIKE 13½   LOADPOT HILL 14   GOWBARROW FELL 10*   WETHER HILL 14½   HIGH RAISE 15   RAMPSGILL HEAD 15

CLOUGH HEAD 6

**Mungrisdale
Common**   *Glenderaterra
                          Valley*
                              ↓   LONSCALE
                                              FELL
                      Burnt   2
                      Horse

Sale How

THE VIEW

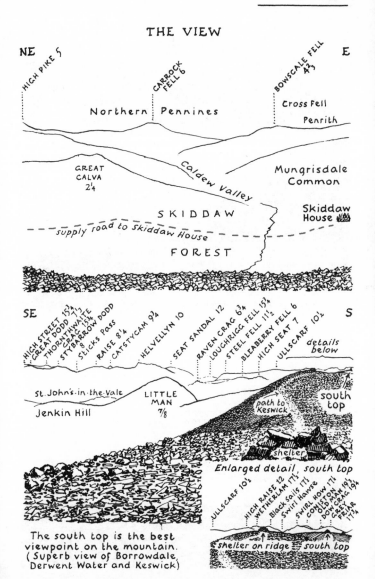

NE

HIGH PIKE 5

CARROCK FELL 6

BOWSCALE FELL 4¾

E

Northern Pennines

Cross Fell

Penrith

GREAT CALVA 2¼

Caldew Valley

Mungrisdale Common

SKIDDAW

Skiddaw House 🏚

supply road to Skiddaw House

FOREST

SE

HIGH STREET 15¼
GREAT DODD 7½
THORNTHWAITE CRAG 15¾
STYBARROW DODD 8
Sticks Pass
RAISE 8¼
CATSTYCAM 9¾
HELVELLYN 10
SEAT SANDAL 12
RAVEN CRAG 6¾
LOUGHRIGG FELL 15¾
STEEL FELL 11½
BLEABERRY FELL 6
HIGH SEAT 7
ULLSCARF 10½

S

details below

St. John's-in-the-Vale

Jenkin Hill

LITTLE MAN 7/8

path to Keswick

south top

shelter

Enlarged detail, south top

ULLSCARF 10½
HIGH RAISE 12
WETHERLAM 17½
Black Sails 17½
Swirl How 17½
SWIRL HAWSE
CONISTON OLD MAN 19½
DOW CRAG 19½
GREY FRIAR 17¾

shelter on ridge   south top

The south top is the best viewpoint on the mountain. (Superb view of Borrowdale, Derwent Water and Keswick)

THE VIEW

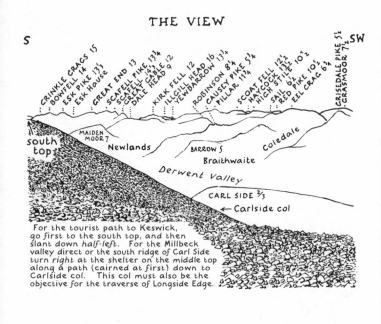

S

CRINKLE CRAGS 15
BOWFELL 14
ESK PIKE 13½
ESK HAUSE
GREAT END 13
SCAFELL PIKE 13¼*
SCAFELL 14½*
GREAT GABLE 9
DALE HEAD 9
KIRK FELL 12
ILLGILL HEAD 16
YEWBARROW 13½*
ROBINSON 8¼
CAUSEY PIKE 5¾*
PILLAR 11¾
SCOAT FELL 12½
HAYCOCK 12½
HIGH STILE 10½
SAIL 6½
RED PIKE 10½
EEL CRAG 6¾
CRISEDALE PIKE 5½
GRASMOOR 7¾

SW

south top

MAIDEN MOOR 7

Newlands

BARROW 5

Braithwaite

Coledale

Derwent Valley

CARL SIDE ⅔

← Carlside col

For the tourist path to Keswick,
go first to the south top, and then
slant down *half-left*. For the Millbeck
valley direct or the south ridge of Carl Side
turn *right* at the shelter on the middle top
along a path (cairned at first) down to
Carlside col. This col must also be the
objective for the traverse of Longside Edge.

W   NW

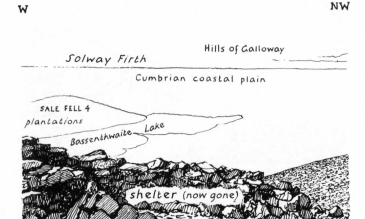

Hills of Galloway

Solway Firth

Cumbrian coastal plain

SALE FELL 4
plantations

Bassenthwaite Lake

shelter (now gone)

THE VIEW

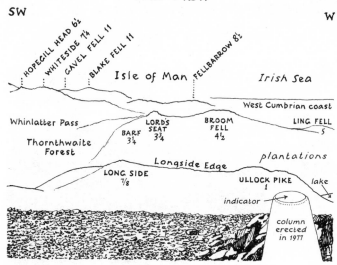

SW   W

HOPEGILL HEAD 6½
WHITESIDE 7¼
GAVEL FELL 11
BLAKE FELL 11
FELLBARROW 8½

Isle of Man   Irish Sea

West Cumbrian coast

Whinlatter Pass

Thornthwaite Forest

BARF 3¼
LORD'S SEAT 3¾
BROOM FELL 4½
LING FELL 5

Longside Edge   plantations

LONG SIDE 7/8

ULLOCK PIKE 1   lake

indicator

column erected in 1977

NW   N

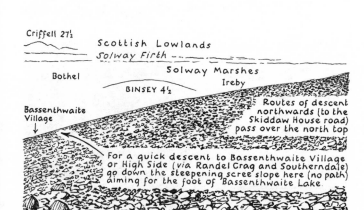

Criffell 27½

Scottish Lowlands
Solway Firth

Bothel

Solway Marshes
Ireby

BINSEY 4½

Bassenthwaite Village

Routes of descent northwards (to the Skiddaw House road) pass over the north top

For a quick descent to Bassenthwaite Village or High Side (via Randel Crag and Southerndale) go down the steepening scree slope here (no path) aiming for the foot of Bassenthwaite Lake.

Skiddaw Little Man 2837'

'Little Man' on Ordnance Survey maps

SKIDDAW ▲   Skiddaw ● House

CARL ▲   ▲ SKIDDAW
SIDE   LITTLE MAN

Millbeck ●

Applethwaite ●

● Keswick

MILES

0 1 2 3 4

from the weir, Mill Beck

NATURAL FEATURES

Skiddaw's Little Man is situated fully one mile from its High Man and forms a distinctive peaked summit with independent routes of ascent, commanding the most magnificent panoramic view of the heart and soul of Lakeland and controlling a major watershed — and on these grounds is treated here as a separate fell and deservedly given a separate chapter.

The Little Man is so fine a mountain that it is less than justice that its name must forever acknowledge subservience to the parent Skiddaw.   And 'Little' indeed! — the top soars half-a-mile above the valley. From the base of the steep and shattered western face three scree-covered buttresses rise out of the general angle of slope to appear as distinct peaks so far above that the walker here whose mind is saturated with Himalayan literature will irresistably be reminded of Kangchenjunga.   From Carsleddam opposite, at 1700, the whole face is displayed in truer perspective, and the buttresses are seen to lose their identity below a single towering summit, the likeness now being more that of K2. (It is taken for granted that Himalayan enthusiasts are blessed with a little imagination). The west face is quite tremendous.

In complete contrast all other slopes of the fell, the stony rift of How Gill excepted, are smooth and grassy or heathery, rarely exhibiting rock although everywhere steep. The Little Man has a second and lower summit, a 'Lesser Man', prominently in view and often mistaken for the Little Man or even Skiddaw itself on the usual line of climb from Keswick via the back of Latrigg.

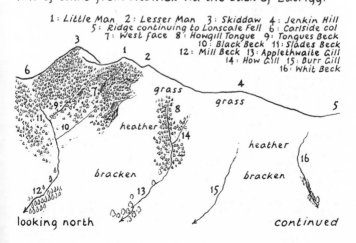

1: Little Man   2: Lesser Man   3: Skiddaw   4: Jenkin Hill
5: Ridge continuing to Lonscale Fell   6: Carlside col
7: West face   8: Howgill Tongue   9: Tongues Beck
10: Black Beck   11: Slades Beck
12: Mill Beck   13: Applethwaite Gill
14: How Gill   15: Burr Gill
16: Whit Beck

grass

grass

heather

heather

bracken

bracken

looking north

continued

NATURAL FEATURES

continued

The lofty ridge from which the summit rises is of geographical importance, forming the watershed between the Eden and the Derwent catchment areas — and it is interesting to note that the common boundary is more clearly defined on the elegant lines of the Little Man than on the broader slopes of Skiddaw.

The gathering grounds of the Eden are shaded on the diagram; all other territory shown drains into the Derwent.

Alone of the Skiddaw summits on the main ridge the Little Man feeds the Eden (via the Caldew) *exclusively* on its eastern flank; the eastern waters of Skiddaw High Man *partly*, and of Lonscale Fell *wholly*, feed the Derwent.

The deep intrusion of the Eden system into Skiddaw Forest strongly emphasises the superior altitude of the Skiddaw massif, which is the hub of the Northern Fells — geographically, that is, not geometrically.

The fall from the summit of Little Man to the valley is so unremitting on all sides that in no place do the slopes halt sufficiently to contain a tarn, or even patches of wet ground. Walking on the fell is dry and pleasant even after much rain.

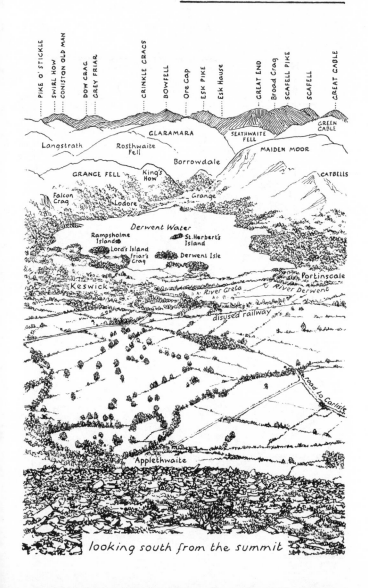

PIKE O' STICKLE · SWIRL HOW · CONISTON OLD MAN · DOW CRAG · GREY FRIAR · CRINKLE CRAGS · BOWFELL · ORE GAP · ESK PIKE · ESK HAUSE · GREAT END · BROAD CRAG · SCAFELL PIKE · SCAFELL · GREAT GABLE · GREEN GABLE

Langstrath · GLARAMARA · Rosthwaite Fell · SEATHWAITE FELL · MAIDEN MOOR

GRANGE FELL · King's How · Borrowdale · CATBELLS

Falcon Crag · Lodore · Grange

Derwent Water

Rampsholme Island · St. Herbert's Island

Lord's Island · Derwent Isle

Friar's Crag

Keswick · River Greta · River Derwent · Portinscale

disused railway

road to Carlisle

Applethwaite

looking south from the summit

MAP

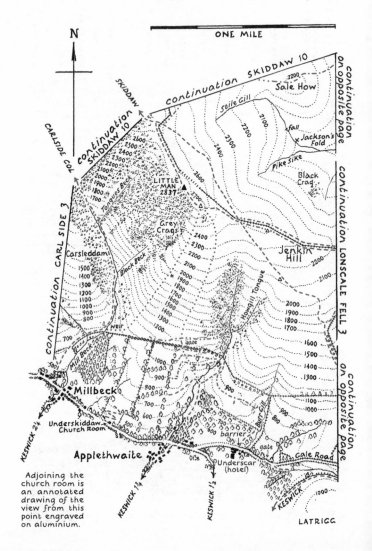

ONE MILE

N

continuation SKIDDAW 10

continuation SKIDDAW 10

Sale How

Stile Gill

x fall

Jackson's Fold

CARLSIDE COL

SKIDDAW

continuation SKIDDAW 10

Pike Sike

Black Crag

2600
2500
2400
2300
2200
2100
2000
1900
1800
1700

LITTLE MAN 2837

continuation on opposite page

continuation LONSCALE FELL 3

Too Gutherscale Beck

2700

continuation CARL SIDE 3

Grey Crags

Jenkin Hill

Carsleddam

2400
2300
2200
2200
2100
2000

1500
1400
1300
1200
1100
1000
900
800

Black Beck

2000
1900
1800
1700
1600
1500
1400
1300
1200

Howgill Tongue

2000
1900
1800
1700

700

weir

1600
1500
1400
1300

1000
900
800

Mill Beck

1100
1000

Millbeck

600

900

Bottt Gill

barrier

gate

Gale Road

Underskiddaw Church Room

KESWICK 2¼

Applethwaite

Underscar (hotel)

continuation on opposite page

KESWICK 1¾

KESWICK 1½

KESWICK

1000

LATRIGG

Adjoining the church room is an annotated drawing of the view from this point engraved on aluminium.

MAP

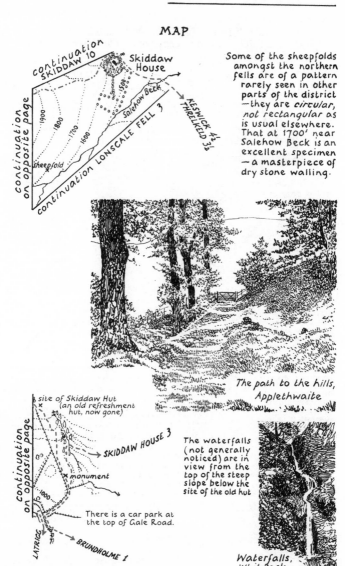

continuation
SKIDDAW 10

Skiddaw House

continuation on opposite page

Salehow Beck

KESWICK 4½
THRELKELD 3½

1900
1800
1700
1600
1500

sheepfold

continuation LONSCALE FELL 3

Some of the sheepfolds amongst the northern fells are of a pattern rarely seen in other parts of the district — they are *circular*, not *rectangular* as is usual elsewhere. That at 1700' near Salehow Beck is an excellent specimen — a masterpiece of dry stone walling.

The path to the hills, Applethwaite

continuation on opposite page

site of Skiddaw Hut (an old refreshment hut, now gone)

SKIDDAW HOUSE 3

× monument

1000

LATRIGG

BRUNDHOLME 1

There is a car park at the top of Gale Road.

The waterfalls (not generally noticed) are in view from the top of the steep slope below the site of the old hut

Waterfalls, Whit Beck

ASCENT FROM MILLBECK
2500 feet of ascent : 1¼ miles

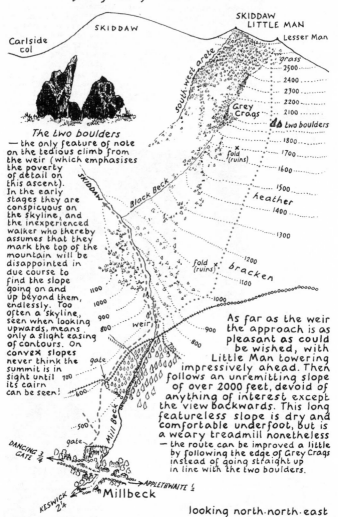

Carlside col

SKIDDAW

SKIDDAW LITTLE MAN

Lesser Man

south-west arête

grass
2500
2400
2300
2200
2100

Grey Craags

the two boulders

1800

1700

fold (ruins)

1600

1500

heather

1400

1300

SKIDDAW

Black Beck

1200

fold (ruins)

bracken

1100

1100

1000

1000

1100

900

800

weir

900

800

gate

700

600

Mill Beck

500

gate

DANCING GATE 3/4

APPLETHWAITE 1/2

KESWICK 2¼

Millbeck

The two boulders
— the only feature of note on the tedious climb from the weir (which emphasises the poverty of detail on this ascent). In the early stages they are conspicuous on the skyline, and the inexperienced walker who thereby assumes that they mark the top of the mountain will be disappointed in due course to find the slope going on and up beyond them, endlessly. Too often a skyline, seen when looking upwards, means only a slight easing of contours. On convex slopes never the summit is in sight until its cairn can be seen!

As far as the weir the approach is as pleasant as could be wished, with Little Man towering impressively ahead. Then follows an unremitting slope of over 2000 feet, devoid of anything of interest except the view backwards. This long featureless slope is dry and comfortable underfoot, but is a weary treadmill nonetheless — the route can be improved a little by following the edge of Grey Craags instead of going straight up in line with the two boulders.

looking north·north·east

ASCENT FROM MILLBECK (VIA THE SOUTH-WEST ARETE)
2500 feet of ascent : 1¾ miles

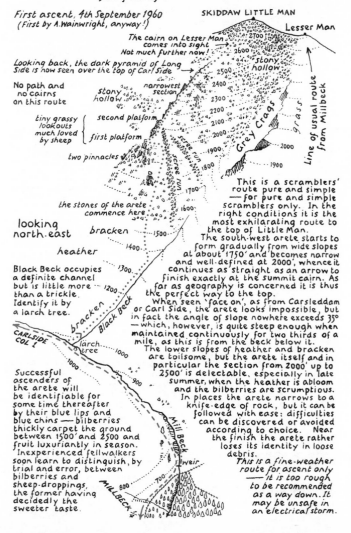

First ascent, 4th September 1960
(First by A.Wainwright, anyway!)

SKIDDAW LITTLE MAN

Lesser Man

The cairn on Lesser Man
comes into sight
Not much further now!

2700
2600
2500

stony
hollow

Looking back, the dark pyramid of Long
Side is now seen over the top of Carl Side →

No path and
no cairns
on this route

narrowest
section

stony
hollow

2400
2300
2200
2100
2000
1900

Grey Crags

grass

Line of usual route
from Millbeck

tiny grassy
lookouts
much loved
by sheep

second platform

first platform

two pinnacles

scree run

2000
1900

the stones of the arete
commence here

1800
1700
1600

looking
north·east

bracken

1500

heather

1400

Black Beck occupies
a definite channel
but is little more
than a trickle.
Identify it by
a larch tree.

1300
1200

CARLSIDE
COL 1

1100

larch
tree

bracken

Black Beck

1000

Successful
ascenders of
the arete will
be identifiable for
some time thereafter
by their blue lips and
blue chins — bilberries
thickly carpet the ground
between 1500' and 2500 and
fruit luxuriantly in season.
Inexperienced fellwalkers
soon learn to distinguish, by
trial and error, between
bilberries and
sheep-droppings,
the former having
decidedly the
sweeter taste.

900

Mill Beck

800
700

weir

MILLBECK 1¼
1000

This is a scramblers'
route pure and simple
— for pure and simple
scramblers only. In the
right conditions it is the
most exhilarating route to
the top of Little Man.
The south-west starts to
form gradually from wide slopes
at about 1750' and becomes narrow
and well-defined at 2000', whence it
continues as straight as an arrow to
finish exactly at the summit cairn. As
far as geography is concerned it is thus
the perfect way to the top.
When seen 'face on', as from Carsleddam
or Carl Side, the arete looks impossible, but
in fact the angle of slope nowhere exceeds 35°
— which, however, is quite steep enough when
maintained continuously for two thirds of a
mile, as this is from the beck below it.
The lower slopes of heather and bracken
are toilsome, but the arete itself and in
particular the section from 2000' up to
2500' is delectable, especially in late
summer, when the heather is abloom
and the bilberries are scrumptious.
In places the arete narrows to a
knife-edge of rock, but it can be
followed with ease: difficulties
can be discovered or avoided
according to choice. Near
the finish the arete rather
loses its identity in loose
debris.
This is a fine-weather
route for ascent only
— it is too rough
to be recommended
as a way down. It
may be unsafe in
an electrical storm.

ASCENT FROM APPLETHWAITE
2450 feet of ascent : 1¼ miles
(2 miles via Howgill Tongue)

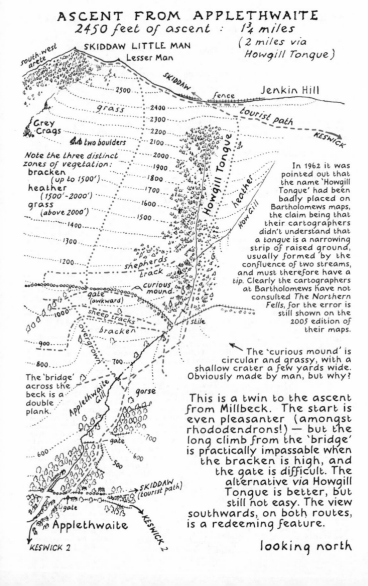

south-west arête

SKIDDAW LITTLE MAN
Lesser Man

SKIDDAW

Jenkin Hill

fence

2500

grass

2400

2300

tourist path

2200

KESWICK

Grey Crags

two boulders

2100

2000

Howgill Tongue

Note the three distinct zones of vegetation:
bracken (up to 1500')
heather (1500'-2000')
grass (above 2000')

1900

1800

heather

1700

1600

Howgill

1500

1400

1300

shepherds track

1200

curious mound

gate (awkward)

1000

sheep tracks

stile

bracken

overgrown

900

800

700

The 'bridge' across the beck is a double plank.

Applethwaite Gill

gorse

700

gate

600

500

600

SKIDDAW (tourist path)

gate

Applethwaite

KESWICK 2

KESWICK 2

In 1962 it was pointed out that the name 'Howgill Tongue' had been badly placed on Bartholomews maps, the claim being that their cartographers didn't understand that a tongue is a narrowing strip of raised ground, usually formed by the confluence of two streams, and must therefore have a tip. Clearly the cartographers at Bartholomews have not consulted *The Northern Fells*, for the error is still shown on the 2005 edition of their maps.

← The 'curious mound' is circular and grassy, with a shallow crater a few yards wide. Obviously made by man, but why?

This is a twin to the ascent from Millbeck. The start is even pleasanter (amongst rhododendrons!) — but the long climb from the 'bridge' is practically impassable when the bracken is high, and the gate is difficult. The alternative via Howgill Tongue is better, but still not easy. The view southwards, on both routes, is a redeeming feature.

looking north

ASCENT FROM SKIDDAW HOUSE
1350 feet of ascent : 2¼ miles

south top
3000
2900
SKIDDAW
2800
SKIDDAW LITTLE MAN
Lesser Man
2700
grass
fence
2600
fence
2500
KESWICK   tourist path
2500
grass
2400

↑ a few iron posts indicate the line of a former fence that went down to the supply road.

2300
2200

Pedestrians on the tourist path will be surprised to see somebody cutting across it. What eccentricity!

Pike Side
Stile Gill
fall
stake
Sale How
2100
✗ sheepfold (Jackson's Fold)
2000
grass
1900

Kilnbain Gill

Very easy grass and very easy gradients give very easy progress. There is nothing of interest. Nobody is likely to drop dead with excitement on this simple, dull climb.

8' stake, Sale How

Slot Gill
✗ sheepfold
heather
1800
1700
1600

Skiddaw House   1500
supply road   HIGH SIDE 5
BASSENTHWAITE VILLAGE 5

Salehow Beck
1500
heather

KESWICK 4½
THRELKELD 3½

looking west-south-west

ASCENT FROM KESWICK

Little Man may, of course, be very conveniently ascended by a short deviation from the tourist path to Skiddaw, and it is quite usual to visit its summit either en route to Skiddaw or on the way down, the latter being the easier and better arrangement.   For a diagram see Skiddaw 11 and 12.

THE SUMMIT

The cairn on Little Man

The summit is small and shapely, but its elegance is rather spoiled by an untidy cairn. The top is mainly grassy and has no features of interest near at hand but its deficiencies are more than made good by the superb view. There is space enough around the cairn for perambulation, but it is obvious that the slopes west and south fall away very steeply, curving over out of sight almost at once. The cairn on the lower summit ('Lesser Man') is adorned by an elaborate arrangement of fence-posts.

DESCENTS: By passing over the summit of Lesser Man and going down the rougher ground beyond the broad highway from Skiddaw is joined at a fence. But consider as a quiet alternative gaining the valley at Applethwaite or Millbeck by way of the wide shoulder descending west of south. Avoid a false start on this latter route by first going over Lesser Man and then immediately swinging downhill to the right. Do not attempt to descend directly from Little Man's cairn: steep screes bar the way here (from Lesser Man nothing worse than grass, a belt of heather and an expanse of bracken is met). Bear *right* for Millbeck and *left* for Applethwaite on approaching the cross-wall at 1200' (but avoid the Applethwaite route when the bracken is high).

The cairn on Lesser Man

RIDGE ROUTES

To SKIDDAW, 3053': 1 mile : NNW, then N

Depression at 2680': 400 feet of ascent

This must be done for the sake of prestige ; safe in mist.

Turn down north after a last look at the view, which is better from here than from Skiddaw, and follow the fence across a depression to join the tourist path, whereupon directions become superfluous.

To LONSCALE FELL, 2344': 1½ miles : ESE : Depression at 2180' 175 feet of ascent : An easy walk

Go down over the lower summit to the point where the tourist path meets the fence. With the latter as company proceed ahead across the flat top of Jenkin Hill and take a beeline for the objective. On Lonscale Fell continue beyond the cairn to have a look at East Peak.

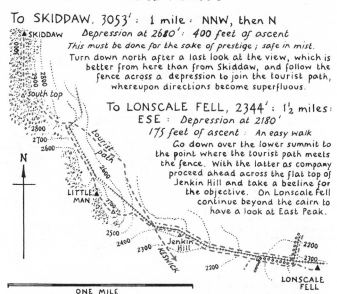

ONE MILE

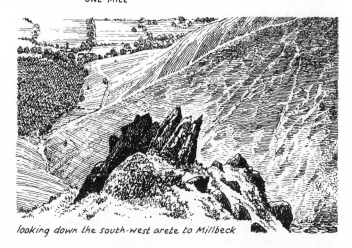

looking down the south-west arête to Millbeck

THE VIEW

There will never be general agreement on the answer to the question: which is the finest view in Lakeland?

Some views depend for their appeal on beauty of foreground, Tarn Hows for example; some on their intimate detail of a particular and pleasing feature, such as Castle Head's view of Derwent Water; some on colour and interesting arrangement, such as those from Ashness Bridge and Loughrigg Terrace. Other scenes have drama as their theme, Scafell Crag from Mickledore for example; popular, too, are the unforgettable birds-eye views from such heights as Great Gable and Great End, while many folk favour the most extensive prospects, as seen from Scafell Pike, Bowfell and Helvellyn. Opinions differ according to individual preference.

But for a classic view of the heart of Lakeland from a position on its perimeter Skiddaw Little Man must have majority support as the one place above all others. This viewpoint is detached and distant, and situated high above the wide Vale of Keswick, so that the mountain skyline beyond is seen across a great gulf, as if being approached by aeroplane, and sufficiently removed to admit correct perspectives and relationships. From this viewpoint, as the onlooker turns his gaze through the southern arc, the picture unfolds like the canvas of a master. This is Cinemascope *in excelsis*, on a scale never envisaged by Hollywood, a vast scene on a screen as wide as the heavens. And all of it is beautiful, nature's quiet artistry. Men are clever enough to make atomic bombs, and strut about like lords of creation, yet they can't even make a blade of grass or a sprig of heather, let alone build up a landscape like this. Which is as well.

N

W

S

MILES

SKIDDAW
LONG SIDE
CARL SIDE
SALE FELL
BROOM FELL
LORD'S SEAT
LOW FELL
BARF
DODD
BLAKE FELL
WHITESIDE
HOPEGILL HEAD
GRISEDALE PIKE
GRASMOOR
EEL CRAG
SAIL
OUTERSIDE
SCAR CRAGS
CAUSEY PIKE
CATBELLS
RED PIKE
HIGH STILE
ROBINSON
HINDSCARTH
DALE HEAD
HIGH SPY
HAYCOCK
SCOAT FELL
PILLAR
KIRK FELL
GREAT GABLE
BASE BROWN
YEWBARROW
SCAFELL
SCAFELL PIKE
GREAT END
ESK PIKE
BOWFELL
CLARAMARA
CRINKLE CRAGS
GREY FRIAR
DOW CRAG

THE VIEW

Principal Fells

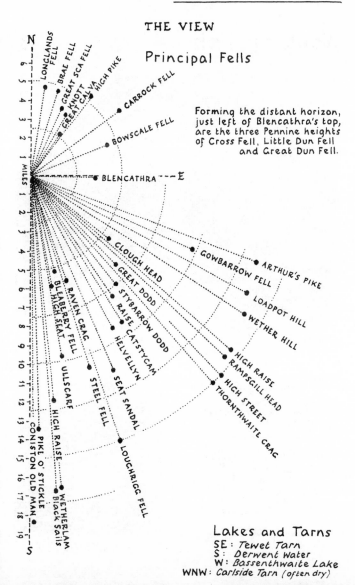

Forming the distant horizon,
just left of Blencathra's top,
are the three Pennine heights
of Cross Fell, Little Dun Fell
and Great Dun Fell.

N

6
5
4
3
2
1

MILES

LONGLANDS FELL
BRAE FELL
GREAT SCA FELL
KNOTT
GREAT CALVA
HIGH PIKE
CARROCK FELL
BOWSCALE FELL
BLENCATHRA - - - E

CLOUGH HEAD
GOWBARROW FELL
ARTHUR'S PIKE
GREAT DODD
LOADPOT HILL
RAVEN CRAG
BLEABERRY FELL
HIGH SEAT
STYBARROW DODD
WETHER HILL
RAISE
CATSTYCAM
HELVELLYN
HIGH RAISE
RAMPSGILL HEAD
ULLSCARF
SEAT SANDAL
HIGH STREET
STEEL FELL
THORNTHWAITE CRAG
HIGH RAISE
CONISTON OLD MAN
PIKE O' STICKLE
LOUGHRIGG FELL
WETHERLAM
Black Sails

S

Lakes and Tarns
SE : Tewet Tarn
S : Derwent Water
W : Bassenthwaite Lake
WNW : Carlside Tarn (often dry)

Souther Fell

1713'

from Mungrisdale,
obviously

(Telegraph poles removed from this view without permission of the P.O. Engineers)

Souther
is pronounced *Souter*

Mungrisdale
is pronounced *Mun-grize-dl*
with the emphasis on *grize*

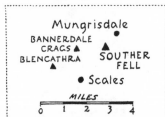

Mungrisdale
BANNERDALE
CRAGS ▲
BLENCATHRA ▲ SOUTHER
FELL
● Scales

MILES
0   1   2   3   4

from Scales Fell

NATURAL FEATURES

Souther Fell, taking the form of a long ridge, extends Blencathra to the east and curves northwards to its extremity, where there is an abrupt fall of altitude to the fields of Mungrisdale — and no more high ground thereafter until, far beyond the broad valley of the Eden, the dark wall of the Pennines closes the horizon. Thus Souther Fell, although of little merit as a climb and of unattractive appearance, occupies an important position as a cornerstone of the Northern Fells, having an extensive view out of proportion to its modest height.

An unusual geographical feature is revealed by a study of the map. Although the fell has slopes facing all points of the compass the whole of its drainage is conducted by a single stream, the Glenderamackin, which encircles its base almost completely like a great moat, with the narrow Mousthwaite col serving as drawbridge.

Blencathra, over the south ridge of Bannerdale Crags, from a cairn on Souther Fell

The River Glenderamackin

The course of the Glenderamackin is remarkable. Starting as a trickle from a marsh below the col linking Bannerdale Crags and Blencathra, it soon gathers strength and aims purposefully for a gap in the hills to the south, eager to be away from its desolate place of birth and join other waters in a tranquil and pleasant passage through Lakeland—for are not the streams of Lakeland the most beautiful of all? But, alas, it cannot find a way across the gap: a low barrier of land, Mousthwaite Col, defeats this object and turns the young river east, and then—a greater disappointment—Souther Fell thrusts across the route. Now there is no alternative but to go due north, and indications suggest that the Eden Valley, and not Lakeland, is destined to receive its waters. But, almost by a freak, it is prevented by a slight and otherwise insignificant eminence at Mungrisdale from entering the Eden catchment area, and here it is again turned to the south. Hope revives. Perhaps, after all, it may be permitted by friendly contours at least to join some tributary of Ullswater? But no, better still: after almost encircling Souther Fell a sudden glorious view of Lakeland opens up to the west, the way thereto at last being clear, and lying through sylvan meadows and rocky gorges and woodlands and great lakes. Now the Glenderamackin is no longer a neglected beck. It has become a river and men to cross it must build bridges. It has acquired a stately loveliness, a leisurely flow—it is a Lakeland river and therefore is beautiful. Artists will paint its picture, and cows stand in its waters.

An ambition has been realised, but it so nearly wasn't!

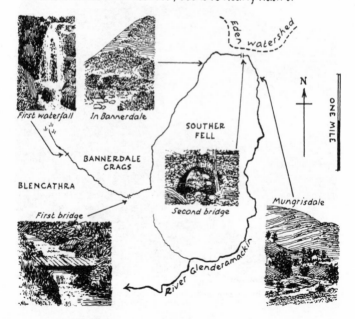

First waterfall

In Bannerdale

Eden watershed

SOUTHER FELL

N

ONE MILE

BANNERDALE CRAGS

BLENCATHRA

Mungrisdale

First bridge

Second bridge

River Glenderamackin

MAP

At the point marked 'H' on the map the path passes under a holly tree. The amount of headroom shows clearly that the path was made by sheep and not by people.

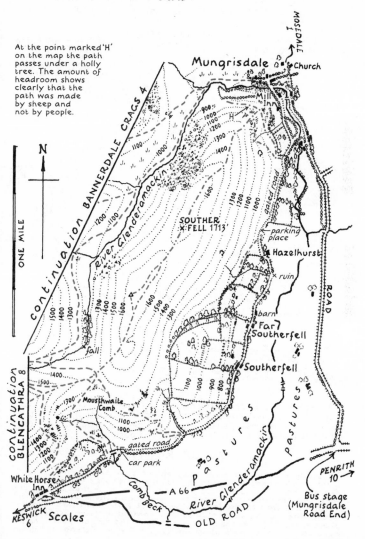

ASCENT FROM MUNGRISDALE
950 feet of ascent : 1¼ miles

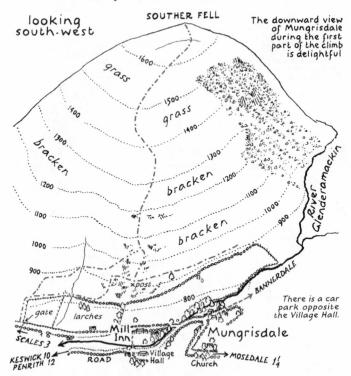

looking
south-west

SOUTHER FELL

The downward view
of Mungrisdale
during the first
part of the climb
is delightful

grass

1600

1500

grass

1400

1400

1300

bracken

1300

1200

bracken

1200

1100

1000

1100

bracken

900

River Glenderamackin

1000

900

post

800

BANNERDALE

There is a car
park opposite
the Village Hall.

gate   larches

Mill
Inn

Mungrisdale

SCALES 3

ROAD   Village
Hall

Church

KESWICK 10
PENRITH 12

MOSEDALE 1¼

Of the two routes above the intakes the higher is recommended,
but this is virtually impossible to find in descent. If using the
lower route for ascent turn uphill just past a group of larches.
The start of the ascent is marked by a post.

RIDGE ROUTE

A study of the Ordnance map shows that Souther Fell is really
a ridge of Blencathra, a continuation of Scales Fell across the
depression of Mousthwaite Col, and there is thus an obvious link
with that mountain. To reach it, go along the ridge to the col
(which lies well to the left of the direct line) and there join one
of the alternative routes of ascent coming up from Scales (see
Blencathra 25). A separate diagram of the ridge-route is hardly
necessary. There isn't space for one, anyway: the page is full *now*.

ASCENT FROM SCALES
1000 feet of ascent : 2 miles

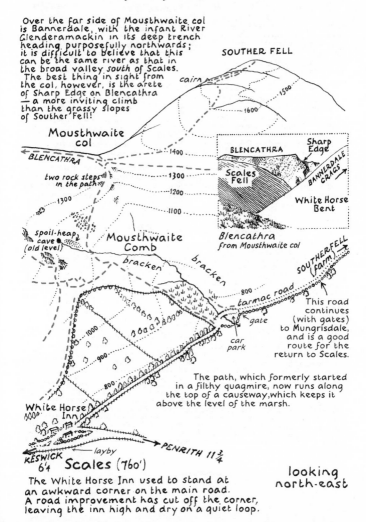

Over the far side of Mousthwaite col
is Bannerdale, with the infant River
Glenderamackin in its deep trench
heading purposefully northwards;
it is difficult to believe that this
can be the same river as that in
the broad valley *south* of Scales.
The best thing in sight from
the col, however, is the arête
of Sharp Edge on Blencathra
— a more inviting climb
than the grassy slopes
of Souther Fell!

SOUTHER FELL

cairn

1500

1600

Mousthwaite
col

← BLENCATHRA

1400

two rock steps
in the path

1300

1200

1100

1300

spoil-heap
cave
(old level)

Mousthwaite
Comb

bracken

bracken

BLENCATHRA

Sharp
Edge

Scales
Fell

BANNERDALE CRAGS

White Horse
Bent

*Blencathra
from Mousthwaite col*

SOUTHER FELL

SOUTHER FELL
(farm)

800

tarmac road

This road
continues
(with gates)
to Mungrisdale,
and is a good
route for the
return to Scales.

gate

car
park

1000

900

800

The path, which formerly started
in a filthy quagmire, now runs along
the top of a causeway, which keeps it
above the level of the marsh.

White Horse
Inn

← KESWICK
6¼

— layby

→ PENRITH 11¾

Scales (760')

The White Horse Inn used to stand at
an awkward corner on the main road.
A road improvement has cut off the corner,
leaving the inn high and dry on a quiet loop.

looking
north-east

THE SUMMIT

The top of the fell is an undulating grass ridge at around 1600 feet for half a mile. The highest point is a grassy hillock — one of several in the vicinity — which is identified by an embedded stone. The main cairn is situated 150 yards south-west of the south summit. It is surprisingly well built in view of the lack of suitable stones in the area. Souther Fell is used for hang-gliding and paragliding by the Cumbria Soaring Club.

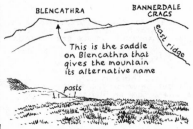

BLENCATHRA

BANNERDALE CRAGS

east ridge

This is the saddle on Blencathra that gives the mountain its alternative name

posts

The north peak of Blencathra (to the right of the Saddle in the illustration) is named on Ordnance Survey maps as Atkinson Pike.

DESCENTS, both to Scales and Mungrisdale, are best made along the ridge (no easy matter in mist). The Bannerdale slope is rough and steep, and the Glenderamackin at its base cannot be forded. The eastern slope is gentler but obstructed by dense bracken.

The Spectral Army of Soutra Fell

This is no legend.

This is the solemn truth, as attested on oath before a magistrate by 26 sober and respected witnesses. These good people assembled on the evening before Midsummer Day 1745 at a place of vantage in the valley to the east to test incredulous reports that soldiers and horsemen had been seen marching across the top of Souter Fell (Soutra Fell was probably its name in those days). They saw them all right: an unbroken line of quickly-moving troops, horses and carriages extending over the full length of the top of Souter, continuously appearing at one end and vanishing at the other — and passing unhesitatingly over steep places that horses and carriages could not possibly negotiate, as the bewildered observers well knew. The procession went on until darkness concealed the marching army. Next morning the skyline was deserted, and a visit to the summit was made by a party of local worthies, fearful that the expected invasion from over the border had started (this was the year of the '45 Rebellion). There was not a trace of the previous night's visitors. Not a footprint, not a hoofmark, not a wheel rut in the grass. Nothing.

There was no doubting the evidence of so many witnesses, and yet it was equally certain that the marching figures had no substance. Scientists and students of the supernatural had no solution to offer. The only explanation ever given was that some kind of a mirage had been seen, probably a vapourous reflection of Prince Charlie's rebels, who (it was discovered on enquiry) had that very evening been exercising on the west coast of Scotland... This beats radar!

THE VIEW

Souther Fell is the most easterly of the northern group and enjoys an uninterrupted prospect across the valley of the Eden to the Pennines. The Lakeland scene is confined to an interesting view of the Patterdale country east of Helvellyn and a delightful vista southwest in a frame of neighbouring fells. Blencathra dominates the picture.

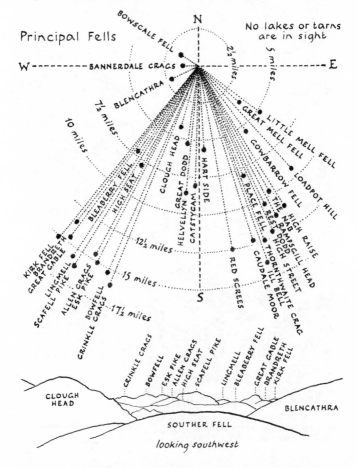

Principal Fells

No lakes or tarns are in sight

looking southwest

Ullock Pike

2230'

from Southerndale

- ● Bassenthwaite
- ● High Side
- ● Ravenstone
  - ▲ SKIDDAW
  - ▲ ULLOCK PIKE
  - ▲ LONG SIDE
    - ▲ CARL SIDE
  - ● ▲ DODD
  - Little Crosthwaite

Keswick ●

MILES
0 1 2 3

NATURAL FEATURES

South-east of Bassenthwaite village, pleasant pastures rise to form, at the top intake wall, a wide shoulder of rough fell, and this in turn runs south and climbs as a narrowing ridge to a dark and symmetrical peak. The ridge, curved like a bow, is known as the Edge, and the dark peak is Ullock Pike. As seen on the approach from Bassenthwaite this slender pyramid is one of the simplest yet finest mountain forms in Lakeland, but its outline commands little attention from other directions, whence it is seen to be no more than a hump at the end of a greater and elevated ridge springing out of the stony bosom of Skiddaw. The western flank falls roughly to Bassenthwaite Lake, the lower slopes here being afforested, and this aspect of the fell is familiar to frequenters of the district; the less well known eastern flank, concealed from the gaze of tourists, drops even more steeply to the upland hollow of Southerndale. Streams are few, the fell drying quickly like the ridged roof of a building, which it resembles.

Watches

Astride the lower level section of the Edge, not far above the intake wall and directly overlooking the footbridge in Southerndale, is a strange and interesting congregation of upstanding rocks, huddled together as though assembled in conference, and suggesting, at first sight, a Druids' Circle. The formation is natural, however, but unusual and (being in the midst of grass) unexpected. Large-scale Ordnance maps give the equally intriguing name of WATCHES to this place.

MAP

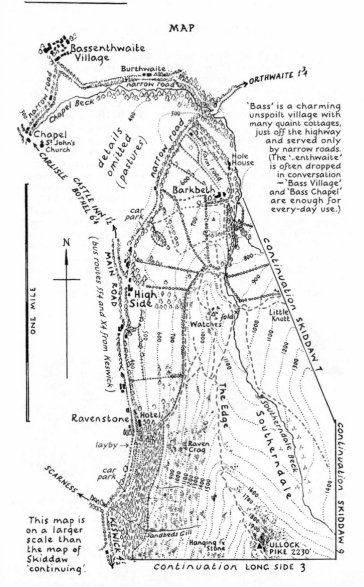

'Bass' is a charming
unspoilt village with
many quaint cottages,
just off the highway
and served only
by narrow roads.
(The '..enthwaite'
is often dropped
in conversation
— 'Bass Village'
and 'Bass Chapel'
are enough for
every-day use.)

This map is
on a larger
scale than
the map of
Skiddaw
'continuing'.

CONTINUATION LONG SIDE 3

Ullock Pike from Chapel

Access to Ullock Pike : the Drove Roads

The lower slopes of Ullock Pike, skirting the public roads from which the ascent must be made, consist of a continuous belt of fenced pastures and plantations, and it is not easy in the absence of walkers' paths and signposts to determine a line of access to the prominent ridge (the Edge) rising to the Pike. The one hopeful breach is provided by the farm-road leading up to Barkbeth (name on gate).

It is unnecessary, however, to disturb the little community of Barkbeth (including the farmyard livestock), for there is a public bridleway that goes past Hole House and comes out at the back of Barkbeth (not the front, as indicated on Ordnance Survey maps). Alternatively, walkers may prefer to approach from the little hamlet (bus stop) of High Side, using the Orthwaite road, which there leaves the main road: at the first car park (¼ mile) bear right through a gate and turn right in 150 yards, following a line of thorn trees. The path ultimately swings away to the left, passing through three more gates to the open fell beyond the intake wall at the narrow entrance to Southerndale, the Edge then rising on the right. On this route of approach the walker is out of sight and earshot of Barkbeth and the farmyard livestock: a small hillock (Barkbeth Hill) intervenes and ensures privacy.

300 yards along the Orthwaite road from High Side, at the top of the first straight rise, is a gate in a recess of the hedge on the right. The gate is now completely disused and overgrown, but it marks the start of a drove road, used for bringing sheep down from Southerndale, and now difficult to trace. The reason it avoids Barkbeth is that it serves Southerndale flocks owned by other farms. The pleasant pastures through which it passes up to the intake wall are often occupied by sheep. On the rough fells sheep are at home, need no fences, and do not stray, but in the lower pastures they are less at ease and will stray given the opportunity. Therefore it is important that all gates should be fastened securely. A habitually solitary walker always closes gates, instinctively; a party is often careless, leaving the duty to each other instead of delegating it to one member.

Another green 'road' comes down to Ravenstone, and may also be used as a means of access (see page 6) but is less attractive.

The yellow posts encountered in the forest mark the route of the Sandbed Gill Trail, which starts and finishes at the tea room in Dodd Wood.

ASCENTS FROM BASSENTHWAITE VILLAGE AND HIGH SIDE

2000 feet of ascent : 3¼ miles (from Bassenthwaite Village)
1900 feet : 2½ miles (from High Side)

ULLOCK PIKE

LONG SIDE

Carlside col

The head of Southerndale

1900
1800
1700
1600
1500

heather

Southerndale Beck

The Edge

1100

Above the intake wall
the Edge may be gained
easily at any point.

"...... by heather tracks
wi' heaven in their wilds"
The last quarter-mile

fold

Watches

grass

1000

gate

900

RAVENSTONE
intake wall

gates

800

boulder

700

The top appears
so clean-cut and
well-defined on
the ascent that,
on reaching it,
a second and
higher top
just beyond
comes as a
surprise.

hawthorns

600

500

Barkbeth

gorse

High Side

ram road

ORTHWAITE 2

500

car park

BASSENTHWAITE
VILLAGE 1¼
CASTLE INN 1½

MAIN ROAD
KESWICK
6

The rising ground above the
Orthwaite road leads naturally
to the Edge, the long north
ridge of Ullock Pike, a
splendid line
of approach
along a
narrowing
and elevated stairway: a
short, enjoyable climb, with
superb views from the small
peaked summit.

Chapel Beck

Burthwaite

Bassenthwaite Village

looking south-south-east

ASCENT FROM RAVENSTONE
1850 feet of ascent : 1¼ miles

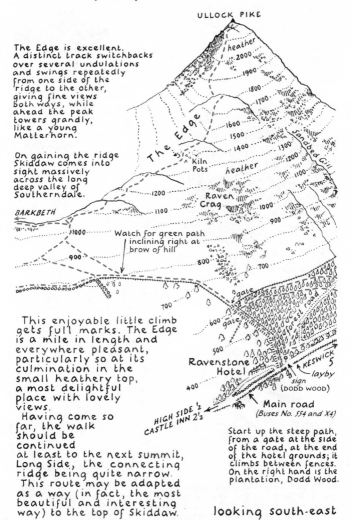

ULLOCK PIKE

heather
2000
1900
1800
1700
1600
1500
1400
1300
1200
1100

Sandbed Gill

The Edge

Kiln Pots

heather

Raven Crag

1000
900

BARKBETH
1000
900

Watch for green path inclining right at brow of hill

800
700

1200
1100

600
700
gate

forest road

gate
500

Ravenstone Hotel

KESWICK 5
layby
sign (DODD WOOD)

400

Main road
(Buses No. 554 and X4)

HIGH SIDE ½
CASTLE INN 2½

The Edge is excellent. A distinct track switchbacks over several undulations and swings repeatedly from one side of the ridge to the other, giving fine views both ways, while ahead the peak towers grandly, like a young Matterhorn.

On gaining the ridge Skiddaw comes into sight massively across the long deep valley of Southerndale.

This enjoyable little climb gets full marks. The Edge is a mile in length and everywhere pleasant, particularly so at its culmination in the small heathery top, a most delightful place with lovely views.
Having come so far, the walk should be continued at least to the next summit, Long Side, the connecting ridge being quite narrow. This route may be adapted as a way (in fact, the most beautiful and interesting way) to the top of Skiddaw.

Start up the steep path, from a gate at the side of the road, at the end of the hotel grounds; it climbs between fences. On the right hand is the plantation, Dodd Wood.

looking south-east

THE SUMMIT

The neat domed summit, upholstered in heather and crossed by a narrow track, is just the sort of place to make one wish it could be parcelled up and taken home for the back garden. There is a low cairn. Just

The highest point

below the top, north, the ridge halts at a false summit, which is nothing more than a little platform but from below appears to be the highest point of the fell.

The true summit from the false one

DESCENTS: Both flanks of the fell are very rough, that dropping into Southerndale being initially craggy and the Bassenthwaite side steepening lower down. The best way off is down the Edge, a splendid line of descent, there being a track good enough to follow in mist.

RIDGE ROUTE

To LONG SIDE, 2405'
⅓ mile : SE
Depression at 2185'
230 feet of ascent
An enjoyable ten minutes

The route follows the rim of Longside Edge, where a distinct but narrow track has been worn in the heather. The walking is quite easy, but there is one spot where anyone striding along with eyes on the distant view might step over the brink of a rocky cleft.

Hanging Stone

The 2½" and 6" Ordnance maps give prominence to a 'Hanging Stone' on Ullock Pike 400 yards west of the summit, but it is hardly worth searching for, being merely an unremarkable block anchored to the lip of a small crag. It attracts attention only when seen from below.

THE VIEW

The praises of some Lakeland views are sung to excess, but here is one rarely mentioned yet ranking with the best. True, Skiddaw looms very large nearby but in other directions the prospect is superb, ranging from the exciting skyline across the southern horizon to the distant hills of Galloway beyond the wide coastal plain of Cumbria and the Solway Firth.

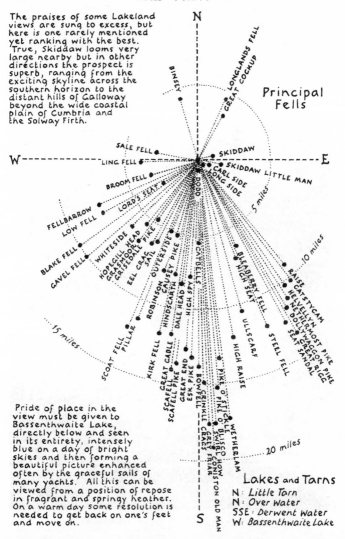

Principal Fells

Pride of place in the view must be given to Bassenthwaite Lake, directly below and seen in its entirety, intensely blue on a day of bright skies and then forming a beautiful picture enhanced often by the graceful sails of many yachts. All this can be viewed from a position of repose in fragrant and springy heather. On a warm day some resolution is needed to get back on one's feet and move on.

Lakes and Tarns
N: *Little Tarn*
N: *Over Water*
SSE: *Derwent Water*
W: *Bassenthwaite Lake*

Bassenthwaite, from Ullock Pike

Some Personal notes in conclusion

Well, that's another finished.

Up to two years ago I hadn't known the northern Fells intimately, and the remoter parts I had known merely as names on the map. Imaginative and romantic names, many of them: Arm o' Grain, Red Cloverloth, Frozen Fell, Ward Steel, Balliway Rigg, Thief Gills, Trusmadoor, Whitewater Dash, Brandy Gill, Black Nettle Hause, Candleseaves Bog, and others. Significantly, these names, foreign-sounding in Lakeland, are all of wild places in the hills, and it would seem that many of them can be attributed to the mining prospectors who first explored these uplands some five or six centuries ago, giving identity to the various landmarks. Down in the surrounding valleys, though, the dalesfolk adopted traditional Lakeland names for their farms and local features — 'thwaite', 'dale' and 'beck' occurring everywhere.

The era of mining activity has largely passed, barytes being the only mineral now being won, and the hills are quiet again. The creatures of the high places are undisturbed. Even in summer, few walkers visit the tops. In winter the Blencathra pack roam the fellsides occasionally. Both summer and winter, Pearson Dalton crosses the hills with his dogs, twice a week making the journey between his home at Fell Side and the lonely Skiddaw House, where he is shepherd. The only sounds are the call of the birds, the cries of sheep, the murmur of streams, the wind rustling the coarse bents and heather. There are no false notes in this peaceful symphony, no discords, no harshness. This is a land of solitude and silence.

On the southern fringe of the group Skiddaw and Blencathra are, however, old favourites. Skiddaw is climbed by the popular path from Keswick every day of the year, often by scores and sometimes by hundreds of people. And Blencathra is deservedly a much-visited peak. These two apart, the only other fell on which I saw another person in the whole of my walks, and then at a distance, was Carrock Fell, and this happened on three different occasions. As for the rest — nobody, not a soul, not once. I felt I was preparing a book that would have no readers at all, a script that would have no players and no public. Nevertheless, these were glorious days for me — days of absolute freedom, days of feeling like the only man on earth. No crowds to dodge, no noisy chatter, no litter. Just me, and the sheep, and singing larks overhead. All of us well content.

I must not eulogise the northern Fells too much. These lonely hills do not compare at all for grand scenery and situations with those of Wasdale and Langdale and Borrowdale. (But Blencathra and Carrock Fell and the Ullock Pike ridge of Skiddaw are very definite exceptions that would rank high in any company). Generally, they are not in the same class. From a walkers point of view, Caldbeck Fells are NOT 'worth all England else.' But they have one great attraction the others are fast losing — for the walker who prefers solitude, for the naturalist, they offer undisturbed enjoyment at

all seasons of the year. They are a
perfect Bank Holiday refuge. They
are just right, too, for the aged hiker
who can no longer force his jaded legs
up Rossett Gill or around Mickledore
— here, on gentler gradients, is a new
lease of life for him.

Skiddaw Forest, magnificent walking
country very reminiscent of Scotland,
is under a threat. Engineers have their
eyes on this vast gathering ground,
and possibly an impounding reservoir
will occupy the floor of this basin, or
the Caldew valley, before long. If it
does, this book will badly need revision.
Why can't these high and mighty public
bodies be content with surplus water only
(goodness knows, there's plenty!), piping
it to reservoirs built in their own areas?

I must mention the grand people of
the little communities around the base
of these fells, especially in the remote
north. Holiday-makers have made very
little impact here. Sturdily independent,
here are folk, unspoiled by 'tourism',
whose roots go deep in their own soil.
Ever alert for sights and sounds on the
fellsides or in the valley fields, their
work is their life. It is a pleasure to

be in their company, an honour to be in their confidence. John Peel was not the only worthy character raised in these parts.

All my walks during the past few years have ended at Keswick Bus Station, where there is a splendid open view of the mountains between Borrowdale and Bassenthwaite, a tremendously exciting array of sharp peaks and lofty ridges. Sometimes, in winter, I have seen them as a black silhouette, or silvered by moonlight, against the fading colours of the western sky; and, in summer, purpling in the dusk of evening with a skyline edged in gold. These are the north-western Fells, which I have long considered the most delectable of all. Envy me my next two years, for this is the area next on my programme. Ready Easter 1964, old Kruschev willing.

I thank those readers who helped to restore the cairn on Pike o' Blisco. A correspondent now tells me that the fine column on Lingmell has been wantonly thrown down. I hardly like to mention it, but........... do you mind? Next time you're passing?

Autumn, 1961   AW.